Exploring Biblical Theology

Exploring Biblical Theology

A Systematic Study of the Word of God
in Understandable Language

by Hobart E. Freeman, Th.D.

Faith Ministries & Publications
Post Office Box 1156
Warsaw, Indiana 46581 U.S.A.

230
F85

ISBN 1-878725-65-3

Printed in the United States of America

Acknowledgment

We wish to acknowledge the
many brothers and sisters in
Christ who lovingly contributed
their time and effort for the
transcribing, editing, and
proofreading of this book.

Table of Contents

Preface   xv

Introduction   1

Chapter One: God's Eternal Plan   5
Predestination   5
Election   11
    Causative and Permissive Decrees   13
    Predestination or Fatalism: Why Pray?   14
Execution of God's Plan: Creation   15
    God's Special Creation—Man   17
        The Nature of Man   19
            Man as Body, Soul, and Spirit   19
            The Origin of the Soul   22
Execution of God's Plan: Providence   24
    Providence—Preservation   25
        Theories Opposing God's Preservation   26
    Providence—Government   27
    Providence—Concurrence   29
    Providential Control   29
        Preventive Control   30
        Permissive Control   31

Directive Control   31
Determinative Control   32

Chapter Two: Revelation and Inspiration   33
The Doctrine of Revelation   33
Preservation of the Revelation   34
Methods of Revelation   35
The Doctrine of Inspiration   36
Inspiration in Relation to Scripture   36
Revelation and Inspiration: Oral Utterances   37
Inspiration—God-breathed   38
The Writers' View of Their Writings   40
The Nature of Inspiration   41
Theories Regarding Inspiration   42
The Biblical View of Inspiration   45
The Extent of Inspiration   46

Chapter Three: The Doctrine of God   51
Various Concepts of God   52
The Existence of God   57
Natural Theology   58
General Revelation   59
The Purpose of General Revelation   63
Special Revelation   63
God's Self-existence   65
God's Nature—His Personality   66
God's Nature—Spirit   67
God's Nature—His Unity   68
God's Nature—His Triunity   70
The Godhead   73
God's Transcendent Attributes   74

God's Eternalness 75
   The Relationship Between Time and Eternity 76
God's Sovereignty 77
God's Immutability 79
God's Omnipresence 83
   Space in Relationship to God and Man 84
God's Omniscience 88
God's Omnipotence 90
   God's Self-limitation 92
God's Infinity 94
God's Moral Attributes 95
   God's Holiness 95
   God's Righteousness 97
   God's Faithfulness 99
   God's Patience 100
   God's Love 101
   God's Grace and Mercy 106
   God's Glory 107
Christology: The Doctrine of Christ 109
   The Personality of Christ 110
   The Human and Divine Natures of Christ 110
      Heresies Regarding the Human and
        Divine Natures of Christ 110
   The Deity of Christ 111
   The Humanity of Christ 116
   The Unity of Christ 118
      The Results of Christ's Unity 121
   The Work of Christ 122
   Christ as Prophet 122
   Christ as Priest 123
   Christ as King 125

The States of Christ   126
The Preexistence of Christ   126
The Incarnation of Christ   127
    The Kenosis Experience of Christ   128
    The Purpose and Necessity
        of the Incarnation   130
    The Virgin Birth   132
The Exaltation of Christ: The Significance
    of His Resurrection   136
    The Importance of the Resurrection   137
    The Certainty of the Resurrection   138
        Rationalistic Theories of the Empty Tomb   139
        The Jewish View of the Empty Tomb   141
        The Scriptural Proof of the Resurrection   141
    The Ascension of Christ   143
        The Purposes for Christ's Ascension
            and Exaltation   144
    The Restitution of All Things   145
    The Climax of Christ's Exaltation:
        His His Second Coming   146
The Doctrine of the Holy Spirit   147
The Personality of the Holy Spirit   147
The Deity of the Holy Spirit   149
The Work of the Holy Spirit   150
    Clarification of Terms Regarding
        the Holy Spirit   154

Chapter Four: The Doctrine of Sin   159
The Nature of Sin   162
The Object of Sin   163
The Universality of Sin   164

The Consequences of Sin   165
The Extent of Sin's Effect Upon Man   166
   Man's Spiritual State Before God   167

Chapter Five: Doctrine of Redemption   169
The Extent of Redemption   171
   Theories Regarding Methods of Salvation   172
   The Biblical View of Salvation   173
The Doctrine of Atonement   173
   The Necessity for the Atonement   174
   Views of the Atonement   176
The Doctrine of Grace   180
   Is Grace Dispensational?   182
   The Difference Between
      the Dispensations of Law and Grace   184
   Unscriptural Attitudes Toward Law and Grace   184
   Sins Against God's Grace   186
Predestination and Election in Relation
   to Redemption   187
Calvinism and Arminianism   189
The Calling   191
   The General Calling   191
   The Special Calling   191
The Doctrine of Faith   194
   The Nature of Faith   194
   The Definition of Faith   195
   Saving Faith   196
   Saving Faith Versus Intellectual Assent   196
   Saving Faith Versus Believism   198
   The Relationship Between Faith and Reason   199
The Doctrine of Repentance   201

The Doctrine of Regeneration   203
  Evidences of Regeneration   204
The Doctrine of Conversion   205
The Doctrine of Justification   206
  The Moral Basis for Justification   207
The Doctrine of Imputation   209
  Aspects of Imputation   211
The Doctrine of Sanctification   211
The Doctrine of Union With Christ   215
The Doctrine of Crucifixion With Christ   218
The Doctrine of Adoption   218
The Doctrine of Eternal Security   219

Chapter Six: The Doctrine of the Church   223
The Nature of the New Testament Church   225
  Views Regarding the Nature of the Church   225
The Revelation of the Church   229
The Beginning of the Church   229
The Purpose of the Church   230
Views of the Organization of the Church   231
Reasons for the Rapid Spread of the Church   232
The Rise of the Formal Church Organization   233
The Government of the Church   236
Theocratic Government in the Church   237
The Authority of the New Testament Church   237
The Practice of the New Testament Church   239
  The Application of Theocratic
    Principles of Government   239
  Church Discipline   242
    Causes and Procedure for Discipline   244
    The Discipline of Heretics and Deceivers   246

Church Discipline of Family Members 247
The Discipline of an Elder 250
Receiving Members Into the Church 252
The Requirements for Participation in Fellowship 252
The Church Offices 254
The Importance of the Pastor and Deacon 257
The Office of Elder 257
The Qualifications for an Elder 259
The Duties of the Elder 261
The Authority of the Elder 262
The Number of Elders 263
The Permanence of the Office of Elder 265
The Ordination of Elders 267
The Office of Deacon 268
The Duties of a Deacon 268
The Selection, Appointment, and
Number of Deacons 269
The Qualifications for a Deacon 270
The Office of Deaconess: Scriptural
or Unscriptural? 271
The Ordinances of the Church 272
Water Baptism 273
The Communion of the Bread and Cup 276
The Lord's Supper 278
Washing of the Saints' Feet 281

Chapter Seven: Doctrine of Last Things: Eschatology 285
Death 285
The Intermediate State 287
The Doctrine of Antichrist 290

The Second Advent   295
  The Time of Christ's Return   296
  Signs of Christ's Return   300
  The Second Advent in Relation to the Millennium   301
Summary of End-Time Events   302
The Millennium   303
The Doctrine of Resurrection   305
  Theories Concerning Resurrection   307
The Doctrine of Judgment   308
  The Destination of the Wicked After Death   310
The Kingdom of God   316
  Views of the Kingdom   316
  God's Universal Kingdom   319
    God's Method of Ruling   320
  God's Mediatorial Kingdom   321
    God's Rule: Judges   322
    God's Rule: The Kingship   323
    The Division of the Kingdom   324
    The Kingdom in Prophecy   325
    The Nature of Kingdom Prophecy   326
    The Prophetic Kingdom in Relation
      to the New Testament Kingdom   327
  Israel's Rejection of the Kingdom   330
The New Heavens, New Earth, and New Jerusalem   337
Life in the Eternal State   338
  Things Which Will Be Absent   338
  Things Which Will Be Present   341

Subject Index   345
Bibliography   364

Preface

The Christian Church has been well supplied throughout its history with a wealth of materials written about the doctrines of the Faith. The shelves of Christian bookstores and seminary libraries are lined with Bible surveys, systematic theologies, manuals on ethics, books on interpretation of Scripture, the prophets, and countless other topics. In fact, many of these resources are part of the foundation of truth from which the author drew in preparing for the teachings contained in these pages.

With such an abundance of material already available, it is not unreasonable to ask why we are presenting another book on systematic theology. What will this work contribute to the subject that is not already adequately covered elsewhere? The answer is twofold.

First, this book will fill a need for teaching which can be understood easily by the average Christian who has no theological training. God gave Dr. Hobart Freeman a special gift for presenting profound truths in simple terms. However, this text is more than an introduction to the subject of biblical theology. It is a concise, yet comprehensive, presentation of all the doctrines of the Bible in an organized, readable fashion.

Second, this present generation is characterized by religious errors which were not present when the classical theology works were assembled, making it essential that an up-to-date warning be sounded. While some modern errors are simply resurrections of ancient ones, they still should be exposed afresh, so the believer will know to avoid them.

Being a systematic approach to theology, this book follows a clear and logical order in presenting the truths of God's Word. It begins with an overview of God's eternal plan. Then it moves into the ways God has revealed Himself to man, and presents the deep realities of the Godhead, and all of His wonderful attributes.

Next, it looks to the subject of mankind's sin and its consequences, and the plan of redemption which was promised, predicted in prophecy, and provided by Jesus Christ. The doctrine of the church is then covered in great detail, and the book culminates with the triumph of God over all opposition and the fulfillment of the Christian's total redemption for all eternity.

This work has been transcribed and edited from an extended series of teachings on biblical theology spanning several years. The author has gone on to be with the Lord, but it is our prayer that this endeavor will be a source of much blessing and insight, and that it will encourage and motivate many to explore the Book of Books, and to come to know its Author.

Introduction

The importance of a study of Christian theology or the doctrines of the Christian faith cannot be overemphasized. If Christianity is true, then it is not just a religion among the world's religions, as so many seem to think; but it is *The Religion*, for Jesus said, "I am the way, the truth and the life: no man cometh unto the Father, but by me" (John 14:6). According to the Bible itself, *Christianity* is the only valid religion; therefore, every Christian, especially a minister, should feel it is his duty to make a systematic study of its doctrines, as well as its principles.

There are many ways to study the teachings of the Scriptures, such as historically, systematically, and inductively. Experience has proven that the most effective way to acquire a useful working knowledge of the Word of God is by a systematic study of its theology or its doctrines.

The Scriptures themselves urge such a comprehensive study. "Study to shew thyself approved unto God, a workman that needeth not to be ashamed, rightly dividing the word of truth" (II Timothy 2:15). "All scripture is given by inspiration of God, and is profitable for doctrine, for reproof, for correction, for instruction in righteousness: That the man of God [the Christian] may be perfect, throughly furnished unto all good works" (II Timothy 3:16-17).

Many people today, including some ministers, have little interest in doctrinal teaching, that is, the doctrinal studies of the Christian faith. Most seminaries are producing religious administrators instead of men of the Word and prayer.

Some people want to confine religion to the realm of emotional feeling, or to an inspirational sermonette on Sunday morning, or to busyness with church work. True religion is not free from emotion and feeling, of course; but if these do not arise from a sound doctrinal knowledge of the Word of God as a foundation, they will prove empty and worthless in the end. The same thing can be said of religious activity within the church, much of which has no real basis in Scripture.

Christianity is a religion of *truth*. The gospel itself consists of certain definite *facts* which one must understand and believe in order to be saved. These facts are called *doctrines*. A man can no more have salvation apart from a knowledge of certain doctrinal truths about Christ than he can have salvation apart from Christ. The Scriptures themselves say this, for example, I Corinthians 15:1-4. "Moreover, brethren, I declare unto you the gospel which I preached unto you, which also ye have received, and wherein ye stand; By which also ye are saved, if ye keep in memory what I preached unto you, unless ye have believed in vain. For I delivered unto you first of all that which I also received [Notice the following doctrinal truths about Christ], how that Christ died for our sins according to the scriptures; And that he was buried, and that he rose again the third day according to the scriptures." Paul was setting forth certain truths that the Christian must know and believe according to the Word of God in order to be saved.

Romans 10:13-14 says, "For whosoever shall call upon the name of the Lord shall be saved. How then shall they call on him in whom they have not believed? and how shall they believe in him of whom they have not heard? and how shall they hear without a preacher?" In other words, someone must go to them with the word of truth; thus, Christianity is based upon certain doctrinal facts, and not mere sentiment, or activity, or emotion. A knowledge of the truth is essential to genuine salvation. How could someone believe unless he hears—unless someone goes to him and teaches him the doctrinal truths about Christ and the will of God? The importance of learning and holding fast to correct doctrine is stressed throughout the Scriptures, for example, Acts 2:42; Romans 16:17; Ephesians 4:11-14; Colossians 2:8; I Timothy 3:2; 6:20; II Timothy 4; Titus 1:9.

Approximately ninety times in the Scriptures Jesus is said to be a *teacher*; that is, He is said to teach or to be a *teacher of truth*. Paul, the apostles, the prophets, and the priests were called teachers. A person cannot teach others what he does not know, nor can he contend for a faith about which he has no revelation. There is no such thing as biblical Christianity apart from correct doctrine.

Chapter One

God's Eternal Plan

In this initial teaching concerning the great doctrines of the Christian faith, a study will be made of the *Plan of God*, which is sometimes called the *Decrees of God*. The meaning and nature of God's decrees will be examined first, then the execution of His plan in creation and providence. God's decrees are essentially one comprehensive plan, covering all His works, and embracing even the actions of men.

Predestination

In the Scriptures this eternal plan is also called *predestination*, and it is God's sovereign, eternal plan by which He foreordained all things that come to pass. Nothing could ever happen that God did not foreordain. His eternal plan included all events—creation of the universe, man, and angels. It included Adam's fall into sin, the plan of redemption, the rise and fall of nations, and the crucifixion of Christ. In fact, it included all events of history. Even the movements of the earth, the planets, the stars, and the elements of nature were predestinated by God.

Although God's plan is unconditional, eternal, and sovereign, and not dependent on man's choices or actions,

He is *not responsible* for, *nor the cause* of, sin or evil. His predestination of all things included man's free choices and actions. God had to predestinate man's freedom to choose evil as well as to choose good, or man would just be like an animal or a robot, and not be able to glorify God in his right choices. These facts will be dealt with later in this study in greater detail, where ample support from the Scriptures will be given.

The truths of election, predestination, and God's eternal plan are all brought together in one passage. "According as he hath chosen us in him before the foundation of the world" (Ephesians 1:4). The believer was elected before the earth was created, before he was ever born. "Having predestinated us unto the adoption of children by Jesus Christ" (verse 5). Then verse 11 reveals God's eternal plan: "In whom [Christ] also we have obtained an inheritance, being predestinated according to the purpose [His plan] of him who worketh all things after the counsel of his own will." As has been stated, predestination is God's eternal plan by which He foreordained all things that come to pass.

In Scripture God's eternal plan is shown to be *unconditional*. God worked out His plan or purpose "after the counsel of his own will" (Ephesians 1:11). He did not have to ask anyone about it. He did what He wanted to do. His plan is *eternal* according to Ephesians 3:7-11, and also Acts 15:18, which says, "Known unto God are all his works from the beginning of the world." In other words, He planned everything, and He knew the outcome, because He predestinated all events that come to pass.

His eternal plan is also *sovereign*. For example, Daniel 4:35 says, "And all the inhabitants of the earth are reputed as nothing: and he [God] doeth according to his will in the army of heaven, and among the inhabitants of the earth: and none can stay his hand, or say unto him, What doest thou?" The fact that His plan is sovereign is also set forth in Psalm 135:6 which says that God did as He pleased in heaven and in earth.

The Scriptures show that predestination of all things *included man's free choices and actions*. Notice that God predestinated the events in the following passages, yet man freely chose to act as he did.

Genesis 50 is the account of Joseph, who was sold by his jealous brothers into slavery. When Jacob died, Joseph's brothers thought he might try to exact vengeance upon them; but Joseph said: "Fear not, for am I in the place of God? But as for you, ye thought evil against me; but God meant it unto good, to bring to pass, as it is this day, to save much people alive. Now therefore fear ye not" (Genesis 50:19-21). Evidence of God's eternal plan can be seen in Joseph's statement, "Ye thought evil against me; but God meant it unto good." The selling of Joseph into slavery and his rise to power in Egypt were all included in God's eternal plan. God predestinated that event, but Joseph's brothers *freely chose* to act as they did. Predestination did not rule out their freedom.

In Isaiah 10:5-12 the Assyrians went against Israel in battle to conquer and destroy the nation. God sent them against the Israelites as punishment for their sins; but as far as the Assyrians were concerned, they freely chose to do what they did. In Isaiah 10:5-7 God said, "O Assyrian, the rod of mine anger, and the staff in their hand is mine indignation. I will send him against an hypocritical nation [Israel], and against the people of my wrath will I give him a charge, to take the spoil, and to take the prey, and to tread them down like the mire of the streets. Howbeit he [the Assyrian] meaneth not so, neither doth his heart think so; but it is in his heart to destroy and cut off nations not a few." God was sending Assyria to fulfill His eternal plan to punish sin, but Assyria *freely chose* to conquer and plunder.

This truth is seen again in Acts 2:22-23, speaking of the crucifixion of Christ. Peter, on the day of Pentecost, said, "Ye men of Israel, hear these words; Jesus of Nazareth, a man approved of God among you by miracles and wonders and signs, which God did by him in the midst of you, as ye yourselves also know. Him, being delivered by the determinate counsel and foreknowledge of God, ye have taken, and by wicked hands have crucified and slain." Clearly, God's Word sets forth the truth of predestination, as well as the free choices of man.

God by His own will and by His foreknowledge predestinated the crucifixion of Christ on behalf of sinners, but Peter charged Israel with the guilt of having crucified Him. God predestinated it, therefore, it had to come to pass; but the Jews *freely chose* to do what they did. From man's side, he makes the free choice, because the free choices have been predestinated.

"For of a truth against thy holy child Jesus, whom thou hast anointed, both Herod, and Pontius Pilate, with the

Gentiles, and the people of Israel, were gathered together [now, notice this], For to do whatsoever thy hand and thy counsel determined before to be done" (Acts 4:27-28). Here again, it is evident that God predestinated the events; but man chose to act *freely* in what he did.

This principle of man's *choice* is true in the matter of *redemption*. The Scriptures teach that God predestinated and elected those who would believe as a part of His eternal plan from before the world began, but His plan also decreed that they must exercise faith and freely choose to believe and receive the Lord Jesus Christ. From God's side, He predestinates and elects; from man's side, he must respond to the gospel when he hears it.

This is seen, for example, in II Thessalonians 2:13-14. Paul said, "But we are bound to give thanks alway to God for you, brethren beloved of the Lord, because God hath from the beginning chosen you to salvation through sanctification of the Spirit and belief of the truth: Whereunto he called you by our gospel, to the obtaining of the glory of our Lord Jesus Christ." Both election and man's *free response* are seen there in the same passage. How does God bring it about? He said, "through belief of the truth." Even though a person has been predestinated and elected to be saved, he must respond to the gospel when he hears it.

It is very important to see that God's eternal plan had to be unconditional. If any part of the plan was conditioned upon what man might or might not do, then the whole plan of God would have been conditional and uncertain of fulfillment. In other words, the crucifixion of Christ would not

9

have been certain. No event is isolated or stands alone. For God to decree one event as certain (for example, the crucifixion of Christ), then that would make *all events certain*. Otherwise, God would not be sovereign, but dependent upon what man or the devil might do or not do to hinder His plan. However, the Scriptures declare that God is dependent upon nothing or no one. Examples of this have already been given, such as Daniel 4:35; Isaiah 14:27; 46:10; Acts 15:18; Ephesians 1:11.

God already knows what He is going to do. In Romans 9:15-18 Paul said that God does with men as He wills, and no man can presume to ask Him why He does this or that. That would be like a little ant on the ground saying to a man when he is getting ready to walk by him, "Who do you think you are, treading on my territory?" Proverbs 19:21 and 16:33 show how men make plans, but *God determines the outcome* of those plans. In other words, God works all things according to the counsel of His own will. It has previously been stated that predestination includes all things, all events, but it does not make God responsible for man's wrong choices.

There is nothing that man or Satan can do to take God by surprise because His plan has already been decreed. Nor can anything change or suspend God's eternal plan; for even man's free choices, man's plans, and man's actions are included in God's plans. Again, this is made abundantly clear in the betrayal of Jesus by Judas in Luke 22:21-22. Jesus said, "But, behold, the hand of him that betrayeth me is with me on the table. And truly the Son of man goeth, as it was determined." In God's great eternal plan He determined the crucifixion; however, Jesus put the responsibility for it on Judas when He said, "Woe unto that man by whom he is betrayed."

Predestination and *foreordination* actually mean the same thing. To predestinate an event is to foreordain it to come to pass. They signify the *certainty* of a future event—the surety that it will come to pass. Recall the definition of predestination that was given, which includes the term foreordination. Predestination is God's eternal plan by which He foreordained all things which come to pass. In Ephesians 1:11 it is stated that God works all things according to His own purpose, "after the counsel of his own will." God does not have to ask anyone, because He is sovereign and His plan is eternal.

Another term is *foreknowledge*. This signifies the perfect knowledge of God from eternity of the certainty of all events that will ever occur. This is clearly taught in Acts 15:18. "Known unto God are all his works from the beginning of the world." Nothing can take God by surprise. Nothing will be changed or suspended, because even apparent changes were included in God's eternal plan.

Election

Election is the sovereign choice by God of His people from before the foundation of the world. Romans 8:30 says the elect will be effectually called, justified, and glorified. "Moreover whom he did predestinate, them he also called: and whom he called, them he also justified: and whom he justified, them he also glorified." Verse 33 says, "Who shall

11

lay any thing to the charge of God's elect?" Election is not based upon God foreseeing who would believe and then choosing them for that reason. This would mean that God saw that the Christian would believe, and salvation would be based upon works and not upon His grace.

Foreknowledge and election have nothing to do with God foreseeing what man will do, but what He will do. God has "saved us, and called us with an holy calling, not according to our works, but according to his own purpose and grace, which was given us in Christ Jesus before the world began" (II Timothy 1:9). Compare that with Ephesians 1:4-11 and Romans 9:11-13, which show that God chose the Christian before the foundation of the world according to His own purpose.

It is theological nonsense to say, as some people do, that God foresaw what a man might do under certain circumstances; that is, He saw all the possibilities, then He foreordained all the possible choices. This, some believe, leaves man's freedom intact; but that thinking is erroneous because it is impossible to foresee probabilities. *Only actualities can be foreseen.* Thus, the predestination of all things before they occur is God's way of making sure that they happen. "Known unto God are all his works from the beginning of the world."

It should be a great source of encouragement and comfort for the Christian to know that God predestinated all events. Without the certainty that Christ would be crucified and would shed His blood for the redemption of mankind, it might not have happened as it did. If God had not had perfect control of all events leading to the Cross, perhaps they might not have occurred; the devil might have overcome Jesus, or maybe the Jews would not have crucified Him.

Causative and Permissive Decrees

There are two kinds of decrees: causative and permissive. In a *causative decree* God causes an action. Whatever He predestinates, He will personally cause to come to pass, or He will see that it comes to pass, as in the birth of Jesus and the creation of the world. In a *permissive decree* God permits an action. Permissive decrees are predestinated also, but these events are foreordained to come to pass through the free choices and free actions of men. Examples of this are Adam's fall, the betrayal and crucifixion of Jesus, and Joseph's servitude in Egypt. God's eternal *plan* concerning all events is *certain* of fulfillment, although *man* is *free* in his choices. While a sinner makes his decision freely, God can limit the time, the place, the conditions, the influences, and the circumstances in order to bring to pass His perfect will.

God shows repeatedly in His Word that men and nations make free choices. Then He parts the veil, as it were, and shows that it is He who is bringing to pass His eternal purpose in those actions, whether they are good or evil. God is in control of all history—not the devil, not man, not events—but God alone. In predestination God is making sure that His plans will be forthcoming.

Predestination or Fatalism:
Why Pray?

Predestination is not to be thought of as fatalism. *Fatalism* is blind, unintelligent, inevitable fate. The Scriptures show that *predestination* is based upon the perfect wisdom of a righteous God. Some people say, "If predestination is true, and if all events are bound to come to pass anyway, why should we pray?" This reasoning overlooks the fact that predestination cannot influence man's free choices. God's eternal decrees are not revealed to men in advance, but they only know of them after an event has occurred.

This is clearly seen in the example given previously. Joseph's brothers, out of jealousy, sold him into slavery in Egypt. Years later, Joseph's brothers were afraid he would take vengeance upon them; but he said, "Ye thought evil against me, but God meant it unto good." Neither Joseph nor his brothers knew beforehand that it was God's plan from the beginning to save Jacob and his sons so that four hundred years later there would be a nation (Israel) which He would bring out of Egypt.

Prayer is the means God has established for His children to receive His promises, to benefit others, and to commune with Him. Even though God has foreordained the outcome of all events, He has *included* the Christian's *prayers* in His plan in order to bring the events to pass. He works through the prayers. God has foreordained that a certain event should happen, as well as the means by which it happens; thus, prayer, action, and effort on the believer's part are necessary.

14

In conclusion to this part of the study, it has been shown that God's eternal plan is predestination by which He has predestinated or foreordained all events in heaven and earth that will ever come to pass. The greatest and the least events in history are included in this—from the rise of nations to the fall of a sparrow (Matthew 10:29). Predestination includes the good actions of men (Ephesians 2:10). Even evil acts of men are predestinated (Acts 2:23). Predestination includes life (John 1:9); death (Hebrews 9:27); salvation of believers (I Peter 1:5); and the destruction of the wicked (I Peter 2:6-8). It includes all events (Acts 15:18).

Execution of God's Plan: Creation

In this study of the execution of God's eternal plan, the place to begin is with *creation*. According to the Bible, in the beginning God created or brought into existence, without the use of preexisting materials, the whole visible and invisible universe. This truth is seen in more than one passage in the New Testament. "All things were made by him; and without him was not any thing made that was made" (John 1:3). In Colossians 1:16 Paul said the same thing. "For by him [Jesus] were all things created, that are in heaven, and that are in earth, visible and invisible, whether they be thrones, or dominions, or principalities, or powers: all things were created by him, and for him."

The *God of creation* in Genesis 1:1 is the God, *Jesus Christ*, of John 1 and Colossians 1. Jesus in His preincarnate state is the God who did the creating in Genesis. There was a time, according to Scripture, when the world and the

15

universe did not exist. This fact is seen in John 17:5 when Jesus prayed, "And now, O Father, glorify thou me with thine own self with the glory which I had with thee before the world was." In Ephesians 1:4 Paul said that God has "chosen us in him before the foundation of the world."

A second fact the Scriptures set forth about creation is that the world and the universe were *created by God alone.* Nothing exists that He did not create, whether man, angels, the material of the universe, or Satan before his fall into sin. This was shown in John 1:3, Colossians 1:16, and Genesis 1-2.

Thirdly, the Scriptures reveal that everything was *created out of nothing.* The word of God alone did the creating, without the use of any prior materials. Some theologians dispute this and say it is impossible to create something out of nothing. They argue against the biblical teaching of what is called creation "ex nihilo" or creation "out of nothing." They contend that Genesis 1:1 does not require that men believe God created out of nothing, but that God could have created out of preexisting materials.

In reply to that, the Hebrew does not permit their argument. In normal Old Testament Hebrew usage the verb is always placed at the beginning of a sentence, unless the writer or the Holy Spirit wanted some special emphasis. In Genesis 1:1 the phrase, "in the beginning," stands first. Obviously, to any student of Hebrew, the Holy Spirit is emphasizing that this is the beginning of all things, and that God created all things. Nothing preexisted! The Hebrew verb used in this verse is the term "created." God could have inspired the writer to use other Hebrew terms, such as "formed" or "designed"; but the verb used here is "created."

It should be obvious, even to the liberals and to the skeptics, that only God can create. Man has to use preexisting materials. He forms; he shapes; he designs; he manufactures; but only God can create. It is almost a laughable matter to students of the Bible that scientists are allegedly discovering ways to create new forms of life. However, they do not create new forms of life; they simply shape, design, form, or manipulate something that has already been created by God.

Proverbs 8:26 says that God created even the dust from which He made the earth. The Hebrew literally says, "the beginning of the dust of the earth." Certainly there is no suggestion that God used preexisting materials in John 1:3. In fact it is ruled out. John said that all things were made by Jesus Christ, and there is nothing that is made that He did not make. Hebrews 11:3 clearly shows that God created all things out of nothing. "Through faith we understand that the worlds were framed by the word of God, so that things which are seen were not made of things which do appear."

God's Special Creation—Man

God's eternal plan also included the *creation of man*. "God created man in his own image [a refutation of the theory of evolution], in the image of God created he him; male and female created he them" (Genesis 1:27). Conversely, the *naturalistic evolutionary theory* teaches that millions or billions of years ago life began spontaneously and mysteriously, and from that original living matter, intelligent

17

life has slowly evolved. Of course, this theory does not tell the source of the original matter. The *theistic evolutionists*, which are found within Christendom, believe that God is operating the process of evolution in which man could have arisen from a non-human creature, and when God endowed him with a soul, this act constituted the "creation of man." They also believe that animals have changed from species to species, for example, from reptile to bird.

The evolutionary theory denies the biblical account of the creation of man and his fall into sin from his original state of purity and innocence. Instead, man is said to be inherently good, and is progressively developing morally and intellectually through the evolutionary process. World Wars I and II, together with the declining moral conditions of the twentieth century, have done much to discredit this idealistic view of man.

For the Christian the matter of special creation versus evolution was settled by Jesus in Matthew 19, when the Pharisees questioned Him concerning marriage and divorce. He told them that in the beginning God made an original pair, male and female, from which the whole human race has descended. Special creation is also shown in Psalm 8, where it says that God created man and gave him the rule and authority over all the created order, over all nature, and over the animal kingdom. How could man have evolved from animals if from the beginning he was placed over the animal kingdom? Man had dominion until he fell into sin.

The Nature of Man

Regarding *man's nature*, what distinguishes him from the animal creation? Creation in the *"image of God"* is ascribed to no other creature. Only man has an inner nature like the nature of God. Man was created with a *spiritual nature* because of the divine purpose God had for him—he was to have fellowship and communion with God. The existence of man's soul does not distinguish him from the animal creation. The Hebrew Scriptures show that even the animals have souls. The Hebrew term "nephesh chayah" or "living soul," used of man in Genesis 2:7, is the identical term used of animals in Genesis 1:24 and 2:19. When God breathed into man's nostrils the breath of life, this was the impartation of the image of God, and it distinguished man from the animal creation. Being in the image of God makes man a moral, rational, spiritual person or personality.

Regarding man's nature, some teach *dualism*, saying that man consists of only body and soul, that the term spirit is synonymous with soul in Scripture, and that the terms are interchangeable. However, this teaching has no basis in Scripture, because soul and spirit are two different words in both the Hebrew and the Greek, and they are never used interchangeably. On occasion, the sense of the passage may allow use of spirit or soul; but they are not synonymous terms.

Man as Body, Soul, and Spirit

According to Scripture man is *triune* in nature, a *trinity*; he is body, soul, and spirit. Since the three terms are used together in Scripture, they cannot be reduced to two terms, as the proponents of dualism contend. In I Thessalonians 5:23 Paul said, "I pray God your whole spirit and soul and body be preserved blameless unto the coming of our Lord Jesus Christ." This verse shows all three terms used separately; therefore, they cannot be the same. In Hebrews 4:12 Paul said, "The word of God is quick, and powerful, and sharper than any two-edged sword, piercing even to the dividing asunder of soul and spirit." Luke 1:46-47 and Isaiah 26:9 also distinguish between soul and spirit.

Everyone knows what the body of flesh is, but what is the soul? What is the spirit? First, the *soul* is seen in Scripture to be the *seat* of the emotions, appetites, desires, and affections, such as love, hate, and joy. See I Kings 11:37; Deuteronomy 6:5 and 12:20.

Secondly, in Scripture the *soul* is the *person* himself. Sometimes it is translated as "his life." "And Esau took his wives, and his sons, and his daughters, and all the persons of his house, and his cattle, and all his beasts, and all his substance, which he had got in the land of Canaan; and went into the country from the face of his brother Jacob" (Genesis 36:6). The term translated "persons" is the Hebrew term "nephesh," which is translated as "soul" in other passages, such as Genesis 46:18; 12:13; Psalm 23:3. "These are the sons of Zilpah, whom Laban gave to Leah his daughter, and these she bare unto Jacob, even sixteen souls" (Genesis 46:18). In the Old Testament the term "nephesh" is often translated as "me" or "myself" or "the person himself."

What is the relationship between the soul and spirit? The *spirit* is the *life principle* which comes from God (Zechariah 12:1). Man is *not spirit*, but he *has spirit* from God. Man *is soul* according to Genesis 2:7. "God formed man of the dust of the ground, and breathed into his nostrils the breath of life; and man became a living soul." Only God is Spirit and is contrasted in Isaiah 31:1-3 with animals, which are flesh.

Animals have souls but they are not spiritual; only man has a spiritual soul because of the inbreathing of God's image. God breathed His spiritual image into man whom He had created from the dust, and man became a living soul. Thus, this simple equation: body + spirit = soul. A man's body plus his spirit, which comes from God, makes him a living soul or person. So man is not spirit, although he does have a spiritual nature.

At His resurrection Jesus received a new, glorified body, which will be His for eternity. He vividly contrasted the nature of this glorified body with that of a spirit in Luke 24:36-43 when He appeared to His disciples, who, in their surprise, thought a spirit had come into their midst. The Lord calmed their fear with His words of comfort and offered to let them touch Him—to feel for themselves that He was flesh and bone, and not a spirit. He did not say flesh and blood, because flesh and blood shall not enter the Kingdom of God. In I Corinthians 15 Paul said that in the resurrection Christians will have a spiritual body of flesh and bones, but it will be spiritual material.

Man's nature is not spirit; even Jesus Himself in the flesh said He is not spirit. He was spirit before the incarnation, but now He is glorified man in a glorified body. In I Corinthians 15:42-44 Paul said, "So also is the resurrection of the dead. It is sown in corruption; it is raised in incorruption: It is sown in dishonour; it is raised in glory: it is sown in weakness; it is raised in power: It is sown a natural body; It is raised a spiritual body. There is a natural body, and there is a spiritual body." In Hebrews 1:7 Paul said the angels are spirits. God created man a little lower than the angels (Psalm 8:5; Hebrews 2:7,9), implying that man is not spirit. Because man's nature is spiritual, made in the image of God, he has the capacity to worship and fellowship with God once he is regenerated. Man may worship in spirit (John 4:23) as a Spirit-filled Christian, but this is not speaking of his nature.

The Origin of the Soul

There are several views with regard to the *origin* of the *soul*. For example, there is the view that the soul preexisted, the creationism view, and the view of traducianism. The *preexistence view* teaches that men's souls preexisted before their creation, formation, or birth; however, that is clearly refuted by Scripture. Genesis 2:7 shows that God created man out of the dust of the earth; He breathed life into man's nostrils, and at that point man became a living soul. His soul had no existence prior to that.

Those who hold to the *creationism view* believe that parents transmit only biological life; that God creates a new soul, which He implants at the moment of conception, at some time in the womb, or at birth. This view confuses the soul with the spirit and overlooks the fact that children have many personality traits of their parents—not merely physical traits, but mental and character traits. This must mean that the parents transmit more than mere biological life through procreation.

The creationism view is that of the abortionist, and states that the child is not a person, not a human being, until he breathes the breath of life at birth, at which time he receives a soul. The abortionists misuse the account of Adam in Genesis 2:7, "And the Lord God formed man of the dust of the ground, and breathed into his nostrils the breath of life; and man became a living soul." They say that man becomes a living soul when he begins to breathe; but they cannot use the experience of Adam, because he alone, of all men, came into existence fully formed. They overlook the fact that Adam did not come through the womb of a mother. God imparted to Adam the seed of life (Genesis 1); and from that time until the present, human life has been continuous. Genesis 3:20 says that Eve became the "mother of all living." For a detailed study on the errors of the abortionists, see the author's book, *Every Wind of Doctrine*, which deals in detail with the errors and unscripturalness of *abortionism*.

The Scriptural view is called *traducianism*, a term derived from the Latin word meaning "to transmit" or "reproduce." This view teaches that the parents transmit the total person—body and soul—through *procreation*. The Bible shows that when God created the original pair, He gave them the power of procreation of full persons, not merely their bodies. God created the species or the human race in Adam, then perpetuated the race through man's procreative powers which He gave him. For example, in I Corinthians 15:22 Paul said, "In Adam all die," which means the human race is in Adam, and they die because Adam sinned. Paul said in Romans 5:12 that sin entered the world through one man; therefore, death is passed upon all men. All have sinned like their first parents.

The Scriptures show that *persons* are in the *loins* or *seed* of their parents. God considered unborn Levi, who was the son of Jacob, to be present in the seed of Abraham. "And as I may so say, Levi also, who receiveth tithes, payed tithes in Abraham. For he was yet in the loins of his father, when Melchisedec met him" (Hebrews 7:9-10). God saw him as a person while he was still in Abraham's seed. In Jeremiah 1:5 God told Jeremiah, the prophet, that He knew him before he was ever formed in the womb. In Romans 9:11-13 Paul clearly said that God knew Jacob and Esau and what He would do toward them before they were ever born.

Genesis 46:26 speaks of Jacob going into Egypt with his family. "All the souls [persons] that came with Jacob into Egypt, which came out of his loins, besides Jacob's sons' wives, all the souls were threescore and six." Persons were in the loins of Jacob; persons were in the loins of Abraham; persons were in the loins of Adam.

Execution of God's Plan: Providence

The second aspect of the execution of God's plan is called *providence*. God not only created the world but He also preserves and sustains it. Providence is the activity of God by which He preserves, sustains, and directs all creation to fulfill

His eternal purpose. This study will explain the three aspects of providence: preservation, government, and concurrence.

Providence—Preservation

Preservation is the continuous work of God by which He upholds and sustains all that He created. God finished His creative work on the sixth day according to Genesis 2:2, but He did not cease all of His activity. In John 5:17-20 Jesus said, "My Father worketh hitherto, and I work." This continuous work is called preservation. Evidence of this truth may be seen in the prophet's prayer in Nehemiah 9:6, "Thou, even thou, art Lord alone; thou hast made heaven, the heaven of heavens, with all their host, the earth, and all things that are therein, the seas, and all that is therein, and thou preservest them all." Without this continuous work of preservation, everything would cease to exist (Psalm 104). God preserves and sustains creation through the operation of the *physical laws* of *nature*, such as gravity; through *secondary causes and effects*, the sun and the rain which He sends; and the operation of the *inherent powers* endowed to all living things. Genesis shows that He placed life within the tree, within the fruit, and within man; and they reproduce themselves.

Sometimes He preserves by direct agency through a *miracle*. God preserves life by *providing* for everything He created. "The eyes of all wait upon thee; and thou givest them their meat in due season. Thou openest thine hand, and satisfiest the desire of every living thing" (Psalm 145:15-16).

In Colossians 1:16 Paul said that Jesus Christ created all things in heaven and earth, and in verse 17 he said that by Him all things *consist*, literally "are held together." Acts 14:17 and Matthew 5:44-45 both reveal that God sustains even the unbelieving, unregenerate world by providing food, sunshine, and rainfall.

Theories Opposing God's Preservation

There are some who oppose this fact of preservation. Those who hold to the *self-sustained universe theory* say that God made the universe, and now He is letting it run by itself. They compare it to a man who made a clock, wound it, and then let it run by itself. The only problem with that theory, according to the second law of thermodynamics, is that the universe is slowly running down. This law of physics teaches the degradation of energy; that energy is gradually being lost every moment of time. It is not replacing itself or maintaining itself, but it is actually being lost; therefore, the universe is slowly running down.

The laws of nature do not operate by themselves. They are controlled and sustained by God. The Apostle Paul said in Colossians 1:17, "All things are held together" by Jesus Christ. This is confirmed in Hebrews 1:3 which says that all things are upheld by the word of His power; consequently, God is continuously holding things together and preserving them.

Another erroneous view is the *continuous creation view*, which contends that the world is continuously undergoing a series of new creations; that objects have no separate existence, but that all things are being recreated at each moment of time. The hand is not the same hand that it was a moment ago. The same would be said of a tree, a bird, or a cloud. Of course, that is contrary to Scripture, because Genesis 2:1-3 says that God ceased His creative activity. He continues to work in the sense of preservation, but He ceased His creative activity. According to Hebrews 4:3, God rested after His creative work, that is, He ceased to work. The theory of continuous creation confuses creation with providence, which, according to Nehemiah, are not the same. He spoke of the creative work of God, then he said that God preserved what He created (Nehemiah 9:6).

The theory of continuous creation also denies the secondary cause. Genesis 1 says that God put within the seed of all living things the ability to reproduce. This is not continuous creation; it is procreation. It is the procreative life and power that God has placed within all living things. Continuous creation, moreover, is contrary to logic and experience. For example, if a person fails to brush his teeth, they would decay. Does God recreate less perfect teeth each moment of time? This would be the case, according to this theory; but the Bible teaches preservation.

Providence—Government

Another aspect of providence is *government*, which is the rule of God over the universe. As sovereign King, He rules, controls, and directs all nature, men, and events toward their predestinated purpose. This has already been dealt with in much detail. God works all things "after the counsel of his own will" (Ephesians 1:11). His government is universal (Psalm 103:19). The Scriptures show that God controls the greatest events of history and the most insignificant events, from the rise and fall of nations to the fall of a sparrow. God controls the nations and sets up over them "whomsoever he will" (Psalm 75:5-7; Daniel 4). Both men and animals look to God to give them their meat in due season. "Thou openest thine hand, they are filled with good. Thou hidest thy face, they are troubled: thou takest away their breath, they die, and return to their dust. Thou sendest forth thy spirit, and they are created: and thou renewest the face of the earth" (Psalm 104:27-30).

There is an opposing *theory of partial providence*, which supposes that God is not concerned with insignificant events. Many Christians believe that He is not really concerned with the personal details of their lives and the decisions they have to make. They believe His concern is with the rise and fall of nations, earthquakes, floods, famines, and wars. They do not believe that He is concerned about the automobile accident, the broken leg, the killing of a sparrow, or whether or not they have sufficient income on their present job, and so on. But who can say what is trivial to God? According to Matthew 10:29 Jesus said Himself that He is concerned with the fall of a sparrow. Job 38-41 shows that God's providential control is so all-inclusive that it embraces such events as the roaming of the wild goat in the mountains and the strength of the waves of the sea.

The theory of partial providence is contrary to the Word of God, as shown in Esther 6-7 where the small matter of a king's insomnia saved the nation of Israel from destruction. Because the king could not sleep, he called for the records and the books of the law to be read to him, which resulted in the preservation of the nation of Israel from annihilation. Also, in I Kings 22, the random shot of an unknown archer slew Ahab and thus fulfilled the prediction that Ahab would die in battle.

It would be logical to say that unless God controls the smallest event of history, He could not control the greatest event, because all events are related in some way. Every cause results in an effect. A flood begins with one drop of rain. The shooting of one bullet started World War I. In conclusion it is evident that the partial providence theory is not in line with the Word of God.

Providence—Concurrence

The third aspect of providence is *concurrence*. The verb "concur" means to agree, cooperate, or work together. In theology concurrence is the providential work of God by which He sustains and directs the free actions of men to accomplish His own wise purposes. Man could not live, could not will to do something, could not make a choice, and could not act apart from God sustaining him in those things. Man makes his choice, but the control and the outcome are in the hands of God. God sustains man in his free choices, but that does not mean that God is responsible for those choices.

Providential Control

This study has been dealing with the execution of God's plan with respect to creation and providence, which leads to the consideration of God's *providential control*.

Remember that God's providence must include man's free choices and actions, or His control of history and the fulfillment of His great eternal plan would be impossible. God's providential control has four aspects: *preventive control, permissive control, directive control,* and *determinative control.*

Preventive Control

By His *preventive control* God prevents a certain action from taking place. This may be exercised by God through the laws and customs of man, by speaking to a man through his conscience, through parental control, by moral teaching, and through religious influences. Sometimes God intervenes directly by warning someone in a dream. An example of this control is seen in Genesis 20, where Abraham, fearing for his life, said of Sarah his wife, "She is my sister: and Abimelech king of Gerar sent and took Sarah. But God came to Abimelech in a dream by night, and said to him, Behold, thou art but a dead man, for the woman which thou hast taken; for she is a man's wife. But Abimelech had not come near her: and he said, Lord, wilt thou slay also a righteous nation? Said he not unto me, She is my sister? and she, even she herself said, He is my brother: in the integrity of my heart and innocency of my hands have I done this. And God said unto him in a dream, Yea, I know that thou didst this in the integrity of thy heart; for I also withheld thee from sinning against me: therefore suffered I thee not to touch her" (verses 2-6). Here is seen God's preventive control in a situation in which King Abimelech was not allowed to touch Sarah, Abraham's wife and half-sister.

Permissive Control

A second aspect is God's *permissive control* by which He permits men to work out their own desires (Acts 14:16; Psalm 81:10-14; John 19:8-11). In John 19, when Jesus was not answering his questions, Pilate said, "Knowest thou not that I have power to crucify thee, and have power to release thee? Jesus answered, Thou couldest have no power at all against me, except it were given thee from above." This shows that God permitted Pilate to act according to his desire, but God was controlling and directing the events to accomplish His own purposes.

Directive Control

Thirdly, there is *directive control*. God directs the free actions of wicked men to the end that He wants to accomplish. God's directive control is seen in Acts 2:23 and 4:27-28. The crucifixion of Christ was not just an event that took place by accident, but God exercised His directive control to ensure that it would come to pass. Through the murder of His own Son at the hands of the Jews, God provided an atonement for sin. God does not simply wait to see what will result from man's sin, and then direct that toward His purpose; but He actively fulfills His eternal purpose in what men do. Pharaoh did as he pleased in afflicting Israel, but God hardened his heart so that he would do what he did (Exodus 4:21; 7:13; Romans 9:17-18). Pharaoh made his own free choices; but God accomplished His eternal purpose, and He received glory through it all (Romans 9:17).

Determinative Control

In *determinative control*, God determines or limits men and the devil in their actions. Job 1 and 2 show that God permitted Satan to touch Job's body and his property, but God determined the limits. He did not permit Satan to kill Job. The Christian may also be comforted in knowing that God determines the extent of trials that befall him. In I Corinthians 10:13 Paul said, "There hath no temptation taken you but such as is common to man: but God is faithful, who will not suffer [allow] you to be tempted above that ye are able; but will with the temptation also make a way of escape, that ye may be able to bear it." The trial is not one that might befall an angel, but it is common to man.

Chapter Two

Revelation and Inspiration
The Doctrine of Revelation

Man's quest for God is evident in philosophy, science, and the many religions. But the religion of the Bible is not one of discovery, it is a revelation or self-disclosure of God to man. Only the Judeo-Christian religion is a result of revelation, where God Himself revealed Himself. This is stressed throughout the Word of God. For example, in Psalm 147:19-20 the psalmist said that God revealed Himself only to Israel. "He sheweth his word unto Jacob, his statutes and his judgments unto Israel. He hath not dealt so with any nation: and as for his judgments, they have not known them." In other words, Judaism was based upon revelation and not upon discovery.

This truth is also seen in Christianity. "But as it is written, Eye hath not seen, nor ear heard, neither have entered into the heart of man, the things which God hath prepared for them that love Him. But God hath revealed them unto us by his Spirit" (I Corinthians 2:9-10). In John 16:7, just before Jesus' ascension, He promised to send the Holy Spirit, and that the Spirit would call all things to the disciples' remembrance (John 14:26). In John 16:13 Jesus said that the Holy

Spirit would show them things to come. It was always by revelation. In II Timothy 3:16 Paul said that all Scripture is given by inspiration of God—it is not discovery—it came by revelation from God.

Preservation of the Revelation

In order for the revelation to be transmitted, it had to be *preserved*. Of the thousands of religious books that have been written over the centuries, many, if not most, have been destroyed; yet the Bible remains. There have been attempts down through history to destroy the Word of God, but God has always watched over it. In spite of the fact that Israel as a nation has been scattered and the New Testament church was also scattered, the Old and New Testaments have been preserved.

In Deuteronomy 9, after Moses came down from the mountain where he had received the revelation of God engraved on tables of stone, he saw that the people had rebelled against God and had made a golden calf; therefore, he cast the stones down in his anger and destroyed them. Then, after Moses had dealt with the rebellious people, he said, "The Lord said unto me, Hew thee two tables of stone like unto the first, and come up unto me into the mount, . . . And I will write on the tables the words that were in the first tables" (Deuteronomy 10:1-2). God simply gave the revelation twice.

That was not the only occasion where God repeated the revelation in order to preserve it, nor is it known how many times He may have done this when earlier editions of the Scriptures were destroyed. It occurred again in the experience of the prophet Jeremiah, chapter 36:20-28. When King Jehoiakim heard the prophecy that Jeremiah had given against him and Israel, he was so full of wrath, he cut the scroll containing the prophecy into shreds and threw it in the fire. Notice this interesting statement in verse 27: "Then the word of the Lord came to Jeremiah, after that the king had burned the roll, and the words which Baruch wrote at the mouth of Jeremiah, saying, Take thee again another roll, and write in it all the former words." This is very significant! Jeremiah was to rewrite "all of the former words" that were in the first scroll which Jehoiakim had burned.

God has supernatural ways to preserve His revelation. When the Dead Sea scrolls were discovered at Qumran several years ago, Christendom realized that God had preserved many copies of the Old Testament Scriptures, as well as some other writings. The Romans had tried to destroy the Scriptures, but this Qumran community in Palestine preserved the Scriptures by putting them in earthenware jars, sealing them, and hiding them in the caves near the Dead Sea. The principle of preservation of the revelation is contained in Isaiah 40:8. "The grass withereth, the flower fadeth: but the word of our God shall stand for ever."

Methods of Revelation

As to the *methods* of revelation, God used a variety of ways to reveal what He wanted man to know. Sometimes it was by *direct voice* from heaven. "And the Lord spake unto Moses face to face" (Exodus 33:11). Sometimes the revelation was *written* on "tables of stone, written with the finger of

35

God" (Exodus 31:18). There is also a general revelation of the existence, power, deity, and glory of God in the *created order* itself. "The heavens declare the glory of God, and the firmament sheweth his handiwork." Another form of revelation is found in Numbers 12:1-8, and that is through *dream* and *vision* to the prophets. In Hebrews 1:1 Paul said that God "in divers manners spake in time past unto the fathers by the prophets."

The Doctrine of Inspiration

Supernatural revelation would be meaningless, or at least useless, apart from an anointed interpreter of the revelation. For example, to an uninformed observer who saw the parting of the Red Sea by a great wind, allowing Israel to cross, it would only mean that a wind blew the water back overnight. But the presence of a Moses to interpret that event as a supernatural act of God makes that incident a divine event—a revelation of God's purpose.

God unveiled Himself and His truth through revelation, but He needed a reliable witness to record the revelation. This receiving of divine truth is called *inspiration*. The doctrine of Scripture involves both revelation and inspiration. It is Scripture because it is revealed by God, and it was recorded because men were inspired by the Spirit of God to do so.

Inspiration in Relation to Scripture

What is inspiration in regard to Scripture? God could inspire a person to speak something (a prophet, an apostle, or a Spirit-filled Christian), and it would not be recorded as Scripture. Inspiration is that divine influence by the Holy Spirit upon the writers of Scripture by which their writings were made verbally infallible. By revelation God unveiled Himself in nature, through the Word, and through His acts, making known to man His will and His purpose. The record of this revelation, which was made under the guidance of the Holy Spirit, is the result of inspiration. Revelation involves God giving truth to man. *Inspiration* involves man's *accurate reception* and *recording of this* truth.

Illumination is the ministry of the Holy Spirit in the mind and heart of the believer by which he is enabled to understand the inspired revelation. A man may be illumined in his mind, and yet not be inspired of the Spirit to write something down or to say, "This is Scripture" or "Thus saith the Lord." This subject is also dealt with on pages 44-45.

Revelation and Inspiration: Oral Utterances

Revelation and inspiration are not to be limited to the writing of Scripture. The terms apply also to the *oral utterances* of the prophets and apostles, as well as to the utterances in the body of Christ through the operation of the gifts of the Spirit (I Corinthinans 12-14). This is not to say that tongues with interpretation or the gift of prophecy operating in a charismatic church service are to be compared with the infallibly inspired Holy Scriptures, but that both are given by the same Spirit, and that revelation and inspiration do occur today. There are regulations concerning the operation of the gift of tongues with interpretation and the gift of prophecy in the church. According to I Corinthians 14:29, if a prophet speaks, then the other prophets are to judge the prophecy; however, such tests are not given for the Holy Scriptures.

Inspiration—God-breathed

It is interesting that the term "inspiration" does not actually occur in the Scriptures, although it is popularly used by Christians and in theology. Job 32:8 says, "The inspiration of the Almighty giveth them [men] understanding." Actually, the term used there in the Hebrew is "neshema," which means breath; therefore, it should be translated, as it is in later versions, "The breath of the Almighty giveth them understanding." The term implies inspiration, which is the reason it was translated that way in the King James and Latin Vulgate Versions.

The term "inspiration" also occurs in II Timothy 3:16 in some English translations, but not in the original Greek. The Greek term "theopneustos," which is translated "inspiration," literally means just the opposite—"expiration," "to breathe out"—not "to breathe in." This study will continue to use the term "inspiration" since it has become popularized, but with the understanding of what the Scriptures mean when it is used.

Inspiration means to put thought and feeling and life and power into something. One might say, for example, "The leader's courage inspired the hearts of his men" or "This book inspired me when I read it." Paul said nothing about God breathing something *into* the writers of Scripture, but that He breathed *out* something—namely, His holy Word.

The term clearly identifies the Scriptures with God's own mouth, His own Word. The "breath of God" created (Psalm 33:6; Hebrews 11:3) and produced Holy Scripture. "All scripture is given by inspiration of God, and is profitable for doctrine, for reproof, for correction, for instruction in righteousness" (II Timothy 3:16). The term used in the Bible is actually much stronger and has a deeper meaning than the English word "inspiration." Good religious music or poetry may inspire; but Paul's emphasis was not that the writers were inspired, but that the Scriptures are the very words of God. They are divine; they are infallible.

The Bible says in Hebrews 1:1 that God spoke unto the fathers by the prophets, and then they uttered or wrote what He gave them. God did not endow men with inspiration, and then sanctify what they wrote; but He moved on them to write what He breathed out—the divine, infallible Word.

In Matthew 16 Jesus told the disciples of His soon death and resurrection; but Peter "began to rebuke him, saying, Be it far from thee, Lord: this shall not be unto thee." Then Jesus said, "Get thee behind me, Satan." Peter was inspired there, in a sense, but was inspired by the spirit of Satan to say what he did. Later in his ministry when Peter wrote Scripture, God breathed out His Word to him, so his writings were infallible. It should be obvious that the prophets or writers of Scripture were not always speaking on behalf of God in their daily conversation; but when they prophesied, and when they wrote Scripture, God breathed out His Word to them, and it was "Thus saith the Lord."

The Writers' View of Their Writings

Did the prophets, the apostles, and the writers of Scripture believe they were inspired by God? Moses and the prophets in the Old Testament repeatedly *claimed* they were inspired by God, and that God had revealed His Word to them. They use the phrase, "Thus saith the Lord," hundreds of times. The visions given to Isaiah and to Amos were revelations from God. They spoke with the conviction that the Spirit of the Lord was speaking through them. The Bible clearly shows that the prophets and the writers were *certain* that God had spoken to them and that they were relating His words to Israel.

What was the attitude of the New Testament writers and apostles toward what they wrote and what they spoke? Did they consider themselves inspired by God in the same sense as the prophets of the Old Testament? The answers to these questions are significant because they become the basis of any study of the New Testament.

It is apparent that the apostles considered themselves to be recipients of divine revelation and that they were *spokesmen* for God. They were even willing to die for what they believed, as all of them did, except the Apostle John. The Apostle Paul believed his writings were inspired because his letters are filled with claims of revelation, inspiration, and divine authority. For example, in Galatians 1 he claimed direct revelation for his message, and boldly pronounced a curse on anyone who preached anything different from what was revealed to him.

In Paul's teaching on the gifts of the Holy Spirit and on matters of conduct within the church, he told the Corinthians that those who were spiritual would recognize that he spoke directly from the Lord, and that those who did not recognize that fact were spiritually ignorant (I Corinthians 14:37-38). Paul commanded the Thessalonians to exclude from their fellowship those who would not obey the instructions which he had taught them. He claimed in Ephesians 3:1-5 that his revelation was equal to that given by the prophets. In II Corinthians 13:10 he warned that he spoke for Christ and thus had authority to discipline those who did not obey his teachings.

"For the scripture saith, Thou shalt not muzzle the ox that treadeth out the corn. And, The labourer is worthy of his reward" (I Timothy 5:18). In this verse Paul was quoting from Old and New Testament writings (Deuteronomy 25:4; Luke 10:7), and he referred to both of them as Scripture. In II Peter 3:16 the apostle spoke of the depth of Paul's writings, which the unlearned and unstable twist, "as they do also the other scriptures, unto their own destruction." Apparently Peter regarded Paul's epistles as Scripture.

The Nature of Inspiration

The nature of inspiration is a very important aspect of this study. Inspiration is the supernatural work of God in a man, involving both divine and human elements, which produced an infallible record of the divine revelation.

Theories Regarding Inspiration

There are many erroneous views which deal with the divine-human relationship in inspiration. The *intuition theory*, held by liberals, supposes that God is merely an influence upon man, and that He gives no direct revelation or inspiration to man. Because man is a spiritual being created in the image of God, he is by nature religious and moral; therefore, according to this theory, he intuitively knows moral and ethical principles and can discover truth for himself. Furthermore, they say that all men are inspired, such as Plato, Shakespeare, Gandhi, and Isaiah; but some are inspired to a higher degree. For example, the Hebrews had a genius for religion as the Greeks had for philosophy, and as the Western world has for technology. Hence, they contend that believers are to study the Scriptures, not to find an infallible revelation, but to help them understand moral, ethical, and spiritual principles, even though some of these may be outdated.

In answer to this erroneous teaching, the natural man cannot even understand the things of the Spirit of God, "for they are foolishness unto him: neither can he know them, because they are spiritually discerned" (I Corinthians 2:14). The Scriptures themselves lay to rest any notion that all men are inspired to some degree, because the natural man cannot even understand spiritual matters. He must be born again and have his mind transformed in order to understand biblical truth. According to Exodus 3, Israel's religion came by revelation. She had no inclination toward spiritual matters; nor did she have a genius for religion, as the Greeks had for philosophy. In Deuteronomy 9:4-7 God told the Jews that He did not choose them because they were more religious or more righteous than any other nation. In fact, He said they were a stubborn and stiff-necked people. He chose them solely because of the promise He had made to their fathers, Abraham, Isaac, and Jacob. The intuition theory is disproved by the Scriptures, which show that man can receive spiritual truth through revelation alone.

The *dictation theory* is held by many conservatives, who believe man is a pen, as it were, in the hand of God. Man is only a secretary, and the writers of Scripture recorded what God dictated to them. The writer's own mind, his thoughts, his ideas, and his beliefs were completely suppressed when he wrote Scripture, and God's revelation alone was recorded. They contend that the writer recorded word for word what he saw, heard, or was inspired to write, and was merely the passive agent to whom God dictated His Word.

In reply, there is some Scriptural basis for this view, but it is too limited. The Bible shows that on occasion God spoke, and, in effect, dictated the message that He wanted written or spoken. This may be seen in Revelation 1:10-11 where Jesus said to John, "What thou seest, write in a book." In Exodus 4:12 God said to Moses, "I will be with thy mouth, and teach thee what thou shalt say." Moses was told to go and speak God's words to Egypt and to Israel. In Numbers 22:38 the apostate prophet Balaam admitted that he could only speak the words that God put in his mouth. Although he tried to curse Israel, he said he had to bless because God had put only those words in his mouth. Many times God Himself spoke in the first person. In Isaiah 1:2 God said, "I have nourished and brought up children." He used the first

43

person pronoun because He spoke directly through Isaiah who, in this case, acted as His secretary.

However, the dictation theory is seen to be inadequate for several reasons. It is apparent to any Bible reader that the style of writing differs from book to book and from author to author, reflecting the personality of the writer. For example, compare the writings of Amos, the farmer and herdsman, with those of Isaiah, the prophet. Note the contrast between the writings of Peter, the fisherman, and those of Paul, the theologian. Sometimes the writers reported different details of the same event. One might have a purpose in reporting things he saw, so he included different details. In relating the same record of healing, for example, Matthew told of two blind men in Matthew 20; but Luke only mentioned one of them in Luke 18. There is no contradiction, but verbally there is a difference in the reporting of details. If one were reporting something he saw, he might think it important to include certain details, although someone else might relate other details.

The *illumination theory* is the liberal neo-orthodox view. According to this theory, God illumined the minds and thoughts of the writers to perceive moral and spiritual truth; but He did not inspire the very words of the Bible. The Holy Spirit illumines every believer, they say; but the Scripture writers were illumined to a higher degree. This view also teaches that the Bible is not actually the Word of God, but that it contains the spiritually enlightened viewpoints of its writers, along with many errors and contradictions. Of course, there are no errors or contradictions in God's Word.

In reply to all of this, God does illumine the believer's mind in order to give him an understanding of the truth that has already been revealed in His Word; but it does not give him the revelation of truth; it does not give him Scripture. The Scripture writers claim direct revelation and inspiration, but there is a difference between that and the illumination of every believer's mind. The Bible shows the difference between illumination and inspiration.

II Peter 1:20-21 is an example of inspiration. "Knowing this first, that no prophecy of the scripture is of any private interpretation. For the prophecy came not in old time by the will of man: but holy men of God spake as they were moved by the Holy Spirit."

An example of the illumination of the believer's mind is seen in Titus 2:11-12. "For the grace of God that bringeth salvation hath appeared to all men, Teaching us that, denying ungodliness and worldly lusts, we should live soberly, righteously, and godly, in this present world." Again, in I Corinthians 12:3 Paul said, "No man can say that Jesus is the Lord, but by the Holy Spirit". This does not mean he cannot say those words, but a saving confession can only come by the Holy Spirit when the truth of the gospel has been illumined to him by the Holy Spirit.

The Biblical View of Inspiration

The biblical view of inspiration is called the *Dynamic View*. The Scriptures are the result of a divine-human relationship, as set forth in Hebrews 1:1. "God, who at sundry times and in divers manners spake in time past unto the fathers by the prophets." God did the speaking, but He did it through the prophets or through His instruments. Inspiration is a supernatural work of God in man, involving both divine and human elements, which produced an infallible record of the divine revelation.

The Dynamic View holds all the elements together. God did the speaking, but He did it through His chosen vessels and their personalities. Their individualism is as clearly seen as their inspiration. The Holy Spirit moved on the writers in a dynamic way in harmony with their personalities but not completely suppressing them. God created men as it pleased Him, each man having traits of his own; and through these vessels He spoke His Word, using their lips, their minds, their gifts, their temperaments, and their personalities. Then, He breathed out to them His infallible Word. Another example is Nehemiah 9:30. "Yet many years didst thou forbear them, and testifiedst against them by thy Spirit in thy prophets." Nehemiah was saying that God spoke out against Israel in judgment by His Spirit in the prophets.

In conclusion to this view it should be noted that the inspired Word, the Bible, can be compared to the incarnate Word, Jesus. In the incarnation of Christ the divine and human elements are blended; in the inspiration and the writing of Scripture the divine and human elements also come together into one.

The Extent of Inspiration

In speaking of the extent of inspiration, this does not refer to how much of the Bible is inspired, because there are no degrees of inspiration. It is all inspired! The genealogy of chapter one of Matthew is as inspired as the account of Jesus' birth in chapter two. Chapter one shows Him to be a son of Abraham coming through the line of David; in chapter two, the birth narrative, He is seen to be the Son of God.

Some believe that only the *thoughts* were *inspired*, and that God left the writers of Scripture completely free to choose their own words, their own ideas, and their own expressions. This view is incorrect because it is unrealistic. God reveals His thoughts to man through the media of words, just as man does in communicating with others. If God wished to convey His will and His Word to man in such a way that it could not be twisted and misinterpreted, He would have to inspire the very words. If He merely inspires thoughts, the writers would have to choose what they would say.

The Scriptural view is the *plenary verbal inspiration view*. The term "plenary" means full, complete, entire, or absolute. This means that the entire Scriptures are inspired, not just a part; all Scripture is God-breathed (II Timothy 3:16). "Verbal" means that which is expressed in words; therefore, verbal inspiration means that God inspired the very words of the Bible and not merely the thoughts. Thus, plenary verbal inspiration means that the Scriptures in their entirety are the words of God; therefore, they are infallible and inerrant in the original autographs or manuscripts.

God said to Jeremiah, "Go to all that I shall send thee, and whatsoever I command thee thou shalt speak. . . . I have put my words in thy mouth" (Jeremiah 1:7-9). He said the same thing to Moses in Exodus 4:10-12, "Now therefore go, and I will be with thy mouth, and teach thee what thou shalt say." In Exodus 34:27-28 God told Moses to write the Ten Commandments. In Revelation 1:11 Jesus said to John, "What thou seest, write in a book." God told Ezekiel, "Speak my words" to the people (Ezekiel 2-3). Isaiah 2:1 and Amos 1:1 both speak of the words which the prophets saw. In II Samuel 23:1-2 David claimed to have been anointed and inspired with the very words of God. He said, "The Spirit of the Lord spake by me, and his word was in my tongue."

Critics deny the plenary verbal inspiration view by saying that human agents wrote the Scriptures. Their contention is that all men are fallible; men wrote the Bible; so the Bible is fallible and is not inerrant in all of its words.

In reply, one must distinguish between the prophet and his prophecy, between the writer and his writings. When the Bible speaks concerning inspiration, the emphasis is on the Scriptures themselves, on the writings and not on the writer. For instance, II Timothy 3:16 says that all Scripture is God-breathed, but it does not say a thing about the writer. Paul truly was inspired, but the thrust is upon the Scripture and not the author. "Prophecy came not in old time by the will of man" (II Peter 1:20-21). The emphasis is on prophecy. While the writers were *sometimes* inspired, their writings were *always* inspired. Yes, they were fallible men who could (and did) make mistakes; but their writings were God-breathed and, therefore, infallible. For example, when Peter denied the Lord, he certainly was not inspired of God; but he was inspired when he wrote his epistles.

In summary, the Bible shows that all Scripture is God-breathed; consequently, when a man was writing Scripture, he was motivated and inspired by the Lord and recorded what God said to write.

Chapter Three

The Doctrine of God

When the term *Doctrine of God* is used in theology, it does not suggest that God is a "doctrine." The term simply means the *teaching* about God. The purpose here will be to study the various concepts of God, the being or existence of God, the nature of God, and all of His wonderful attributes. The Scriptures *assume* the existence of God, declaring simply, "In the beginning God" (Genesis 1:1). This is also seen in John 1:1-3. There is no attempt to argue anyone into the acceptance of the fact that God exists. The psalmist asserted that one who denies God's existence is a fool (Psalm 14:1). Compare that with I Corinthians 1.

God has revealed Himself to man in several ways: through creation; through man's conscience; through God's miraculous and providential works; through the inspired Scripture; through direct revelation of Himself to man, such as the way He revealed Himself to Adam in the garden, or to Paul on the road to Damascus; and He has revealed Himself perfectly through the incarnation of His Son, Jesus Christ.

51

According to Romans 1:18-32, however, sinful man has perverted the true revelation which God gave of Himself with the result that man's ideas now range all the way from outright denial of God's existence, atheism, to the worship of the creation instead of the Creator, which is idolatry. This is seen in Romans 1:22-25, "Professing themselves to be wise, they became fools, And changed the glory of the uncorruptible God into an image made like to corruptible man [such as statues], and to birds, and fourfooted beasts, and creeping things. Wherefore God also gave them up to uncleanness through the lusts of their own hearts, to dishonour their own bodies between themselves: Who changed the truth of God into a lie, and worshipped and served the creature more than the Creator."

Various Concepts of God

Men have held various concepts of God, many either perverting the true revelation of God or denying His existence.

Agnosticism is a common form of skepticism with roots in heathen philosophy, which maintains that it is impossible for the human mind to know ultimate reality or to prove the existence of God. Unlike the atheist, who denies outright the existence of God as well as heaven and immortality, the agnostic contends that God's existence cannot be proven; therefore, he suspends all judgment about the question, admitting that he just does not know.

Skepticism is the critical attitude which questions the validity of all claims to any kind of knowledge. The skeptic holds that absolutely no certain knowledge exists about anything because of the incompleteness of evidence, fallacies, man's reasoning, illusions, the deceptions of the senses, and so on. Religious skeptics argue that such concepts as God, immortality, resurrection, soul, spirit, hell, and heaven cannot be demonstrated and proven as factual; consequently, they are to be rejected. Skepticism is to be distinguished from agnosticism in that the agnostic leaves open the possibility of knowledge, at least in theory, while the skeptic denies any such possibility. The agnostic says, "I don't know." The skeptic says, "I cannot know." Skepticism is found in varying degrees: 1) the denial that any absolute knowledge is possible; 2) the denial of the validity of any knowledge that is not derived from sense experience or subject to scientific proof; 3) the denial of any spiritual knowledge concerning God, soul, and spirit.

Atheism is the denial of the existence of God as contrasted to *Theism* which is the belief in God. Frequently, atheism refers to practical atheism or a practical rejection of God instead of the outright denial of His existence. The practical atheist is that individual who wishes to live as if there were no God, so that he can do as he pleases without fear of judgment from some higher power. Therefore, he merely ignores the existence of God. At least in certain areas of his life, a consideration of God does not enter into his plans, thoughts, or decisions. The atheist is actually a materialist, who denies the spiritual dimension and looks upon God and religion as outmoded superstition. He believes that science, reason, and technology can explain everything, including the origin of man and the universe.

Some well known atheists were Karl Marx, the father of atheistic communism, and Friedrich Nietzsche, who first asserted that God is dead. Nietzsche's concept inspired the ridiculous "death of God" theologies of the 1960s which, because they were self-destructive, have themselves died. All arguments of atheism are actually self-defeating. The very fact that man can perceive the idea of God implies that he is aware of the existence of God; that is, the atheist has to already be aware of God to be able to deny His existence. Moreover, for a mere creature to say that there is no God means that the man himself believes that he is a god. Why? Because he would have to be God, omniscient and omnipresent, everywhere in the universe at once, in order to assume that he knows there is no God. Since the existence of God confronts man everywhere, both in the natural realm and in His Word, then the burden of proof rests upon the atheist to prove God's non-existence—and this he finds impossible to do.

Theism is the belief in one personal God who is the Creator and Lord of the universe. The term arose in the seventeenth century to contradict the term "atheism." *Monotheism* is closely connected with Theism, and is the belief in one God alone and the worship of this one God. Deuteronomy 6:4 says, "Hear, O Israel: The Lord our God is one Lord." In Isaiah 45:5-6 God said, "I am the Lord, and there is none else." He is the Creator of the heavens and earth, and He has revealed Himself in nature and in the Scriptures. Monotheism is the belief that there is one living God who is self-existent, eternal, infinite, and perfect.

Henotheism is the belief in or worship of one supreme god among the many gods. For instance, the ancients in the Near East believed that there was a god for each nation, and that their own god was considered to be supreme. Examples of these are Chemosh of Moab, Dagon of Philistia, and Marduk of Babylonia. Many of Israel's neighbors considered Yahweh, the God of Israel, to be the God of the Hebrews only. Henotheism is still current today in many countries. *Monolatry* is the worship of one god. The worshipers believe in the existence of many deities, but the god they worship may or may not be the supreme god.

Pantheism is the belief held by the earliest school of Greek philosophy that God and the material or physical universe are one. God is all things and all things are God. God is nature at work. God is not a personality, but a combination of all the laws, forces, causes and effects, as well as the physical matter of the universe. Pantheism obviously cannot explain the origin or the presence of evil in the universe nor the goal or purpose of the universe.

Polytheism is belief in and worship of many gods or deities. The personification and worship of the sun, the moon, the stars, the wind, animals, or other natural phenomena is a form of Polytheism known as *Naturalism*. The ancient nations of Babylonia, Assyria, Egypt, Greece, and Rome were all polytheistic, as well as the Aztec and Mayan Indians in more recent history. In this present age Shintoism of Japan and Hinduism of India hold to the worship of multiple deities.

Deism, which arose in England in the seventeenth century, is the result of an attempt to harmonize the Bible with scientific reason. Deists say that insight into this harmony would free man from his many so-called superstitious beliefs derived from the Bible. They believe that "God" or some "supreme being" exists totally apart from the universe which He created; that He created a well ordered universe, which He endowed with immutable laws, and which operates by itself without the need of divine intervention. The universe, they say, is like a giant clock which God made, wound up, and left to run by itself, governed only by predetermined physical or natural laws. Further, they contend that man by his own God-given reason is able to know both the existence of a supreme being and what his own moral and ethical duties are.

It is important to know what deists believe, because several are well known in American history, such as Benjamin Franklin, Thomas Jefferson, and Thomas Paine. The deists deny the inspiration of Scripture, miracles, and prophecy as being incompatible with God's unchangeable, immutable laws. They also argue against God's providential concern for man, saying that He is not concerned with healing man when he is sick or providing for his needs. In addition, they oppose the Scriptural doctrine of future rewards and punishments, as well as (in some instances) the denial of the future life itself. Deism never became a widespread religion in America because of its impersonal view of God and its fatalistic outlook on life.

Animism is the primitive concept that everything is inhabited by a spirit; that all natural objects and phenomena have souls or consciousness. This would include trees, animals, storms, rocks, etc.

Fetishism is the belief in or use of an object (fetish) which allegedly is inhabited by a spirit or has magical power. It is a form of idolatry because this object receives unquestioning respect, reverence, and devotion.

Idolatry is the personification of and reverence for a man-made object or image, or for a created object, such as the sun or moon. It is the paying of homage, which only God should receive, to some object or image. Isaiah 42:8 says, "I am the Lord: that is my name: and my glory will I not give to another, neither my praise to graven images." See also Deuteronomy 4:15-19; John 1:18; and Isaiah 44:9.

The Existence of God

Another aspect of the study of God from Scripture is the *Existence of God*. The knowledge of God basically comes from two sources. One is the revelation of God in nature or creation, which is called *general revelation*. "The heavens declare the glory of God; and the firmament sheweth His handiwork" (Psalm 19:1). Paul said in Romans 1 that man can know the power and existence of God by looking at creation. Of course, this does not give a saving knowledge, but it gives a revelation of the existence of God. God also reveals Himself in His Word. This is called *special revelation*.

Natural Theology

There are two views regarding the knowledge of God from nature or creation: the Natural Theology view and the General Revelation view. The *Natural Theology* view denies that God is revealing Himself through nature, but claims that man can deduce certain facts about God from creation; man can prove the existence of God and some aspects of His nature by his unaided reason. A proponent of this view was Thomas Aquinas, who lived in the thirteenth century A.D. Those who have studied any theology will recognize this as the Roman Catholic view. Aquinas taught that man's intellect cannot give him a saving knowledge of God, even though he can develop a theology about God. Certain truths come only by special revelation, such as the incarnation, the Cross, resurrection, and Jesus Christ. According to this view, sinful man can discover God by his reason as he beholds the creation; but it takes grace to find God savingly.

Natural Theology deals with God's existence; whereas, *Christian Theology* deals with the incarnation of God in Jesus Christ. Natural Theology says that man's reason is able to lead him to faith. He can reason from observing creation that there must be a Creator; that things just did not create themselves; but that there is no direct encounter between man and God through nature.

Aquinas actually had two arguments for the existence of God. The first one was based upon "First Cause," and is called *Cosmological Proof* (cosmos—world). Since there is a world; then, man can reason that there must be a God. Why?

Because nothing can be the cause of itself, or it would have existed before itself. Every effect has a cause, and there is a limit to how far back men can look to find the first cause. They cannot go back to infinity; they must begin somewhere—either in an uncaused cause or a first cause. Aquinas said this first cause is God.

His second argument, called *Teleological Proof* (telos—end or purpose), was based upon the design of the universe. The other argument was based upon *First Cause*, but here the emphasis is upon the *final purpose* of creation; that is, he believed that the great intricacies, the comprehensiveness, the design, and the orderliness of the universe argue for a designer. Nature did not arrange itself into this intricate and orderly design, but there must have been a supreme intelligence behind it all to produce such order. Nothing just happened by itself, but there must have been an intelligent will directing all things toward a purpose.

The argument that there is no general revelation must be rejected; but the argument for God's existence based upon first cause, and the argument for God's existence based upon the intricate design of the universe are valid arguments. However, the designer that Aquinas is trying to prove could have been one who was working from preexisting materials, which is not the Designer of Scripture.

General Revelation

One of the ways God reveals Himself is through *General Revelation*. Augustine taught that God reveals Himself through nature. His view of general revelation was called the Ontological (being) view. Augustine, who lived in 354-430 A.D., emphasized this view with respect to man's knowledge of God and general revelation. He said that man's conception of God's existence implies that God does exist; that is, a knowledge of God and the existence of God are related—there is a rapport between knowledge and being. Augustine said that man by his unaided reason could not even know or understand his own world unless God shows him. This general revelation is seen in Acts 14:15-17, also in John 1:6-9 where John said that Jesus Christ illumines or lights every man that comes into the world. In Romans 1:19 Paul said that God supplies whatever knowledge man has of God or the world.

Augustine held that there are two kinds of knowledge, sensual knowledge and spiritual knowledge. Sensual knowledge is knowledge acquired through the sense experiences; spiritual knowledge is self-consciousness and knowledge of God, or God-consciousness. He believed that man was created in God's image, and that he possesses a spiritual nature and a conscience; he is God-conscious. However, he is preoccupied with the sensual and not the spiritual. His eyes are turned outward on the things of this world, and he lacks both the desire and the ability to turn his eyes inward to spiritual truth; consequently, man needs revelation from God Himself.

Aquinas said that faith follows reason. Man can reason up to God; so he can have faith in the existence of God, but not a saving faith. Aquinas said that faith follows reason and completes it; but Augustine believed that reason always follows faith, that reason only operates properly within faith, and only by faith is man able to see and think aright. The reformers also held this view. Calvin, for example, said man can only know God to the extent He speaks to him, whether in nature or in His Word. Luther opposed the Roman Catholic view and taught that there is no natural theology. He said no one could reason up to God. God is giving Himself everywhere to be known. Man has a general knowledge about God because God is continually confronting him in nature, as well as in his conscience.

Another proponent of the Ontological view of general revelation was Anselm, 1033-1109 A.D. He said there is a relation between knowing and existence, or knowing and being. To know or believe God exists must mean that He does exist and is revealing Himself to man. The very fact, he said, that man can conceive of a supreme being implies that He exists. All men have in their minds the idea of an infinite being, while at the same time they recognize that they themselves are finite. They did not conceive this comparison by themselves, Anselm said, so there must be an infinite being greater than themselves who has revealed this truth to them.

Anselm said, "God is that, than which nothing greater can be thought." Since an infinite God is the greatest thing that man's mind can conceive, then God must exist. Of course, it could be said, "I can think of an island, which no more perfect island can be thought of, but that does not mean that it exists in reality." But Anselm would reply, "This proof can only be used to prove God's existence, because God is greater than an island, and only God is that, than which nothing greater can be thought of."

The *Anthropological Argument* of Christianity holds that nothing more clearly points to the existence of an intelligent Creator than man himself, who is able to comprehend and appreciate the creation of which he is a part. In other words, animal creation does not have the capacity to admire a beautiful sunset. They do not notice that the leaves are falling, nor do they appreciate their beautiful colors as they turn to reds and browns in the fall. The very fact that man is intelligent, rational, and spiritual, argues for a Creator who is all of this. Man knows he did not create himself, so whoever created him must be greater; he must be all that man is, and far, far more. Human personality cannot be explained by naturalistic evolution which asserts that life as man knows it developed from inanimate matter. Personality could not have arisen from impersonal matter; creation by a superior personality is the only explanation. "Know ye that the Lord he is God: it is he that hath made us, and not we ourselves" (Psalm 100:3). God is answering the naturalistic evolutionist right in that verse.

The *Moral Argument* says there is an inward compulsion within man's being, called "conscience," that demands that he do right. Man himself would not condemn himself, for he would always seek to justify his conduct. However, when he does wrong, and then admits to himself that he has done wrong, this is evidence that there must be a divine voice from without, which is making these moral demands. This feeling of guilt, this sense of duty, this sense of right and wrong which all have, must come from outside. According to Romans 2:15, it is the conscience bearing witness to the law of God written in man's heart. The conscience tells man to do right, but it is the Christian's responsibility to learn from

God's Word how to do right. Remember here that an ignored conscience will become seared and can no longer hear the voice of God.

The Purpose of General Revelation

In conclusion, what is the purpose of general revelation if it cannot save? 1) God reveals His glory through creation (Psalm 19:1). 2) Creation is a revelation of God's existence (Romans 1:19-20). 3) It renders man without excuse. Man sees the general revelation, but he chooses to pervert what he sees (Romans 1:20-26). The uncultured pagan, when he looks at creation, imagines idols; the cultured pagan looks at creation and imagines evolution.

Special Revelation

Evidence of God's existence is also seen in *special revelation*, such as the Scriptures, Christ's incarnation, and the witness of the Spirit in the heart of the believer. The Scriptures *assume* the existence of God. Nowhere does the Bible seek to argue anyone into faith in the existence of God or into any other kind of faith. The first verse of the first book of the Bible says, "In the beginning God . . ." (Genesis 1:1). That is all man is told, and that is all he needs to be told. God's existence is also assumed in John 1:1, "In the beginning was the Word, and the Word was with God, and the Word was God."

Another example in Scripture that assumes God's existence is Colossians 1:16-17. "For by him were all things created, that are in heaven, and that are in earth, visible and invisible, whether they be thrones, or dominions, or principalities, or powers: all things were created by him, and for him: And he is before all things, and by him all things consist." David said in Psalm 14:1, "The fool hath said in his heart, There is no God." A person who denies God's existence is intellectually and spiritually below the demons and the devil. James 2:19 says that the demons believe in God and tremble. Satan himself acknowledged God's existence in Genesis 3:1 when he said to Eve, "Hath God said?" The Scriptures never attempt to argue anyone into believing that God exists, for only a fool would deny His existence.

The *incarnation* of the Son of God is the supreme revelation and proof of the existence of God. The apostle said in John 1:14, "And the Word [Jesus] was made flesh, and dwelt among us, (and we beheld his glory, the glory as of the only begotten of the Father,) full of grace and truth." Verse 18 says, "No man hath seen God at any time; the only begotten Son, which is in the bosom of the Father, he hath declared him." Additional proof may be seen in John 17:5, where Jesus prays to the Father to restore to Him His glory which He had before the creation of the world.

A third evidence of special revelation is the *witness of the Holy Spirit* to God's reality and existence. According to Romans 8:16, "The Spirit itself beareth witness with our spirit, that we are the children of God." In this way His existence is assumed or proven in the believers. I John 4:13 shows that man has the witness within himself. "Hereby know we that we dwell in him, and he in us, because he hath given us of his Spirit." The witness of the Spirit is also made to the world, according to John 16:7-11, where Jesus said that when

64

the Holy Spirit is come, He will convict the world of sin, because men do not believe on Him.

God's Self-existence

Another aspect of God's existence is His *self-existence*. God not only exists, but He is also self-existent. He is not dependent upon anything outside Himself, but the source of His being is within Himself. God lives by His own life, not depending on anything to give Him life. In John 5:26 Jesus said, "For as the Father hath life in himself; so hath he given to the Son to have life in himself." God is the fountain of life. "For with thee is the fountain of life: in thy light shall we see light" (Psalm 36:9). God's nature is "to be." This is seen in His very name. When Moses asked God, "What is your name?" He said, in effect, call me the one who is—call me "I AM." "And God said unto Moses, I AM THAT I AM: and he said, Thus shalt thou say unto the children of Israel, I AM hath sent me unto you" (Exodus 3:14).

Although God is the ground of His own existence, this does not mean that He is self-caused or self-originated; for God is eternal—without beginning and without end. The Scriptures declare this very clearly. The significance of this is seen in the fact that this makes God sovereign. Since He is self-existent, He alone is free and independent to do what He chooses, and what He chooses is righteous. All of His decrees, His works, and His plan of salvation are wrought according to His own will and good pleasure. "In whom also we have obtained an inheritance, being predestinated according to the purpose of him who worketh all things after the counsel of his own will" (Ephesians 1:11).

God's self-existence also makes Him *self-sufficient*. He did not create because He needed anything outside of Himself, for God was complete and perfect within Himself as Father, Son, and Holy Spirit. He created the world as a "theater" for His glory. According to Isaiah 43, Israel was created for the glory of God. "The heavens declare the glory of God; and the firmament sheweth his handiwork" (Psalm 19:1). The Christian has been redeemed so that he might be "to the praise of the glory of his grace" for eternity (Ephesians 1:6). God's self-existence also means that He is the *source of life*; He has life in Himself. He created man, permitting him to partake of this life and have fellowship with Him, so that man might glorify God and enjoy Him forever.

God's Nature—His Personality

The study of God's nature includes His personality, God as Spirit, God's unity and His triunity. The Scriptures reveal God's *personality* or the evidence that God is a personal God. This is significant in view of the fact that most of the cults deny His personality, making Him "the absolute," "the source of all things," "the first cause," or a principle like "love." On the contrary, the Scriptures represent God as a *personal being*, not as a spiritual principle, or mere influence, or power, or immanent in nature as the Pantheists teach. God has the *attributes* of *personality*. He is a God who acts, a God who speaks, a God who thinks, a God who decrees and wills things to come to pass.

The God of the Bible is *self-conscious*. In Exodus 3:14 God's self-consciousness is seen in that He has the ability to say "I AM." This ability shows that one has the power to know himself and the world around him. It is the mark of personality. An animal, for example, lacks this capacity to think or say, "I am, I exist, and this is a world around me." God is also *self-determining*; and this self-determination is seen in many Scriptures, such as Isaiah 40:13-14 and Ephesians 1:9-11. In Daniel 4:35 the prophet said that God "doeth according to his will in the army of heaven, and among the inhabitants of the earth."

As previously pointed out, God has *self-life*. He is called the "living God" throughout Scripture, for example, Jeremiah 10:10 and I Timothy 3:15. The Scriptures speak of God as a living God, meaning that He is a God who speaks and acts, in contrast to the non-living, non-personal idols or gods that men have made. Life is a requisite for personality. God proves His life by His works and by His activity on behalf of His people.

God's Nature—Spirit

God is also Spirit. The Bible does not define God's essential nature except in this one phrase—He is *Spirit*. "God is Spirit: and they that worship him must worship him in spirit and in truth" (John 4:24). This means that God is a non-material, invisible, personal being who is not bound by the limitations of time or space. Spirit has no weight, size, or shape, and does not occupy space. A being which has no parts cannot be divided and needs no space. In contrast to man, God is pure Spirit.

Those passages of Scripture that speak of God as having eyes, heart, hands, and ears are called *anthropomorphic.* Man's vocabulary and understanding are limited to earthly concepts; so God, who is formless Spirit, has revealed Himself in terms which can be understood, as having eyes, ears, heart, and so forth. This does not mean that God is impersonal or that He is a mere figure of speech. God as "person" can feel love and compassion, although He has no heart. The Scriptures say that He has no ears, and yet He can hear; nothing is done that He does not see, though He has no eyes. "A spirit hath not flesh and bones," Jesus said in Luke 24:39. God is all-wise, all-knowing Spirit. He comprehends all things, but the only way finite creatures can comprehend this is by anthropomorphic analogies.

In Isaiah 31:3 God contrasts His nature as Spirit with that which He created, which is flesh. God, as Spirit, is present everywhere at the same moment; however, this does not mean that He cannot manifest Himself in any form at any one place if He chooses. On the contrary, although His Spirit is everywhere throughout the universe and heaven, the Scriptures declare that He sits upon His throne in the heavens and rules with Jesus Christ at His right hand. He sat upon His throne in Israel. He spoke to Moses "from off the mercy seat that was upon the ark" (Numbers 7:89). He seemed pleased, also, to take upon Himself the form of man which He created. "And God said, Let us make man in our image, after our likeness" (Genesis 1:26f.; see also Philippians 2:7).

God's Nature—His Unity

Another aspect of God's nature is His *unity*, which means that God is one. "Hear, O Israel: The Lord our God is one Lord" (Deuteronomy 6:4). This was in contrast to the other nations who had many gods. The full meaning of the oneness of God as stated in the Old Testament must be understood by the Christian in the light of the full revelation, if for no other reason than that Jesus Christ came calling Himself the Son of God. In fact, He said He was God. To say that God is "one" means that He is the only God (Isaiah 44:6-8). It means He is one essence or nature. He is Spirit—one divine Spirit (John 4:24).

To say that God is one does not mean that this one God cannot manifest Himself eternally in three manifestations as Father, Son, and Holy Spirit. In John 10:30 Jesus said, "I and my Father are one," and in John 17 He prayed to the Father. Thus, they are not the same personality, though they are the same God. To say that God is one means that there is a unity of nature, or essence, or being in God. The one God is one divine Spirit manifested eternally as Father, Son, and Holy Spirit. Modern-day Israel, along with Unitarians and others who deny the deity of Christ, stumble at this truth, confining themselves only to the Old Testament revelation in Deuteronomy 6:4, "Hear, O Israel: The Lord our God is one Lord." But His oneness is a oneness of essence or nature, that is, He is only one God. "I and my Father are one," Jesus said, "he that hath seen me hath seen the Father" (John 10:30; 14:9). Obviously, they are not the same personality, but the same being or nature—God. There is but one God essence, one divine Spirit. The Jews correctly interpreted the meaning of Christ's words when He said, "I and my Father are one," for they said He had claimed equality with God. He did say that He was one with the Father; but He did not say He was the Father, because He prayed to the Father, and He said that the Father sent Him into the world. If He were the one sent, He could not have been the sender. God's oneness means that He is one essence, one divine Spirit.

Religious significance should not be given to the number "one" as the Jews and others do who deny the deity of Christ. His oneness is *not* a *mathematical* oneness. It is not the number one, but a *qualitative* oneness. It is a personal oneness, a *unique oneness* that belongs only to God. There is one divine Spirit which is God. Monotheism and its emphasis in the Old Testament had its necessary purpose—to guard Israel against idolatry. The Israelites did not philosophize about the oneness of God or the nature of God, nor did they try to reason this out. They did not come to this truth by discovery, but God revealed Himself to them as the one God. Because Egypt and some other nations were polytheistic, worshiping many gods, His oneness of nature was in contrast to other religions of the day.

There are no other gods, but this does not mean that Christ is not God. Christ and the Father are one—one essence, one being, one nature, one divine Spirit, but different personalities. God is triune or has tri-personality. "Whosoever denies the Son," Jesus said, "has not the Father." God's unity means the divine nature is undivided, indivisible, and there is but one infinite and perfect divine Spirit.

God's Nature—His Triunity

The doctrine of the *triunity* of God logically follows the study of the unity or oneness of the Godhead. The Scriptures show that in the nature of the one God there are *three distinct personalities* revealed as Father, Son, and Holy Spirit. The doctrine of the triunity or the triune nature of God is a revelation from His Word and cannot be conceived by observing the created order or general revelation.

Some critics point out that the term "trinity" does not occur in Scripture, which is true; but that does not mean that the doctrine of the trinity or triunity of God is not from the Word of God. There are other words used in theology which are not found in the New Testament, yet they support valid principles. For example, the word "atonement" does not occur in the Greek New Testament. The term translated "atonement" in Romans 5:11 is the Greek word "reconciliation," yet that is the basic doctrine of the New Testament and also the church's message. Even though a term may not occur in Scripture, the principle, the teaching, or the idea may be there, as in the case of the triunity or trinity of God.

The tripersonality of God is *not tritheism*, that is, *three separate gods*. There are three eternal personalities—Father, Son and Holy Spirit—but only one divine essence called God. According to Scripture, the three personalities are equal and eternal. There are no earthly analogies to express adequately the truth of the triunity of God. While there have been many attempts to do this, none are adequate. Therefore, it is advisable to take the Scriptures for what they say. God is what He reveals Himself to be in His Word—not what men say He is, not what the Unitarians or the liberals say He is—He is one divine Spirit, eternally manifested as Father, Son, and Holy Spirit. It should be obvious that if God is not what He reveals

Himself to be in His Word, then He is yet unrevealed, and man does not know what He is like.

To find the truth of the triunity of God, the place to begin is where most would probably not look, and that is in the Old Testament. The triunity is not clearly revealed there, yet the Old Testament does lay the foundation for the full revelation which is found in the New Testament. The plurality of the Godhead is suggested in certain passages such as Genesis 1:26. "And God said, Let us make man in our image, after our likeness." Plural pronouns are used there both in the Hebrew and in the English translation. To whom is He speaking? Obviously, to the other personalities in the Godhead. Another suggestion of the plurality of the Godhead is in Genesis 19:24. "The Lord rained upon Sodom and upon Gomorrah brimstone and fire from the Lord out of heaven." The Lord on earth, who appeared as an angel, rained down fire from the Lord who was yet in heaven.

There is also an interesting statement in Isaiah 48:16, which is a prophetic passage speaking of the future Messiah. "Come ye near unto me, hear ye this; I have not spoken in secret from the beginning; from the time that it was, there am I: and now the Lord God, and his Spirit, hath sent me." Notice the triune suggestion. The "me" is the Messiah or the preincarnate Christ who is speaking. The "Lord God and His Spirit" sent the Messiah, Jesus Christ. Certainly this passage is more than a hint about the triune nature of the Godhead!

In the Old Testament the Messiah as God is distinguished from God the Father. This is seen in Isaiah 9:6, 48:16, Zechariah 12:10, 13:7, Psalm 45:6-7, Daniel 7:13-14, Psalm 2.

The Old Testament revelation—while it stresses monotheism and the oneness of God—very carefully lays the groundwork for the New Testament doctrine of the triunity of the Godhead. The Old Testament stressed the truth that God is one God (Deuteronomy 6:4); but this one God has a Son who is called God, and has a Spirit who is designated as the *Holy Spirit* and the *Spirit of God*.

The Godhead

stop

God is revealed as the Father (John 6:27), the Son (John 6:69), and the Spirit (Acts 5:3,4,9). These three as the one God are called in theology the *"Godhead."* There are many erroneous views about the Godhead. Some make God one in the sense that the Father became the Son, and He later became the Holy Spirit. He was the Father in the Old Testament, they say, the Son in the New Testament, and in the church age He is now manifest as the Holy Spirit. While God truly is one, it is not a mathematical oneness; it is qualitative, as was pointed out previously.

There are people who deny the deity of Christ or the personality of the Holy Spirit. They deny that God is three eternal personalities. It has already been stated that God is not what men may say that He is, but He is what He reveals Himself to be in the Scriptures. The Bible clearly shows God to be one divine essence, one divine Spirit, who manifests Himself from all eternity as Father, Son, and Holy Spirit. There was never a time when He was not Father, Son, and Holy Spirit, nor shall there ever be.

Both the unity and the distinctions in the Godhead are seen throughout the New Testament, and certainly they are suggested in the Old. The *distinction* between the divine personalities in the Godhead can be seen in such passages as John 3:16 and Galatians 4:4, where the Father sent the Son into the world. The Father, Son, and Spirit are distinguished in John 15:26 where Jesus said that after He had returned to heaven, He and the Father would send the Holy Spirit. The *unity* of the Godhead is seen in Ephesians 4:4-6. "There is one body, and one Spirit, even as ye are called in one hope of your calling; One Lord, one faith, one baptism, One God and Father of all, who is above all, and through all, and in you all." There the Spirit, the Lord Jesus, and God the Father are distinguished, but it says clearly that they are all one.

The Scriptures also show two truths regarding the revelation of the Godhead. Since God is one, there is no real distinction between having God with man, having Christ in man, or having the Holy Spirit indwelling man, because the three are one God. This fact can be seen in John 14:15-26. The Scriptures also differentiate between the three personalities. The Father is the source or the ground of all things (I Corinthians 15). The Son is the Creator and Redeemer (Colossians 1). The Holy Spirit is the agent of all life, both in the creation of the world and in the regeneration of the sinner.

God's Transcendent Attributes

God also reveals Himself in His attributes, which are the inner perfections of His nature. These fall into two categories. Some of God's attributes emphasize His transcendence or perfections which are not found in man, such as His eternalness, immutability, omnipresence, omniscience, and omnipotence. There are other attributes of God where some analogy can be found in regenerate man, such as His wisdom, love, holiness, and mercy.

God's Eternalness

The Bible states that God alone is eternal (Deuteronomy 33:27; I Timothy 1:17); He exists from all eternity (Psalm 90:2); He has neither beginning nor end (Revelation 1:8); and He has life without end (Revelation 4:10). Only God can claim this unique distinction. All else had a beginning, however ancient, and will have an end.

Eternalness is that perfection of God which expresses His complete transcendence with respect to time. Transcendence means "to be above and independent of," that is, to completely surpass man and everything created. Time has no effect on God; He created it. God cannot be too late or too early in His actions. He cannot grow any older; He was never young. These are "time" concepts and they do not apply to God. Even His name which He revealed to Moses expresses His eternalness. Moses asked, "What is your name?" God answered, "My name is," then He gave the Hebrew verb, "To Be." "I AM, the one who is." Men give names to their gods or their concept of deity, but God describes Himself as the source of life or existence. He is "I AM."

The Relationship Between Time and Eternity

It would be helpful for the believer to know something of the relationship between time and eternity, so that he could understand the eternalness of God. Only God is eternal. He gives eternal life, but man does not have eternity within him as God does. God's eternality is one of His attributes which shows that He is so unlike man. What is the relationship between time and eternity? Time is created; eternity is not. Eternity is not "simply" uncreated time, but it stands by itself. Time and the universe began together. One cannot exist without the other. Eternity is not "everlasting" time because time is a finite concept—a finite portion of infinite eternity. Time had a beginning and it will have an end.

The blessed hope of the believer is that he will partake of God's immortality (I Corinthians 15). John 3:16 says, "For God so loved the world, that he gave his only begotten Son, that whosoever believeth in him should not perish, but have everlasting life." He gives everlasting life to the one who believes. There will be no night in the eternal state—only *day*. "And the gates of it shall not be shut at all by day: for there shall be no night there" (Revelation 21:25).

Since God is eternal, He does not change (Malachi 3:6). Change implies finiteness, which means to be subject to the limitations of time. Unlike God, man's whole existence is governed by time. The changes that constantly occur in man's experience are described in Ecclesiastes 3:1-8.

Although God as Spirit is not subject to the limitations of time, it is real to Him, at least with reference to man, because He created it. Time cannot be erased or ignored, as if it does not exist. It can cease, and one day will cease; but it is not ignored by God. Time was created by God when He created the universe, because time is necessary to measure the changes that constantly take place. The moment God created the first particle and the space to contain it, time and change began. God established a relationship of movement among the heavenly bodies by which man would be able to measure time. This is clearly seen in Genesis 1. Time and the physical universe began together because one could not exist without the other. To create something is to give it a beginning, and time is the result of creation.

Eternity is the "measure" of God's existence. It is continuous, not broken into seconds, minutes, hours, days, weeks, months, and years. Peter said in II Peter 3:8, "One day is with the Lord as a thousand years." This comparison is only saying that God is not bound by man's time concept. Time is a creation of God, but God's eternalness is a part of His nature or being, an expression of God's life. It is not the period or duration within which God lives His life, as man lives in time, but eternity is *in God*. To say that God inhabits eternity, as Isaiah does in Isaiah 57:15, expresses that God alone is eternal, and that eternity is within God.

God's Sovereignty

God's *sovereignty* assures the Christian of the ultimate triumph of the Lord Jesus Christ over Satan. This attribute also guarantees the absolute fulfillment of all of God's Word and His promises. God's sovereignty is the "golden thread" which is evident throughout the Scripture. For example, God's providence, election, predestination, foreknowledge, grace, redemption, and salvation all prove divine sovereignty. The dictionary defines a "sovereign" as one who possesses original and supreme jurisdiction and power, and is subject to nothing or no one. Obviously, this term can be applied only to God. Earthly kings, to be sure, are called "sovereigns," and their kingdoms are called "sovereignties"; but only God, in the final analysis, is sovereign. It is He who gives the power to the kings to rule, even though they may consider themselves sovereigns. To say that God is sovereign is simply to say that God is God. Any attempt to deny the sovereignty of God, as the Arminians do, is simply to say that God is not God. If man does not have a sovereign God, he does not have the true God.

The Scriptures call God the "almighty God," the "only God," the "King of kings," and the "Lord of lords." He is said to work all things after the counsel of His own will. "In whom also we have obtained an inheritance, being predestinated according to the purpose of him who worketh all things after the counsel of his own will" (Ephesians 1:11). He does as He desires in the armies of heaven and earth (Daniel 4:34-35). The Bible says He is absolutely sovereign in His choice of those whom He saves (Romans 9:15-21). For additional insights into this subject, see the author's book, *Divine Sovereignty, Human Freedom, and Responsibility in Prophetic Thought.*

God's Immutability

If God is eternal and sovereign, He cannot be subject to change. God is described in Scripture as "the Father of lights, with whom is no variableness, neither shadow of turning" (James 1:17). He said of Himself, "For I am the Lord, I change not" (Malachi 3:6). God's *immutability* is that perfection which describes His *unchangeableness* in His being, in His decrees and plans, in His Word, and in His will. The Scriptures say in Hebrews 13:8, "Jesus Christ the same yesterday, and today, and for ever." He does not change; His Word or His promises do not change. "God is not a man, that he should lie; neither the son of man, that he should repent [or change His mind about anything He has ever said]: hath he said, and shall he not do it? or hath he spoken, and shall he not make it good?" (Numbers 23:19.) Such biblical texts show that God remains forever faithful to Himself and to His Word; and as a consequence, He is faithful to His decrees and His promises that He has made to His people.

God's immutability *does not mean* that He is *immovable* or *static*. Man cannot understand God's unchangeableness merely from his earthly experience of unchangeableness, which to him often speaks of immobility, being static or dead. The immutability of God does not mean that He is inactive or emotionless or passionless, but His immutability is the unchanging essence of His being and nature. The Bible says, "God is love," and this love is changeless, unwavering, and eternal, as are all of His other attributes. God does not change His mind, His purpose, or His decrees; they are eternal. He does not change His being; He does not increase, decrease, or grow older. He does not change His counsel. In all of these things, God is unchanging, unchangeable.

God's activity and works show that He is not static. Before creation there was only the Godhead; there were no angels or men, and there was no universe. Since the time when God finished His creative work, He has been taking care of that which He made, showing that He is active in providence. He sustains and preserves all He has created. He is not the disinterested god of Deism, nor the "universal mover" of Greek philosophy. When God created the universe, this changed the order of God's realm; but there was no *change in God.*

God's redemptive activity is seen from the beginning, (Genesis 3:15), and it will continue to the end. History bears clear testimony to the reality of God's activity in wrath and judgment against sinners, as well as against nations. For example, consider the exile of Israel and the destruction of Babylon. God's activity in deliverance is evident in the Exodus account, and is also seen today in the testimony of the deliverance of His children from sickness, accident, harm, and death.

God's activity may also be seen in His response to the prayers of faith and intercession. God is moved to action by prayers, as any believer who prays in faith can testify. This does not mean that the Christian's prayers change God's mind, His will, or His purpose; but prayers are an important part of God's purpose. Proof of this is that the prayer of faith brings changes in man's circumstances. The Christian's intent is not to change the will of God, but to pray in line with His will and to receive answers. "And this is the confidence that we have in him, that, if we ask any thing according to his will, he heareth us: And if we know that he hear us, whatsoever we ask, we know that we have the petitions that we desired of him" (I John 5:14-15).

In passages such as Ezekiel 22:29-31 and Isaiah 59:16, God was asking for intercessors to intercede on behalf of the sinful nation of Israel, so that He might turn from His wrath and spare Israel from judgment, or at least to postpone it. Such intercession does not change God's mind, will, or purpose because God has ordained that men should intercede, and He has promised to answer prayers that are made according to His will. Jesus said in Mark 11:24, "Therefore I say unto you, What things soever ye desire, when ye pray, believe that ye receive them, and ye shall have them." James 1:5-8 says that when the believer prays he is not to doubt that he will receive the answer. This means that God has included all prayers of faith and all intercessions in His plans and purposes. For God to respond to such prayers He does not have to change His mind, His decrees, His decisions, or His purposes, because the Christian's prayers are included in the outworking of God's will for his life and for the church. For further insight into the appropriating of God's promises, see the author's book, *Faith for Healing*.

Included in God's unchangeable plans is the fact that some *promises* or *prophecies* are *conditional*. In Jeremiah 18 God said if He pronounced judgment upon a nation for its sins, and later the people repented, He would turn from His wrath. Or if He said He would bless a nation, and afterward the people did evil in His sight, He would turn from His blessing and pronounce wrath upon them. In John 15:7 Jesus said, "If ye abide in me, and my words abide in you, ye shall ask what ye will, and it shall be done unto you." Notice the condition, *if*. In such cases God does not change His mind or purpose, but His action toward man is determined by man's response to His conditional promises or prophecies. In Deuteronomy 28 God promised blessings to those who obeyed Him, but if they disobeyed they would be under His curses. He does not change His mind in those cases, but His immutable counsel stands. He will act toward man as man obeys or disobeys Him.

God's activity was also seen in the incarnation of Christ. This is the greatest proof that God is not static or unchangeable. He is immutable in His being, His nature, and His attributes; but in the incarnation God changed His form from Spirit to flesh. He did not give up being God, because Jesus, the Logos, the Son of God, simply changed His mode of existence from pure Spirit to taking on human flesh. This may be seen in Philippians 2:6, "Who, being in the form of God, thought it not robbery to be equal with God." The Greek says, "He emptied himself, and took upon himself the form of a servant, and was made in the likeness of men." Of course, He only emptied Himself of the form of God (Spirit) in order to take on the form of man. God's unchanging love motivated Him to change His form by taking on human nature so He could die in the Christian's place as the sinless Son of God. Jesus "took on him the seed of Abraham" (Hebrews 2:16).

God's Omnipresence

The *omnipresence* of God is that perfection of God by which He is personally present everywhere in heaven and earth at the same time. This is seen, for example, in Jeremiah 23:23-24. "Am I a God at hand, saith the Lord, and not a God afar off? Can any hide himself in secret places that I shall not see him? saith the Lord. Do not I fill heaven and earth? saith the Lord." In Psalm 139:7-10 David asked, "Whither shall I go from thy spirit? or whither shall I flee from thy presence? If I ascend up into heaven, thou art there: if I make my bed in sheol [the place of departed spirits], behold, thou art there. If I take the wings of the morning, and dwell in the uttermost parts of the sea; Even there shall thy hand lead me, and thy right hand shall hold me." Also see I Kings 8:27-66; Isaiah 66:1; Amos 9:1-4; Acts 17:27-28.

How can God be present everywhere at the same time? Because God is Spirit, He is not limited by space and distance. When God created the universe, space was created to contain the things which He had made—the sun, the moon, the stars, and all living things. A body must occupy space whether it is celestial or human. It would be impossible for it to exist without space. God, however, does not have a body, so He does not occupy space. All created objects have some measure of spread—even a microscopic speck—but uncreated spirit requires no space. It is difficult to conceive of anything which has no parts and requires no space; but when one considers what space is—mere emptiness—it can hardly be essential to God's existence!

God as Spirit cannot be divided, having a part on earth, a part on Mars, a part in believers' hearts, and a part in heaven. God said through Jeremiah, "I fill heaven and earth." This is not to be confused with Pantheism, which teaches that "God is in everything" and "everything is in God," that His presence fills the universe as smoke fills a room or water fills a bottle. On the contrary, God's omnipresence means that there is no part of space in this universe where God is not actively and personally present.

Some might raise the questions, "If God does not occupy space, where is heaven?" "If Christ has a glorified body and is seated at the right hand of God in heaven, does not this imply that even a glorified body occupies space?" "What of the countless angels? Where are they?" "Where are Satan and the demons?" "Where are the departed dead?" "Where are heaven and hell?"

Space in Relationship to God and Man

To answer such questions it is necessary to define space in two aspects: in relationship to man and in relationship to God. Space, as it pertains to man, may be defined as that form of reality in which created objects can exist. Space is necessary for objects to maintain their separate identity, for without space all things would become one. Two objects cannot occupy the same space at the same time. For example, when a woman bakes a cake, she may have fifteen ingredients. They are all separate; but when she mixes them together, they lose their separate identity, and they occupy the same space. God has given man a body and has given him space, because space is needed to maintain his individual identity.

God's domain, on the other hand, is entirely in another dimension, one which does not need space. His realm cannot be easily understood by man because it is completely different from space and time as he knows it. The spiritual dimension permeates the created dimension; it was already present when God created finite, "visible" space.

The fact that the spiritual realm permeates the earthly is well illustrated in II Kings 6, where the king of Syria sent an army to capture Elisha the prophet. Elisha, by his visions, had learned all the secret plans of the king of Syria and had informed the leaders of Israel so that she would not be ensnared by Syria. One day Elisha's servant saw this army surrounding them in retaliation, and he was afraid; but Elisha said, "Fear not: for they that be with us are more than they that be with them. And Elisha prayed, and said, Lord, I pray thee, open his eyes [the servant's], that he may see. And the Lord opened the eyes of the young man; and he saw: and, behold, the mountain was full of horses and chariots of fire round about Elisha." The spiritual dimension, with the chariots, angels, and the army of the Lord, was already present; but it took spiritual vision to see it. The servant learned that the spiritual dimension permeates the physical. This is the reason the Bible can say that God *fills* heaven and earth; that He is everywhere present at the same time.

It should be understood that God's dimension is spiritual, but this does not mean that it is merely spacelessness. There is some form of distance or separateness even in the spiritual dimension between God and His creation, between angels and other spirit beings. Remember, as stated previously, the absence of distance would mean loss of identity.

God indwells and fills the Christian, but this is different from the Hindu concept of absorption in the deity. For God to maintain His identity, and man his, there must be some form of separateness even in union. It is difficult to explain by analogy because it is spiritual. Man dwells in a realm where all he can comprehend is space and objects that occupy space. Thousands of demons possessed the man in Mark 5. They were not affected by the limitations of space, but they maintained their own personal identities and names. The man said, "My name is Legion: for we are many." Spirit beings do not occupy space, so there can be an innumerable host of demons in one individual. It is not unusual, even today, for those in a deliverance ministry to cast numerous demons out of a person, each of the spirits identifying itself by name.

Spiritual space (that is, distance in the spiritual dimension) is that actuality which enables God to maintain His personal identity and His separateness from all of His creation. God does not need space; but, at the same time, there is some form of separation even in the spiritual dimension. Keep in mind that God's dimension is not mere spacelessness. While there is a real distinction between all things in God's dimension, it is not to be compared to the space/time dimension in which man lives. In the spiritual realm space is *distinctional* rather than *geographical*.

The behavior of light can be used as an analogy to describe spiritual space. Light does not occupy created space. As two light beams converge, both can pass through the same location at the same time. It is impossible for material or created objects to do this. A person could direct three beams of light to the same location (or ten, or one hundred, or ten thousand), yet each keeps its personal distinction—its apartness. Space does not separate the beams of light any more than it separates spirit beings, but space is the reality of their personal individual existence.

The dimensions of New Jerusalem are given in Revelation 21 in terms of *"cubits"* and *"furlongs"*—earthly concepts. However, since New Jerusalem will be a spiritual city, not occupying space as man knows it, the elect will have to wait to comprehend its actual appearance. As an analogy to show the reality that spiritual things do not occupy space, consider the many thoughts, ideas, and facts which can abide in the human mind. All of these are separate and do not occupy space because the thought realm is in a different dimension.

One needs to think of God's omnipresence as God's personal presence. God is everywhere at one and the same time because He is Spirit, and Spirit is not limited by space. God does not have to *go* anywhere to *be* everywhere at the same time. He is omnipresent as Spirit. Dimensions such as length, height, breadth, and separation between things are real in the spiritual realm; but all of these terms must be understood in the sphere in which they are used.

God's Omniscience

Another attribute of God is His *omniscience*, which means having all wisdom; God is all wise. The Bible says in I John 3:20, "For if our heart condemn us, God is greater than our heart, and knoweth all things." God's omniscience is His perfect knowledge of all things past, present, and future. It is His infinite knowledge, and includes His ability to apply that knowledge with perfect wisdom. God possesses all knowledge within Himself; He does not have to learn it or acquire it from without, as man does.

God's knowledge is *immediate* and does not come from thinking or reasoning, but He possesses His knowledge of all things *from eternity*. All of God's attributes are aspects of His nature; therefore, He does not have to exert some effort to know and remember. Thus, it is not so much that God has omniscience, but that He is omniscient. The Apostle James said that God knows all things. "Known unto God are all his works from the beginning of the world" (Acts 15:18).

God's knowledge embraces every sphere. It is seen to be perfect in Job 37:16. "Dost thou know the balancings of the clouds, the wondrous works of him which is perfect in knowledge?" His knowledge includes understanding of the whole universe (Psalm 147:4-5 and Job 38). It includes perfect knowledge of the animal order (Job 39-41). "Are not two sparrows sold for a farthing? and one of them shall not fall on the ground without your Father" (Matthew 10:29). God's knowledge embraces all of the works of men (Psalm 33) and the thoughts of men (Acts 15:8 and Psalm 139).

God's omniscience and His omnipresence are insepar-able. He is present everywhere at the same time, so He knows all things. That statement may be turned around. He knows all things because He is everywhere present at the same time. This truth is clearly presented in Psalm 139.

God's knowledge is not limited to the *present*, but He also foreknows all *future* events. He can know the future be-cause He is not limited by time as man is. Man must wait for events to occur before he can acknowledge their reality, but God has always known all things. Fulfilled prophecy is ob-jective proof of God's knowledge of the future. "Therefore the Lord himself shall give you a sign; Behold, a virgin shall conceive, and bear a son, and shall call his name Immanuel" (Isaiah 7:14). In the Hebrew it actually says, "Behold, a virgin has conceived, and has already borne a son." In other words, it was prophesied in a form of the verb called the "perfect state," as if it had already happened, even though it would be seven centuries before its fulfillment.

What God's knowledge does not include should be mentioned. Omniscience deals only with what is *actual* and *possible*, not with what is impossible or absurd, for these can-not be known. For example, God has no knowledge of round squares, dry water, white darkness, or two times two equals five. These are self-contradictory or ridiculous and are, therefore, not objects of knowledge.

God's *wisdom* is an aspect of His personal knowledge, but it is not identical with it. It is really the other side of the same coin. "O the depth of the riches both of the wisdom and knowledge of God! how unsearchable are his judgments,

89

and his ways past finding out!" (Romans 11:33.) The wisdom of God is so far above man's wisdom that it is incomprehensible. I Corinthians 12:7-8 speaks of a "word of wisdom" which is one of the gifts of the Holy Spirit. That wisdom comes from God.

Wisdom is the application of knowledge to the correct attainment of some goal. God's wisdom is His perfect judgment and discernment based on His perfect knowledge. Because God is all-wise, He chooses the highest ends and the best means possible. "O Lord, how manifold are thy works! in wisdom hast thou made them all: the earth is full of thy riches" (Psalm 104:24).

God's wisdom is not simply a greater degree of something that man possesses. Man's wisdom is often the source of his pride and his rebellion to God, as shown in I Corinthians 1:18-31. The wisdom of man is contrasted there with the wisdom of God, and is seen to be in a totally different realm or dimension. Perfect judgment and discernment based upon perfect knowledge are qualities completely lacking in man.

God's Omnipotence

Another attribute of God, and a very important one, is His *omnipotence*, which means that He is all powerful. God's omnipotence is that perfection which enables Him to do whatever He wills, and to accomplish it with or without the use of means. His omnipotence is closely related to His sovereignty. All of God's activity is according to His own will and according to His own purpose. "In whom also we have obtained an inheritance, being predestinated according to the purpose of him who worketh all things after the counsel of his own will" (Ephesians 1:11). "Ah Lord God! behold, thou hast made the heaven and the earth by thy great power and stretched out arm, and there is nothing too hard for thee" (Jeremiah 32:17). "With God all things are possible" (Matthew 19:26). "He hath done whatsoever he hath pleased" (Psalm 115:3).

When the Scriptures say that nothing is impossible with God, it should be understood that God's power does not include that which is self-contradictory. God cannot, for example, create a stone too heavy for Him to lift. He cannot make a three-sided rectangle or create two mountains without an intervening valley. His omnipotence is not the power to do that which is contrary to His character or nature. God cannot sin (James 1:13). God cannot lie (Numbers 23:19). God cannot deny Himself (II Timothy 2:13). God cannot die (Isaiah 57:15). God cannot justify a sinner without satisfying the demands of His law against the sinner (Romans 8:3-4).

God's omnipotence is not mere physical power; but it is the unique ability to do all that He wills to do, whether it is to create a world out of nothing (Hebrews 11:3) or to save a sinner. As stated previously, God's omnipresence is His power to be everywhere at the same time. Such is the case with all of His attributes; they all interact with His power. Thus, one attribute of God cannot be separated from another. God's omnipotence is that perfection by which He is able to maintain all of His other perfections, such as holiness, righteousness, faithfulness, truthfulness, love, grace, justice, and sovereignty.

Man is unable to reason up from his earthly concept of power, supposing it to be like God's, and to equate it with His, except that God possesses His power to a greater degree. His power is not merely an attribute; it is God, Himself. God does not have power; God is power! He is omnipotent. The power of God arises from the fact that God is God.

God's Self-limitation

God's omnipotence includes that power which enables Him even to limit Himself on some occasions in the exercise of that power. God has perfect freedom of power; therefore, He can limit His power if He so chooses. When God determined to create beings having freedom of choice, He gave them freedom to say "yes" or "no" to Him; thus, He imposed upon Himself a measure of *self-limitation*. Paradoxically, this self-limitation reveals His omnipotence or His power. For a righteous and holy God to tolerate creatures with wills of their own, who are now in rebellion against Him, requires a greater power of restraint than the power He would exercize to annihilate them.

Nebuchadnezzar, Alexander the Great, and Hitler conquered more territory and people than they could rule or hold in subjection. This is not so with God, for He has the power to rule all of creation. When He limits Himself, He is revealing His great power to be able to do that. Furthermore, this self-limitation is not of necessity, but is freely chosen by God. He did not need to create beings to whom He would grant freedom; but in so doing He brought into existence wills and activities which would repeatedly stand against His will and His works, but only in the temporal realm. God's omnipotence is not hampered even slightly by man's freedom, since it is He who wills to uphold the exercise of the human will, and He can cause man's freedom to cease at any time.

Daniel 4:35 says, "And all the inhabitants of the earth are reputed as nothing; and he doeth according to his will in the army of heaven, and among the inhabitants of the earth: and none can stay his hand, or say unto him, What doest thou?" It would be impossible for anything God created to be an ultimate threat to His sovereignty, because, as God, He is absolutely sovereign.

Self-limitation is not to be thought of as some weakness of character. Every parent limits himself when dealing with a disobedient child. A good father disciplines and corrects in love. He may spank or withhold some blessing in order to correct a child, but he would not wield his full power in that discipline.

Another example of self-imposed restraint is the manner in which a mature Christian deals with an unsaved person or with a new convert. He does not immediately present him with the depth of understanding of God's Word he possesses, nor does he necessarily present to him testimony of all of his experiences the Holy Spirit has given him, such as healings, visions, or the miraculous. With the weak he would be weak, in the sense that he would try to meet the immature person on his own level and gradually teach him the deeper things of the Word of God.

In God's self-limitation He chose to limit Himself when He created man; but it is a temporary limitation, because there will be universal admission to the sovereignty of God on the final day. Paul said in Philippians 2:10-11, "That at the name of Jesus every knee should bow, of things in heaven, and things in earth, and things under the earth; And that every tongue should confess that Jesus Christ is Lord, to the glory of God the Father." The act of bowing to Jesus Christ and acknowledging His Lordship does not imply universal salvation, but that every created being will have to acknowledge His Lordship. Even Satan's power is only temporary and is divinely limited.

God's Infinity

God's *infinity* is that absolute perfection which characterizes all of His attributes as being limitless and perfect. In other words, He is subject to no limitations. With reference to time, God's infinity is His eternalness. With reference to space, God's infinity is His omnipresence. With reference to His wisdom and knowledge, God's infinity is His omniscience. He knows all. "Great is our Lord, and of great power: his understanding is infinite" (Psalm 147:5). The term translated there as "infinite" literally means in the Hebrew "without number." Paul said in Romans 11:33, "O the depth of the riches both of the wisdom and knowledge of God! how unsearchable are his judgments, and his ways past finding out!" "Be ye therefore perfect, even as your Father which is in heaven is perfect" (Matthew 5:48). "As for God, his way is perfect: the word of the Lord is tried: he is a buckler to all those that trust in him" (Psalm 18:30).

Since God is infinite in power, in wisdom, in knowledge, and in truth, He is also infinite in His faithfulness to fulfill His Word to the believer. Psalm 119:90 says, "Thy faithfulness is unto all generations: thou hast established the earth, and it abideth." In Hebrews 10:23 Paul encouraged the Christians, "Let us hold fast the profession of our faith without wavering; (for he is faithful that promised)." The Bible shows that it is sin to limit God in any way. "Yea, they turned back and tempted God, and limited the Holy One of Israel" (Psalm 78:41). God rejected Israel because they limited Him.

God's Moral Attributes

God's metaphysical attributes are primarily those perfections that are incommunicable, such as His being, His existence, His sovereignty, His eternalness, His immutability, His omnipresence, and so on. The *moral attributes* are those qualities of God's character that He possesses largely in relation to His creation, such as love, patience, and mercy. They are also to be found to some degree in His creation, that is, in angels and man.

God's Holiness

The two most frequently mentioned moral attributes of God are His holiness and His love. The Scriptures repeatedly say God is holy. His *holiness* is the perfection by which He is by nature morally separate and unique from all other creatures. This is seen in the terms that are employed both in the Hebrew and the Greek, which literally mean "to be set apart," "to be separate." The term that is used in reference to

God in the Hebrew speaks of God's separateness or His apartness from what He created. Of course, in the moral sense, it refers to God's absolute purity of nature.

In what sense is God holy with regard to the basic meaning of apartness or separateness? The answer lies in His moral uniqueness, His moral otherness, His moral transcendence, and His absolute purity. "Thou art of purer eyes than to behold evil, and canst not look on iniquity" (Habakkuk 1:13). "Yea, the stars are not pure in his sight" (Job 25:5). "Who is like unto the Lord our God, who dwelleth on high, Who humbleth himself to behold the things that are in heaven, and in the earth!" (Psalm 113:5-6.) God has to bow down, as it were, to even behold the creation. Holiness with respect to God means His total separation from sin and evil, as well as from all that is created.

Holiness so exclusively belongs to God that the term "Holy" becomes a synonym for the name of God in Scripture. "For thus saith the high and lofty One that inhabiteth eternity, whose name is Holy; I dwell in the high and holy place, with him also that is of a contrite and humble spirit, to revive the spirit of the humble, and to revive the heart of the contrite ones" (Isaiah 57:15). In Isaiah 6:3 the seraphim stand before the throne of God, constantly saying, "Holy, holy, holy." They could have just pronounced His name, because His name is Holy. Isaiah repeatedly called God "the Holy One of Israel" (Isaiah 1:4). In religious systems some men may call their leaders "His Holiness," but the Bible reserves that title for God alone.

God's holiness is also the motivation for His wrath against sinners. When man loses respect for God's holiness, he loses understanding of his own moral depravity. Because of His holy nature, God cannot permit sin to exist in His universe. Consequently, men cannot violate His holy order and sin with impunity. God is absolutely Holy; therefore, He requires holiness of His children. "But as he which hath called you is holy, so be ye holy in all manner of conversation; Because it is written, Be ye holy; for I am holy" (I Peter 1:15-16). The same thing is said in Leviticus 19:2. In Hebrews 12:14 Paul said, "Follow peace with all men, and holiness, without which no man shall see the Lord." Such Scriptures show that God is deeply concerned about the holiness of His creation. If men do not conform to His holiness, then He will judge them accordingly.

God's Righteousness

Another of God's moral attributes is His *righteousness*. God deals with creation according to righteousness and justice. The terms in both Greek and Hebrew mean "to be righteous or just." The original Hebrew has a moral and religious connotation which means "to be straight or firm" or "to conform" to some proper standard or norm. Isaiah 28:17 says, "Judgment also will I lay to the line, and righteousness to the plummet." Here Isaiah is using carpenters' terminology; judgment will be laid to a line and righteousness must conform to a certain standard.

God's righteousness is His own moral holiness, His sinlessness, His perfection of character, which is the standard and norm for all men. This is revealed in the Old Testament law, and in the New Testament Scriptures, and of course, perfectly through Jesus Christ. God Himself is the standard or norm of righteousness to which man must conform, as set forth in Deuteronomy 32:4. "He is the Rock, his work is perfect: for all his ways are judgment: a God of truth and without iniquity, just and right is he." "Ye shall be holy: for I the Lord your God am holy" (Leviticus 19:2). "Be ye therefore perfect, even as your Father which is in heaven is perfect" (Matthew 5:48). In Matthew 6:33 Jesus told His hearers, "Seek ye first the kingdom of God, and his righteousness."

In the Old Testament when a person took an oath he always swore by a greater entity than himself. God, however, because of His perfect righteousness, could swear to nothing higher, so He swore unto Himself (Hebrews 6:6-18). The righteousness of a Christian should not merely be a definition of his character, but it should also be expressed in his deeds. Believers are to do righteous deeds because God does righteousness (Deuteronomy 32:4).

Righteousness and justice are the two aspects of God's holiness. God's *righteousness* is His own conformity to His own sinless, holy nature, which conformity He also demands of His creation. God's *justice* is His absolute fairness in His treatment of His creatures with respect to how they conform to His standard, which is God Himself. Remember, this standard is expressed in Old Testament law as, "Love your neighbor as yourself" and "Love God with all of your heart." It is revealed in the New Testament through Jesus Christ, who said, "I am the way, the truth and the life: no man cometh unto the Father, but by me" (John 14:6). Jesus never pointed to anyone other than Himself or His Father. God is righteous and He demands righteousness of His people. Because God is just, He visits conformity with reward, or non-conformity with punishment. In Genesis 18:23-25 Abraham said, "Shall not the Judge of all the earth do right?" Romans 2:4-6 shows that God does right toward all of His creation, and He judges man according to his works.

How can man possibly conform to the strict demands of the law? The standard of righteousness which is required by God as revealed in His holy law can only be fulfilled by the Christian through faith. Paul said that when a person has faith in Jesus Christ, the righteousness of the law is fulfilled in him (Romans 3:20-22 and 8:1-4). Further, he can fulfill the righteousness of the law by loving his neighbor as himself (Romans 13:8-10). God not only requires righteousness, but He has provided a way that this righteousness can be fulfilled; not by works of righteousness—but by faith in His Son. All works of faith are works of righteousness.

God's Faithfulness

Another attribute is God's *faithfulness*. He is righteous and just; therefore, He is faithful. In II Timothy 2:13 Paul said, "He abideth faithful: he cannot deny himself." In Hebrews 10:23 Paul said, "Let us hold fast the profession of our faith" because God "is faithful that promised." In I Thessalonians 5:23-24 the apostle relates that God is faithful to complete and preserve His work in the believer. In Matthew 5:18 and Isaiah 40:8, He is seen to be faithful to His Word. Deuteronomy 7:9 says God is faithful to His covenants. Numbers 23:19 says, "God is not a man, that he should lie;

neither the son of man, that he should repent: hath he said, and shall he not do it? or hath he spoken, and shall he not make it good?"

God's faithfulness means that He is steadfast, reliable, and trustworthy; He is faithful to all that He has said. God's righteousness means that He is faithful and true to Himself—to His perfect holiness. God's justice means that He is faithful in His dealings with His creation. If He has promised to punish sin and iniquity, He will do that. If He has promised to reward those who have faith in Jesus Christ and obey Him, He will do as He promised.

God's Patience

Another attribute of God is His *patience*. He is called the "God of patience" in Romans 15:5. God's patience is shown in His *mercy*. His long-suffering or patience with His creatures restrains Him from breaking forth in immediate wrath when man sins and disobeys Him. God gives man time to turn to Him in repentance. "The Lord is not slack concerning his promise, as some men count slackness; but is longsuffering to us-ward, not willing that any should perish, but that all should come to repentance" (II Peter 3:9). God demonstrated His patience and justice in the days of Noah, according to I Peter 3:20, when He waited 120 years for man to repent while Noah built the ark.

God's patience is not meaningless delay nor does it show indifference to man's sins. His patience is purposeful because it gives man time to repent; but the time will come when His patience will come to an end, in the sense that the day of judgment will fall upon all of those who do not take advantage of His offer of forgiveness and salvation.

God's long-suffering is not only seen in His mercy but also in His *wrath*. He sometimes endures sin, disobedience, rebellion, and wickedness until man's cup of iniquity becomes full; then, His judgment reveals His power and righteousness. "What if God, willing to shew his wrath, and to make his power known, endured with much longsuffering the vessels of wrath fitted to destruction: And that he might make known the riches of his glory on the vessels of mercy, which he had afore prepared unto glory?" (Romans 9:22-23.)

God's Love

The *love* of God and His holiness are His two most mentioned attributes in the Scriptures. All of His perfections express holiness or love in some way. For example, God's holiness required man's atonement; God's love provided it. The basic text would be I John 4:8b, "God is love," with John 3:16, "For God so loved the world, that he gave his only be-gotten Son, that whosoever believeth in him should not perish, but have everlasting life."

There are two terms in the Old Testament that need to be mentioned. One is "ahabah," which means "uncondi-tioned love." It is unqualified love, and it is motivated by nothing in the object that is loved. For example, it is *God's election love* for Israel and for the church. The other term, "chesed," means "mercy," "loving-kindness," or "steadfast love." It is *covenant love*, emphasizing the mutual concern, devotion, and faithfulness that should exist between two parties who make a covenant together.

In the New Testament there are two terms for love. The Greek term used for *natural affection* and *emotional love* is "phileo." *Unconditioned spiritual affection* is "agapao," and speaks of love which is based solely upon the will of the person who does the loving. For example, it is God's love (agapao) toward man which is seen in the gift of His Son (John 3:16).

To manifest this same "unconditioned" love is Jesus' requirement for His children in Matthew 19:19, "Thou shalt love thy neighbour as thyself." "But I say unto you, Love your enemies, bless them that curse you, do good to them that hate you, and pray for them which despitefully use you, and persecute you" (Matthew 5:44). This is called "unconditioned" love because it is not based upon any good in the person receiving the love. It has to be unconditioned love for a Christian to be able to love those who hate and mistreat him, for there is nothing in his enemies that would cause him to love them; but he can love them because he has the love of God in his heart.

What is the meaning and significance of God as love? God's love is *unconditioned* and *eternal*. The nature of God's love is seen most clearly when contrasted with man's love ("phileo"), which is basically natural affection or emotional love. Man's love is sometimes called "eros," which is natural, physical love, as contrasted with "agapao"—spiritual, personal love. Man's love for an object is determined by its value, whether it be for a material object or for a person. In vivid contrast, the love of God *creates* the value of the object.

No man ever purposely goes out and looks for a har-
lot, a drug addict, an alcoholic, or a gambler to marry. He
would avoid someone that he knows would give him problems; but God does just the opposite in His choice—He
chooses whom the world rejects. Why? "That no flesh
should glory in his presence" (I Corinthians 1:26-29). For
example, God chose Israel, not because she was righteous or
some great nation; but He chose her in spite of the fact that
she was not any of those things.

God said to Israel, through Moses, "For thou art an
holy people unto the Lord thy God: the Lord thy God hath
chosen thee to be a special people unto himself, above all
people that are upon the face of the earth. The Lord did not
set his love upon you, nor choose you, because ye were more
in number than any people; for ye were the fewest of all
people: But because the Lord loved you, and because he
would keep the oath which he had sworn unto your fathers,
hath the Lord brought you out with a mighty hand, and redeemed you out of the house of bondmen, from the hand of
Pharaoh king of Egypt" (Deuteronomy 7:6-8). God told the
Israelites that they were the fewest people on earth, but He
chose them anyway because of His promise to the patriarchs.

Moses continued speaking to the Israelites in Deuteronomy 9:4-6. "Speak not thou in thine heart, after that the
Lord thy God hath cast them [these nations] out from before
thee [from the promised land], saying, For my righteousness
the Lord hath brought me in to possess this land: but for the
wickedness of these nations the Lord doth drive them out
from before thee. Not for thy righteousness, or for the up-
rightness of thine heart, dost thou go to possess their land:

but for the wickedness of these nations the Lord thy God doth drive them out from before thee, and that he may perform the word which the Lord sware unto thy fathers, Abraham, Isaac, and Jacob. Understand therefore, that the Lord thy God giveth thee not this good land to possess it for thy righteousness; for thou art a stiffnecked people."

The same truth is taught in the New Testament in Romans 5:6-10. "While we were yet sinners, Christ died for us." "For ye see your calling, brethren, how that not many wise men after the flesh, not many mighty, not many noble, are called: But God hath chosen the foolish things of the world to confound the wise; and God hath chosen the weak things of the world to confound the things which are mighty; And base things of the world, and things which are despised, hath God chosen, yea, and things which are not, to bring to nought things that are." For what reason? "That no flesh should glory in His presence" (I Corinthians 1:26-29).

God's love is for the unlovable, the rebellious, the unworthy sinner; thus, God's love is not motivated by the value of the object. The prophet Ezekiel described what man looks like, in this case Israel, in the sight of God—nothing but a repulsive mass of corruption, yet He chose to love her anyway (Ezekiel 16:1-14). There is no value in mankind, nothing worthy of God's love. Man is nothing but sinful, weak, rebellious, carnal, and unlovely; but when God fixed His eternal love upon him, that created the value in His sight. That does not imply that man has any inherent worth; but God loves His children as adopted sons because of their relationship to the One He loves, Jesus Christ, who is of inestimable value.

The *motive* for God's "agapao" love is within Himself, in His nature; God is love. God's love is not mere emotional affection. It is not prompted merely by some utilitarian consideration, but God loves because God is love. The greatest expression of His love is seen in the gift of His Son for sinners (John 3:16).

God's love is *self-giving*, not conditioned, as human love is, with selfish concern. God did not need man, but He created man to enjoy Him and to share in His love and blessings. God was self-sufficient within the triune Godhead; yet because of His loving and giving nature He wishes to share Himself and His love with others. In the eternal choice of Israel or the church, God demonstrated His self-giving love. Paul said in II Corinthians 8:9, "For ye know the grace of our Lord Jesus Christ, that, though he was rich, yet for your sakes he became poor, that ye through his poverty might be rich."

God's love is *eternal*. He did not begin to love His children after He created them, but the Bible says that He created them to be objects of His love. In Romans 5:8 Paul said that while men were yet sinners, God showed His love toward them by giving His Son, Jesus Christ. In Jeremiah 31:3 the prophet said, "The Lord hath appeared of old unto me, saying, Yea, I have loved thee with an everlasting love: therefore with lovingkindness have I drawn thee." In Ephesians 1:3-5 Paul related that God predestinated His elect before the foundation of the world to be adopted as His sons and to receive salvation.

God's unconditional love is supposed to produce a like *response* in His children. His love went out to them (I John

4:9-11); therefore, the believer's love is to go out to others. Love is the greatest of the Christian virtues according to I Corinthians 13. It is the fulfilling of the righteousness of the law, according to Romans 13:8-10. In summation, if a man loves God and his neighbor, he will not sin against either of them. According to I John 1, love is proof of the new birth.

God's Grace and Mercy

Grace and *mercy* are attributes of God which express His love, according to Ephesians 2. God's grace is His *unmerited favor* toward sinners, and mercy is the *application* of that grace. The three terms—grace, faith, and mercy—are used in Ephesians 2:4-8: "But God, who is rich in mercy, for his great love wherewith he loved us, Even when we were dead in sins, hath quickened us together with Christ, . . . For by grace are ye saved through faith; and that not of yourselves: it is the gift of God." The divine order is this: 1) Because of God's eternal *love*, 2) He had *mercy* upon man, which was 3) expressed as *grace* 4) through the gift of *faith* 5) unto his *salvation*. God's attitude of love is revealed as undeserved kindness or mercy which He bestows upon man. Man's response: 1) He believes, 2) repents, 3) confesses, and 4) obeys.

By grace, God bestows other undeserved things upon His children, such as supernatural gifts and ministries (Romans 12; Ephesians 4:7-16). Good works are by His grace (II Corinthians 8:7; 9:6-8). The grace of God is the undeserved favor that He bestows upon the elect which results in blessings in this life and salvation for eternity.

God's Glory

Another aspect of God that is dealt with under attributes, which is really not an attribute in itself, is *God's glory*. His glory is a revelation of all of His other perfections. The word "glory" in the Hebrew means that which is "heavy" or "weighty." In the Greek it means "honor," "reputation," or "fame." Whether the term is applied to man or to God, it speaks of that which makes the person weighty, big, great, or important; or deserving of respect, honor, or praise. God is glorious because of all of His perfections.

God's glory is expressed in the Scriptures in relation to His creation. As His perfections are manifest, so is His glory. But man does not need to see His perfections for Him to be glorious, because He had glory before He ever created the universe. This fact is seen, for example, in John 17:5. "And now, O Father, glorify thou me with thine own self with the glory which I had with thee before the world was." Before creation, God was glorious in Himself, and He manifested His glory to Himself, that is, within the triune Godhead—the Father to the Son, the Son to the Spirit, the Spirit to the Father and the Son.

It is impossible for man to see God, but He can see His glory in several ways. 1) His glory is seen in *creation*. Psalm 19:1, "The heavens declare the glory of God; and the firmament sheweth his handiwork." 2) He shows His glory in His *supernatural manifestations*, such as the revelation of Himself in a cloud in Exodus 16:10. Leviticus 9:23-24 says, "The glory of the Lord appeared unto all the people. And there came a fire out from before the Lord, and consumed upon the altar the burnt offering." 3) He is also glorified through His *works* or His *miracles*. In John 2:1-11 Jesus' first miracle was turning water into wine. "This beginning of miracles did Jesus in Cana of Galilee, and manifested forth his glory; and his disciples believed on him." Even in the present day, miracles are manifestations of the glory of God. Man is simply an instrument through whom God manifests His glory by the gifts He has set in His church, such as miracles, prophecy, and healings (I Corinthians 12; Romans 12). 4) The glory of God is manifest supremely *in* and *through Jesus Christ*. The Apostle John said in John 1:14, "And the Word was made flesh, and dwelt among us, (and we beheld his glory, the glory as of the only begotten of the Father,) full of grace and truth." Although God is invisible, He manifests His glory visibly unto His creation. The day will come when the redeemed will behold the glory of the Son of God. Jesus prayed in John 17:24, "Father, I will that they also, whom thou hast given me, be with me where I am; that they may behold my glory." 5) God's *saints* will be *glorified*, according to Romans 8:17-30. "When he shall appear, we shall be like him" (I John 3:2b).

God's glory is the revelation of Himself in His wisdom, power, holiness, love, mercy, truth, and grace. In fact, His creation exists to see His glory and to give Him glory, according to Isaiah 42:5-12. Psalm 150 exhorts that all creation should praise the Lord, and concludes with, "Let every thing that hath breath praise the Lord. Praise ye the Lord."

Christology: The Doctrine of Christ

The next area of this study in theology is called *Christology* or the *doctrine of Christ*. The scope of this subject will include three aspects: the personality of Christ, the work of Christ, and the states of Christ.

Jesus Christ and His work occupy a central place in the entire body of Scripture. God created the universe by Him; He redeemed man through Him; and the Father is revealed in Him. Everything that the Father has said or done in relation to this world has been through His Son, Jesus Christ—either in His preincarnate state, through His ministry while He was on earth, or at present at the right hand of the Father.

The study of the doctrine of God dealt with the Godhead—eternal Father, eternal Son, eternal Holy Spirit—one God, eternally manifested as Father, Son, and Holy Spirit. Whatever was learned about the nature of God would apply equally to His three manifestations. Because of the different offices or work that each personality has undertaken on behalf of or in relation to creation, it is important to examine the personality and work of both Christ and the Holy Spirit. One should avoid the mistake of thinking that the work and personalities of the Godhead are so separated that he logically ends up thinking there are three gods, as the Jews charge. This would be incorrect, for the Father, Son, and Holy Spirit cannot be separated either in their nature or being, but only in their personal, eternal, distinct manifestations.

The Personality of Christ

The study of the personality of Christ deals with what is called the "person of Christ." Actually the New Testament Greek does not use the term "person," although it is sometimes translated that way. The term that occurs in the Greek is "hupostasis," which means the "foundation or substance" of something, that which has "real existence," the "nature" of something. In Hebrews 1:3 Paul revealed that Jesus is the exact substance or nature of God. This text will use the term "personality" when speaking of the Godhead, because "person" implies that God is a person as men are persons; but He is distinct from man—He is Spirit.

The Human and Divine Natures of Christ

When Jesus took on humanity, He became a human personality; but He was also divine. He was one personality with *two natures*, and in this He stands unique. "Great is the mystery of godliness: God was manifest in the flesh" (I Timothy 3:16). In the early church councils a man was considered a heretic if he denied either of these facts: that the human Jesus was the divine eternal Son of God; or that the divine eternal Son of God became human. Both of these truths must be adhered to in order for a person to be a Christian.

Heresies Regarding the Human and Divine Natures of Christ

Throughout church history many heresies have arisen concerning the person of Christ. Some of these accepted the

110

humanity of Christ, but denied His deity. The Jewish leaders said Jesus was only a man and was guilty of blasphemy because He made Himself God (John 10:33). This error is called the *Judaistic Heresy*. There was a group in the first century called the Ebionites, who denied the virgin birth. They taught that the Holy Spirit was a female spirit that wedded itself to Christ when He was adopted at His baptism. Their heresy is called *Ebionism*. The heresy of *Arianism* denied the triunity of the Godhead, the deity of Christ, His equality with God, and His eternality. *Docetic gnosticism* claimed that the eternal Logos entered Jesus' body at His baptism and left Him when He died; that He only "seemed" to die on the Cross. The *Apollinarians* said that Jesus was human in body and soul, but not in spirit; therefore, they denied His full humanity.

Some heresies were concerning the union of two natures in Jesus. *Nestorianism* said that Jesus was two persons, not two natures in one person. *Eutychianism* or *monophysitism* said that after the incarnation Jesus Christ possessed only divine nature. *Monotheletism* taught that Christ had two natures, but only one will, which was divine. All of these errors are heretical because they oppose the truth that Christ took upon Himself humanity while He remained deity.

The Deity of Christ

The *deity* of Christ is revealed in many ways in the Scriptures.

1) His deity was revealed in His *birth*. Christ was born of a woman, as all men are; but He came into the world in a

very unique way. Luke 1:26-38 tells of the angel Gabriel's appearance to a virgin named Mary. He told her she would bear a son; but the son would be conceived by God Himself, the Holy Spirit, and the child would be called the Son of God. Compare that with Micah 5:2 where the prophet foretold of Jesus' birth in Bethlehem. "Out of thee shall he come forth unto me that is to be ruler in Israel; whose goings forth have been from of old, from everlasting." According to the prophecy, the child to be born had no beginning. His human birth was not His beginning, but the Logos was simply taking on human flesh.

2) His deity is revealed in His *appellations*—His names and titles. The application of divine names and titles to Christ could not be explained unless He was considered to be God. He is called *God* in many places: "In the beginning was the Word [the Logos], and the Word was with God, and the Word was God" (John 1:1). Jesus is called *God* in Hebrews 1:8; Titus 2:13; and I John 5:20. To call Him God would be meaningless if He were not God.

Jesus is called the *Son of God* in many passages, such as John 3:16 and Matthew 17:1-5. The phrase, *son of God*, is also used of *angels* in Job 38:7, and it is used of *Adam* in Luke 3:38, speaking of his having been created by God. Believers are called sons of God in many passages, for example, Romans 8:14 and I John 3:2. When the phrase, "sons of God," is used of angels or men, it speaks of origin or beginning; but when the phrase is used of Christ, it is always used in a unique way—it designates His equality with God and His oneness of essence with God. This may be seen in John 1:1 where Jesus is said to be equal with God because He was with God and was God Himself. Hebrews 1:2-3 shows that the Son was of the same essence as God. "Son of God" also speaks of His relationship to God. Jesus said, "I and my Father are one" (John 10:30).

Another term which speaks of Jesus is *only begotten Son* (John 3:16). This does not refer to His origin, however, because He was the Son of God from all eternity. The term *only begotten* suggests that Jesus had a beginning; but that is a mistranslation in the King James Version. The term in the Greek is "monogenes," which was incorrectly translated from the verb "gennao," meaning "to beget." It should have been translated from the Greek word "genos," which means "kind." Thus, "mono" (one) "genes" (kind) means that He is the only one of His kind; that is, He is unique. The French Bible correctly reads, "His unique Son." John 3:16 should be translated, "For God so loved the world, that he gave his only Son—his unique Son."

The meaning of "monogenes" is seen from its use in Hebrews 11:17 which says, "By faith Abraham, when he was tried, offered up Isaac; and he that had received the promises offered up his only begotten son." Obviously, Isaac was not his only son, because Abraham had other sons. Ishmael was his first son—not Isaac; therefore, Isaac could not have been his *only begotten* son in the sense that he was either the *first* or his *only* son. Isaac was "monogenes" in that he was the son of the promise, Abraham's unique son, the only one of his kind. His uniqueness lies in the fact that he was the one God promised to Abraham *through* Sarah (Genesis 17:15-19; Romans 9:7-9), and also because it was a miracle that a one

113

hundred year old man and a ninety year old woman could bear a child.

Jesus is called *Lord* in Romans 10:9; the *image of God* in Colossians 1:15; and *Emmanuel* in Matthew 1:23 and Isaiah 7:14. He is designated *mighty God* and the *Father of eternity* in Isaiah 9:6. Christ is referred to as the *Holy One* in several passages, and so on.

3) His deity is confirmed in the fact that Jesus *received worship*, which belongs only to God. There are several instances in the Scriptures where men and angels were worshiped, but they invariably rejected such honor from men. When the heathen heard the gospel and saw the miracles, they would occasionally try to worship the apostles as if they were gods. However, the apostles refused the worship (Acts 10 and 14). In Revelation 22:8-9 when John bowed down before the feet of the angel to worship, the angel said, "See thou do it not: for I am thy fellowservant." However, Christ expected, encouraged, and received worship from men. He said of Himself in John 5:23, "All men should honour the Son, even as they honour the Father." In John 9:35-38, after Jesus had healed the blind man, the man said, "Lord, I believe. And he worshipped him." Jesus also received worship from the disciples (Matthew 14:31-33 and 28:9,17).

4) The *apostolic testimony* of Christ's deity is seen in many passages, such as Philippians 2:6, where Paul said that Jesus was equal with God. Paul also cited the Old Testament and said, "Let all the angels of God worship him" (Hebrews 1:6). This is also seen in other passages.

114

5) The deity of Christ was revealed in His *resurrection* and *ascension*. Paul said in Romans 1:4 that Jesus' resurrection proved that He was the Son of God. His deity is further proven by His ascension to an exalted position at the right hand of God, as declared by Peter in Acts 2:33.

6) The deity of Christ is revealed *in the heart of every believer*. This is something that must be experienced, because no one can argue another into the knowledge that Christ is God. This truth must be verified in every Christian's personal experience with Him. It is not by rational proof that those who have received Christ bear this knowledge, but it is evidenced within by His Spirit. According to I Corinthians 12:3, no man can confess that Jesus is the Son of God except by the Holy Spirit. This does not mean that a sinner could not say the words, but he cannot make a *saving confession* except by revelation of this fact by the Spirit of God. Jesus told Peter the same thing in Matthew 16 when Peter confessed, "Thou art the Christ, the Son of the living God." Jesus replied, "Flesh and blood hath not revealed it unto thee, but my Father which is in heaven."

The deity of Christ is also revealed in the following ways:

7) *In His creative and providential works*. "All things were made by him; and without him was not any thing made" (John 1:3; cf. Colossians 1:16-17; Hebrews 11:3).

8) *In His authority to forgive sins*. "When Jesus saw their faith, he said unto the sick of the palsy, Son, thy sins be forgiven thee" (Mark 2:5).

115

9) *In His righteous and sinless life.* "For we have not an high priest which cannot be touched with the feeling of our infirmities; but was in all points tempted like as we are, yet without sin" (Hebrews 4:15; cf. II Corinthians 5:21).

10) *By His miracles.* "If I do not the works of my Father, believe me not. But if I do, though ye believe not me, believe the works: that ye may know, and believe, that the Father is in me, and I in him" (John 10:37-38; cf. Acts 2:22).

11) *In His own claims* of having authority over the law (Matthew 5); as Savior (Matthew 18:11); as Messiah (Matthew 16:16-17); and as the resurrection and the life (John 11:25).

12) *In the claims of others.* "John [the Baptist] answered, saying unto them all, I indeed baptize you with water; but one mightier than I cometh, the latchet of whose shoes I am not worthy to unloose; he shall baptize you with the Holy Spirit and with fire" (Luke 3:16; cf. Mark 3:11; 5:7; 15:9).

The Humanity of Christ

The Word of God gives evidence that Jesus had a real and complete *humanity*. Throughout the history of the church, heretics have denied this truth, and continue to do so today. However, Christ's humanity is clearly revealed in Scripture.

1) He was *born* in the ordinary way that all men are, that is, *of a woman*. "Forasmuch then as the children are partakers of flesh and blood, he [Christ] also himself likewise took part of the same" (Hebrews 2:14). Galatians 4:4 says,

"When the fulness of the time was come, God sent forth his Son, *made of a woman*, made under the law." Jesus is also called a "babe" in Luke 2:12 and a "child" in verse 43. Thus, His *birth* shows His humanity.

2) His humanity is seen in His *growth* and *development*. The record of Luke, chapter 2, shows that He grew and developed physically and intellectually.

3) His *temptations* reveal that He was fully human. Jesus' temptations were real, and as a real human being He had to overcome them. He was tempted by Satan face to face in an attempt to cause His downfall, but Jesus overcame the temptations as a true man and without sin. Why would Satan have bothered if he had not known Christ was truly human? He knew he could not tempt God whose nature was spirit. Paul said in Hebrews 2:17-18, "In all things it behoved him to be made like unto his brethren [human], that he might be a merciful and faithful high priest in things pertaining to God, to make reconciliation for the sins of the people. For in that he himself hath suffered being tempted, he is able also to succour them that are tempted," that is, the Christian in his temptations.

4) His *limitations* and *needs* as a human being show that Jesus had a true humanity. Paul tells in Philippians 2:7 that Christ Jesus emptied Himself of the form of God and took on the form of a servant. As stated previously, that does not mean He ceased to be God. He was still divine Spirit; but at the same time, He had all the attributes of human personality. He knew hunger and thirst; He knew weariness and tears and the need of sleep.

5) His temporal *suffering* and *death* give evidence of His humanity, as shown in Hebrews 2:10 and 5:8. Luke 23:46 and Acts 20:28 speak of His death as a human.

6) His humanity is also revealed in *His own claims.* He claimed to be a man in John 8:40, and the "Son of man" in John 5:27.

7) The *testimony of others* also spoke of His manhood. In I Timothy 2:5 He is called "the man Christ Jesus." In Acts 2:22 and in I Corinthians 15:21 He is said to be a man.

8) Finally, His humanity is revealed in His possession of a *full human nature* with body, soul, and spirit. Matthew 26:12 speaks of His *body;* Matthew 26:38 speaks of His *soul;* Luke 23:46 speaks of His *spirit.* He has a complete or full human nature even though He was Logos, the divine Spirit, Son of God, before His incarnation.

The Unity of Christ

Of vital importance in the study of Biblical Theology is an understanding of the mystery of the *unity of Christ,* which is the inseparable union of two natures, human and divine, in one personality or one being, the Son of God. His two natures are so vitally and inseparably united that He is properly spoken of as the "God-man." A person is a heretic who denies His *full humanity* or His *full deity.* The two ideas may appear contradictory, that is, humanity and deity, flesh and spirit, man and God; nevertheless, the Scriptures declare both are true of this unique personality, Jesus Christ.

An important question is: How can two natures be united in one personality? It should be stated initially that the union of the two natures is beyond human comprehension, and that the Scriptures do not attempt to explain all the mysteries of the Godhead. I Timothy 3:16 says, "Great is the mystery of godliness: God was manifest in the flesh." Even the Apostle Paul considered it a great mystery!

Attempts to explain the mystery by earthly analogies are futile because there are no real analogies about God. The two analogies which follow will suffice to show this. Some say that the union of the human body and soul is analagous to the union of divine and human natures in Christ. Each is distinct, yet they are inseparably related. However, this is not a proper analogy because the soul and body are not two natures but are the elements of only one nature—human.

Another analogy is the union of Christ with the believer, who are said to be one, just as He and the Father are one. This comparison falls short, however, because He is still Christ and the Christian remains himself. While saints are said to be one with their Lord by faith in Him through the new birth, two distinct personalities still exist.

There are two truths which should be made clear regarding Christ's unity: a *double personality* is denied, and a *single personality* is affirmed by the Bible. There is no teaching to suggest that Jesus has a double personality. He is not two persons with two natures, but one personality with two natures. For Him to have two natures does not require a double personality. Scripture shows that the eternal Logos did not take into union with Himself an individual *man* who was already a personality, but He took upon Himself a *human* nature which had no separate existence before His incarnation. In other words, He took upon Himself humanity. Logos became human; He did not simply inhabit a baby born at Bethlehem. In addition to His divine nature He assumed a human nature, which did not develop into an independent or separate personality, because that would have resulted in two persons.

Before His incarnation Jesus was the Logos. After His birth, the one personality was then God-man or divine-human. He possesses all the essentials of both natures. He has both a divine and human consciousness. How this can be is a mystery, yet the Scriptures show it to be true.

It is interesting to notice in the Bible that when Jesus spoke He revealed His two-fold nature, even though He is a single personality. In John 17:5 He prayed, "Father, glorify thou me with thine own self with the glory which I had with thee before the world was." He was born a babe in Bethlehem of the virgin Mary, yet He claimed in this verse to have been preexistent.

Again, in John 3:13 Jesus said, "No man hath ascended up to heaven, but he that came down from heaven, even the Son of man." He spoke as a man, calling Himself a man; however, He often showed by His words that He was divine, that He existed before He took on flesh. In John 8:54-59 Jesus infuriated the Jews who were rejecting Him, when He said that His Father was God. They attempted to stone Him when He said, "Your father Abraham rejoiced to see my day: and he saw it, and was glad. Then said the Jews unto him, Thou art not yet fifty years old, and hast thou seen Abraham? Jesus said unto them, Verily, verily, I say unto you, Before Abraham was, I am." Jesus Christ existed before Abraham was born. Through what Christ said, He revealed His two-fold nature—divine and human.

The Bible says in Acts 20:28 that God purchased the church with His own blood. Since God, as Spirit, does not have blood, Paul was obviously speaking of the fact that Jesus Christ was God, the Logos, who took on humanity. The same truth may be seen in I Corinthians 2:8 and Romans 1:3-4. In I Corinthians 15:47 Paul showed that the man Jesus is the Lord from heaven. Human and divine statements are repeatedly ascribed to the same person.

The Results of Christ's Unity

What are the results of this union of the human and divine? According to Hebrews 2 Christ took upon Himself the seed and nature of man. The Scriptures show that Jesus shall remain eternally the God-man; He forever keeps His humanity. Philippians 3:20-21 says that the bodies of the redeemed will "be fashioned like unto his glorious body." He still has His body, and He is seen in heaven as the Son of man. As the church's intercessor in heaven, Christ intercedes on behalf of the elect. He understands the trials and temptations Christians go through because He suffered the same things; therefore, He can now function as a sympathetic high priest.

The Work of Christ

The Scriptures show that the work of Christ is a three-fold ministry of prophet, priest, and king. His prophetic ministry relates to His message and ministry here on earth. His priestly ministry was His provision of an atonement. His ministry as king speaks of His Lordship and reign. These were three separate offices in the Old Testament, but all were united in Christ Jesus.

Christ as Prophet

Prediction of Christ's prophetic ministry was first seen in the Old Testament in Deuteronomy 18:15-19. God said that He would raise up a Prophet like Moses, who would speak all that He commanded. In John 1:19-23 the Jews asked John the Baptist, "Art thou Elijah?" Then, "Art thou that prophet?" They were referring to "that prophet" described in Deuteronomy 18, the Messiah they were awaiting. John denied that he was the Christ, but said he had been sent to announce His coming.

Jesus *claimed* to stand in the office of *prophet* in Matthew 13:57 when He said, "A prophet is not without honour save in his own country," speaking of Himself. He said the Father sent Him and gave Him the words to speak to the people (John 12:49-50). The *people* evidently *recognized* Him as a prophet, for they called Him a prophet in John 4:19 and 9:17. He was referred to as "that prophet" in John 6:14 and Acts 3:22-23.

The primary *function* of a prophet was his ministry as a *spokesman* for God (Isaiah 6, Amos 7, and Jeremiah 1). In John 8:26-28 Jesus claimed to have been sent by God when He said, "I speak to the world those things which I have heard of him." In John 10:36 Jesus said that God sent Him. In John 20:21 He said, "As my Father hath sent me, even so send I you." A prophet also *foretold* future events, as Jesus did, for example, in Luke 21 and Matthew 24 where He predicted certain events that would take place in the latter days. A prophet also confirmed his own ministry by working miracles and signs, his works sealing his authority. This is apparent in the ministries of Elijah, Moses, and Elisha. Christ as a prophet was proven both by His message and by His miracles (John 5:36).

Christ as Priest

Christ also fulfilled the office of a priest. The prediction of Christ's priestly ministry is recorded in Psalm 110:1-4. In verse 1 David said, "The Lord said to my Lord." Then in verse 4 the Father said to His Son, "Thou art a priest for ever after the order of Melchizedek." Joshua, the high priest, mentioned in Zechariah 3, was a type of Christ. As the prophet spoke for God to the people, the priest acted as a *mediator* on behalf of the people toward God. This function may be seen in Exodus 28-29. The Old Testament priesthood prefigured the priesthood of Christ. Jesus' priestly work is often referred to in the Gospels, as well as in Romans 3:25 and I John 2:2.

The *nature* of the priestly ministry was two-fold. It was *sacrificial* and *intercessory*. The Book of Leviticus sets forth the sacrificial nature of the priestly office (Leviticus 4:34-35). His ministry in the Old Testament was to offer animal sacrifices which the people brought, so their sins could be covered over by the blood of the victim. Christ's priestly ministry was unique because He not only offered a sacrifice for man's sin, but He offered Himself *as the sacrifice* (Isaiah 53). In John 1:29, when John the Baptist saw Jesus, he said, "Behold the Lamb of God, which taketh away the sin of the world." John was speaking of the sacrificial nature of Jesus' ministry on the earth. Hebrews 9 and 10 also show that Jesus' ministry as priest was sacrificial in the offering of Himself as the sacrifice.

Secondly, the priestly ministry of Jesus was *intercessory*. The Old Testament priest made intercession once a year on behalf of the people, entering into the Holy of Holies, where he sprinkled the blood of the atonement upon the mercy seat of the Ark (Leviticus 16). Hebrews 9 and 10 show Jesus functioning in this same way, but in this case He was taking His own blood, rather than the blood of bulls and goats.

The *nature* of Jesus' intercession is that of an advocate. "We have an advocate with the Father, Jesus Christ the righteous" (I John 2:1). An advocate or intercessor is one who speaks to a higher authority on behalf of another, toward whom he is favorably and sympathetically inclined. Jesus acts as an intercessor for the Christian. He is not merely sitting at the right hand of God *praying* for the elect. Better than that—He is their advocate. As such, He does not have to pray to the Father for He is seated in authority with the Father. From the time He presented His blood to the Father (Hebrews 9:24), all He has to do is *speak*, and the Father gives Him whatever He *says*.

The *reason* Jesus Christ can be a sympathetic high priest is stated in Hebrews 2:14-18, where Paul said that Jesus took upon Himself man's human nature so that He could suffer temptation. Verse 18 says, "For in that he himself hath suffered being tempted, he is able to succour them that are tempted." One cannot really know how to sympathize with others or how to intercede for them unless he has suffered the same things. Jesus' priesthood is effective *perpetually*, according to Hebrews 7:25. He is able "to save them to the uttermost that come unto God by him, seeing he ever liveth to make intercession for them."

Christ as King

Christ's kingship has primary reference to His sovereignty over the earth and the entire universe. Because this study of Biblical Theology will deal with the kingship in greater detail under the doctrine of last things, it will only be treated briefly here. The eternal kingship of Christ was *predicted* in many Old Testament passages. Daniel said, "I saw in the night visions, and, behold, one like the Son of man came with the clouds of heaven, and came to the Ancient of days, and they brought him near before him. And there was given him dominion, and glory, and a kingdom, that all people, nations, and languages, should serve him: his dominion is an everlasting dominion, which shall not pass away, and his kingdom that which shall not be destroyed" (Daniel 7:13-14). Other passages which show His kingship are Jeremiah 23:5-6; Psalm 2:6; Isaiah 9:6-7; Micah 5:2; and Zechariah 6:12-13.

In the New Testament also Christ is *said to be king* over an eternal kingdom. Prior to the birth of Jesus, God's angel visited Mary, and said, "And he shall reign over the house of Jacob for ever; and of his kingdom there shall be no end" (Luke 1:33). *Jesus* Himself *said* He was a *king* in John 18:37 and 19:21. This truth is again set forth in Acts 2:30 and Matthew 25:31-34. His kingdom is called the "kingdom of heaven" in Matthew 4:17, the "kingdom of God" in Luke 19:11, and the "kingdom of David" in Mark 11:10.

The States of Christ

Another aspect of the study of the doctrine of Christ is the examination of the states of Christ. There are three divisions or states in which the Son of God has existed: His existence before His birth, His incarnation in the world, and His present exaltation at the right hand of God for all eternity. Of all humanity, Christ is unique in that only He has existed in three states.

The Preexistence of Christ

The Scriptures clearly teach that the Son of God *existed before* His incarnation. For example, in John 17:5, this is clearly seen in Jesus' prayer. "And now, O Father, glorify thou me with thine own self with the glory which I had with thee before the world was." His preexistence has several aspects. As the *Logos* He was coequal with the Father, as seen in John 1:1; "In the beginning was the *Logos* [translated "Word"], and the *Logos* was with God, and the *Logos* was God." John also said in verse 14, "The *Logos* was made flesh, and dwelt among us, (and we beheld his glory, the glory as of the only begotten of the Father,) full of grace and truth."

Christ also preexisted as the *Son of God*. He was and is eternally related to the Father as the Son, even before His birth. Jesus is referred to as God's "unique Son" in several passages. "For God so loved the world, that he gave his only begotten [unique] Son" (John 3:16). See John 1:14,18.

In His preexistent state Christ was the *Creator* of all things (John 1:3; Colossians 1:16-17). At times He appeared as the *Angel* of the Lord in the Old Testament. Proof that these appearances were really God is that the Angel is called "the Lord," and He received worship which is due only to God (Genesis 16, Exodus 3, Judges 13). Paul spoke of Him in I Corinthians 10:4 as the *"Rock"* that was with Israel and preserved her in the wilderness. In I Peter 1:11 Peter said that the *Spirit of Christ* was in the Old Testament prophets before His birth or incarnation.

The Incarnation of Christ

The incarnation of Christ is His second state as the Son of God. The term incarnation is derived from the Latin verb which means "to embody with flesh." In theology the term is used in reference to the Son of God assuming humanity; the divine Logos taking human form and nature upon Himself; the union of the human with the divine.

There were many prophecies in the Old Testament predicting the one who was to come, who would be both human and divine. The incarnation is implied in Genesis

3:15 where He is called the "seed of Eve"—a human; but His divine side is suggested in that He defeats Satan. These two aspects are also evident in II Samuel 7:12-14, where He is called the seed of David, and is also said to be God's Son. Isaiah 9:6 tells of a child who would be born, but this child would be called the "mighty God." The prophet Isaiah fore-told of a son who would be born of a virgin, and His name would be called "Immanuel," that is, "God with us" (Isaiah 7:14). He is a servant of God who suffers and dies according to Isaiah 53; however, in His death He bears the iniquity of His people and secures their justification. In Zechariah 6:12-13 He is called a "man," but He will be King and Priest upon His throne. He is called the "Lord of hosts" in Zechariah 14:17.

The incarnation is *declared* throughout the New Testa-ment as well. God was manifest in the flesh (I Timothy 3:16). The Logos became flesh (John 1:14). The virgin will be with child of the Holy Spirit (Matthew 1:18-23). Emmanuel, "God with us," is born the babe in Bethlehem (Luke 1-2). God sent His Son in the likeness of sinful flesh (Romans 8:3). Christ is the seed of David according to the flesh, but also the Son of God (Romans 1:3-4). Christ is made of a woman, but He is God's Son (Galatians 4:4).

The Kenosis Experience of Christ

Christ was in the form of God in His preexistence; but for deity to become human it was necessary for Jesus to go through the experience of "emptying," which is called *"kenosis"* in theology. The King James Version says in Philip-pians 2:7 that Christ "made himself of no reputation." A

128

better translation of that is "He emptied himself," based on the Greek verb "kenoo," which means "to empty." There are two aspects to Christ's self-emptying: the temporary and the permanent. Jesus Christ temporarily gave up the independent exercise of certain of His divine attributes, such as omniscience, omnipresence, and omnipotence. He never gave up their possession, only their independent use. He had to learn and acquire knowledge like any other human being (Luke 2:40,46,52). He learned obedience by the things which He suffered (Hebrews 5:7-8). He suffered temptations (Matthew 4; Hebrews 2:18; 4:15). He did not know the time of His second coming (Matthew 24:36; Mark 13:32). Jesus had to depend on the power of the Holy Spirit to know and to do His Father's will (Isaiah 61:1; Acts 10:38; John 5:19-20,30; 12:49-50). He experienced hunger (Mark 11:12-13), weariness, pain, and grief. God could not experience any of these things except as He took on human form. He temporarily surrendered His divine glory when He took on humanity, since divine glory could not appear in physical form. He also temporarily relinquished His infinite riches (II Corinthians 8:9). He gave up all that could be recognized as God, and became just a common, ordinary Jew in appearance.

When Jesus emptied Himself of the *form* of God, it was *permanent*. In His kenosis His form as invisible Spirit ceased, and He "was made in the likeness of men" (Philippians 2:7). From the moment of Jesus' conception He became forever human; and since His resurrection He is God-man glorified. John spoke of this form when he said, "We shall be like him" (I John 3:2). Paul refers to this glorified body in Philippians 3:21, explains it in detail in I Corinthians 15:35-50, and said,

"We shall be changed. For this corruptible must put on incorruption" (verses 52-53).

When Jesus emptied Himself of the form of God and took on the form of man, He did not surrender His deity or His equality with God. He said in John 10:30, "I and my Father are one." By analogy, if an earthly king is forced into exile, he does not cease to be of royal blood or lineage, even though he may for a time put aside his royal garments, lay aside his sceptre, and step down from his throne.

The Purpose and Necessity of the Incarnation

The basic purpose for the incarnation was the redemption of sinners by God (Genesis 3:15; Isaiah 53). In John 1:29 John the Baptist said when he saw Jesus, "Behold the Lamb of God, which taketh away the sin of the world." The solemn purpose for the incarnation, which is *redemption*, has largely been replaced within Christian circles by an overemphasis upon the account of Christ's birth—the so-called "Christmas story." The gospel, however, is the *death* of Jesus. While the incarnation is an integral part of God's eternal plan, it was never God's intention that His church should turn the event into a holiday. The roots of Christmas are not to be found in Scripture, but are imbedded in paganism and Roman Catholic tradition. Fundamental Christianity would have nothing to do with its observance until quite recently. Surely if God had established this holiday, the world would have nothing to do with it, as is the case with the communion of the bread and cup, feet washing, and water baptism.

The incarnation was *necessary* for the redemption of men because it is impossible in any absolute sense for mere animal sacrifices and their blood to atone for the sins of men. This fact is set forth in Hebrews 10:1-5. "For it is not possible that the blood of bulls and of goats should take away sins." Therefore, God sent His Son to redeem man. Only another human—one without sin, since a sinner cannot redeem sinners—could act as an adequate substitute for a human being.

There is a grave error being taught, especially in charismatic circles, which states that Jesus became a sinner on the Cross and had to be born again after spending three days in hell. Nothing is more contradictory to the Word of God. A detailed study of this error is given in the author's book, *Did Jesus Die Spiritually?* Paul said in Hebrews 2:14 that Christ took human flesh upon Himself so He could die, in order to redeem the Christian. Hebrews 4:15 says that Jesus was "in all points tempted like as we are, yet without sin." He never became a sinner.

The Son of God as eternal Spirit could not die, could not suffer, could not be tempted; but Jesus Christ (the Logos who became man) could do these things. The divine Logos could not and never did die; that is, even on the Cross the Spirit did not die. At His death in the body, Jesus said, "Father, into thy hands I commend my spirit" (Luke 23:46). Thus, the divine Logos, by virtue of His inseparable union with human nature, could suffer and experience death through this union. Acts 20:28 says that God shed His blood on the Cross. This is God Logos as human, Jesus Christ—shedding His blood.

131

The Virgin Birth

Another aspect of the incarnation is the virgin birth of Christ, which the Bible clearly teaches. A study of the virgin birth is necessary to understand adequately the incarnation itself. In an ordinary conception and birth a new personality begins, but Jesus Christ did not have His beginning in Bethlehem. John said, "In the beginning was the Word [speaking of Jesus], and the Word was with God, and the Word was God.... And the Word was made flesh, and dwelt among us, (and we beheld his glory, the glory as of the only begotten of the Father,) full of grace and truth" (John 1:1,14). Micah 5:2 says that the babe born in Bethlehem was the Eternal One whose goings forth have been from everlasting.

The virgin birth of Jesus Christ was not just another person coming into existence, produced through the union of a husband and wife; but the eternal Logos, the Son of God, was being clothed with humanity. It was invisible Spirit becoming visible by taking on flesh in order that Christ might suffer and be tempted as a man, and then offer Himself as the Lamb of God, as a pure sacrifice on behalf of those He would redeem.

Liberals are unanimous in rejecting the virgin birth of Jesus Christ, saying it was a later invention of His disciples in order to glorify their leader. The liberal and neo-orthodox critics cannot deny that the New Testament Gospels clearly teach the virgin birth; therefore, they attack the Old Testament prophecy which predicts it, trying thereby to discredit the New Testament account. They reason that if they can destroy the validity of the Old Testament prophecy in Isaiah

7:14, then that would call into question the accuracy of the claims in the New Testament Gospels.

The problem of Isaiah 7:14 is quite complex. One modern version of the Bible, which follows liberalism and its denial of the virgin birth, contends that other versions, such as the King James Version, are in error when they translate the Hebrew term in Isaiah 7:14 as "virgin." They contend that the word simply means "a young woman of marriageable age," which is the way they translate the term in this later version. Isaiah's prophecy, they say, speaks of a woman who is already with child. The child which she will bear will be a sign to King Ahaz, and is said to be Isaiah's son, whom he will name Mahershalalhashbaz, which means "the spoil speeds and the prey hastens," speaking of the coming judgment upon Israel for her sins. Critical theologians say that the child is not literally called "Immanuel" as Isaiah 7:14 says, and his birth only signifies that God will be with Israel.

The Hebrew term translated "virgin" in Isaiah 7:14 is "almah." In every case where "almah" is used in the Old Testament, it means an unmarried woman; and in Old Testament Israel, if a woman was unmarried, she was assumed to be a virgin. In the various places where the term is used, it can always mean virgin, and in no case can virgin be denied.

The Septuagint, which is the Greek translation of the Hebrew Old Testament, translates "almah" with the Greek word "parthenos," which definitely means "virgin." These Hebrew and Greek scholars must have believed that "almah" meant virgin, or they would have chosen another word meaning an unmarried woman or a woman of marriageable age. If the term in Isaiah 7:14 did not mean "virgin," then a sign was not given to King Ahaz. Isaiah said, "The Lord himself shall give you a sign," and if this verse does not mean a virgin birth, then what would be the sign? It should settle the matter for any Christian that the Holy Spirit, who inspired both the Old and the New Testaments, inspired the writers to translate the Hebrew term "almah" as "virgin." This matter is covered extensively in the author's book, *An Introduction to the Old Testament Prophets*.

Jesus also testified to His unique origin in Luke 2:48-49. At the age of twelve, Jesus and His parents went to Jerusalem for the feast of the Passover. As His parents were returning home, they discovered that Jesus was not in the company traveling with them, so they returned to Jerusalem, and "they found him in the temple, sitting in the midst of the doctors, both hearing them, and asking questions." His mother asked Him, "Son, why hast thou thus dealt with us?" He answered her by saying, "Wist ye not that I must be about my Father's business?" Jesus and Joseph both knew He was not referring to Joseph as His Father. In John 8:18-19 Jesus said, "The Father that sent me beareth witness of me." The religious leaders asked, "Where is thy Father? Jesus answered, Ye neither know me, nor my Father: if ye had known me, ye should have known my Father also." They knew Joseph, His apparent father; but Jesus said that God was His Father.

An important question to ask is this: Can a person be a true Christian, yet reject the virgin birth? The author attended a seminary years ago where a professor of New Testament, when confronted about this matter, answered, "No, you do not have to believe in the virgin birth to be a

Christian." That is nonsense because the Scriptural claims that Jesus is from God, and not Joseph, are inseparably related to the rest of the Scriptures' claims about Him. They say that He is Savior; He is the Logos; He is sinless; His atoning death redeems those who believe on Him; He was raised bodily from the grave; He is now at the right hand of God; and He will return and judge this world. Salvation is believing and obeying *all* of the gospel, not just that part which one may want to accept. Jesus said in John 8:19 that the Pharisees did not know who His Father was. He said that if they did not believe what He was telling them, they would die in their sins. A person who is truly saved would never say, "I will just believe what I think is essential and the rest is not important." Everything set forth in the Word of God is important.

Liberals say that the virgin birth was biologically impossible, but they neglect the truth that the sinless life of Jesus was just as great a miracle. In fact, belief in the miracle of the virgin birth is necessary in order to explain how Jesus, the man, could live His life without sin, for the Scriptures relate that all men are sinners (Romans 3). Men are without righteousness in themselves; all have sinned and come short of the glory of God. People who struggle with the virgin birth are not really contending so much with this question as with a more basic one—the problem of their unbelief in the written Word of God.

If Jesus were not virgin born, that would mean He had a human father; and if He had a human father, that would mean He was a sinful child of Adam by nature and in need of someone to atone for His sins. The Word of God repeatedly

135

says, however, that Jesus was sinless. In Hebrews 4:15 Paul said that Jesus was "in all points tempted like as we are, yet without sin." Irenaeus in 190 A.D. said that the Christian church, which was scattered over the whole world by that time, had been taught by the apostles to believe in the virgin birth. Others in early church history believed in the virgin birth, including Tertullian, Justin Martyr, Ignatius, and Origen.

The Exaltation of Christ: The Significance of His Resurrection

In dealing with the states of Christ, His preexistence and incarnation have been studied thus far. The next aspect to be examined is His present *exaltation*, beginning with the significance of His resurrection. Why was Jesus raised from the dead? First, His resurrection was necessary for man's *justification*, according to Romans 4:25. "Who was delivered for our offences, and was raised again for our justification." Man would still be in his sins if there were no resurrection. The very fact that God raised Jesus after He had made the offering for man's sins is proof that God accepted that offering. His death reconciled man to God, according to Romans 5:10; and Paul said that without the resurrection of Jesus, "ye are yet in your sins" (I Corinthians 15:17).

A second significance of the resurrection is that it is the very *basis* or heart of the *gospel*. In I Corinthians 15:12-19 Paul clearly said that if there is no resurrection, there is no gospel—there is no hope. Those who deny the bodily resurrection of Jesus Christ deny resurrection for themselves, as well as any hope of salvation. Paul said if Christ was not raised from the dead, there is no redemption for mankind.

Another significance of the resurrection is that it is an essential part of the Christian's *faith* and *confession* unto salvation. The apostle states in Romans 10:9-10 the way to be saved: "That if thou shalt confess with thy mouth the Lord Jesus, and shalt believe in thine heart that God hath raised him from the dead, thou shalt be saved." Believing in the resurrection is as necessary as believing in the virgin birth. A person cannot pick and choose what he will believe from God's Word and still be a Christian. This text shows that it is vital for followers of Christ to both *believe* and *confess* that God raised Jesus from the dead.

Furthermore, the significance of the resurrection of Jesus is that it is the *basis* for *man's resurrection*. If Jesus is not raised, according to Paul, man will not be raised, because His resurrection is the pledge for the Christian (Romans 6:5). This same truth is seen in Romans 8:11; II Corinthians 4:14; I Thessalonians 4:14. The resurrection of Jesus is also the *basis* for the *Christian's new life* as seen in Romans 6:4-23 and Colossians 3.

The Importance of the Resurrection

The importance of the resurrection in the early church is seen throughout the New Testament. Jesus predicted His own resurrection (John 2:19; 10:14-18). After it took place, Jesus rebuked the disciples for their failure to believe He would rise again, showing them from the Old Testament that His resurrection was predicted (Luke 24:25-27,44-45). However, once He had opened their understanding,

137

especially after Pentecost, the believers did recognize predictions of His resurrection in the Old Testament, such as Psalm 16:10, quoted by Peter in Acts 2:27. In fact, the resurrection was the central theme of Peter's sermons in Acts 2 and 3; and Paul quoted Psalm 2 in his sermon at Antioch in Pisidia (Acts 13). Even before Pentecost, one of the qualifications in the selection of an apostle to replace Judas Iscariot was "to be a witness with us of his resurrection" (Acts 1:21-22). The preaching of the resurrection was the cause of the first persecutions of the church (Acts 4:1-3; 5:27-42). This event is mentioned over one hundred times in the New Testament, proving its importance.

The Certainty of the Resurrection

The certainty that the resurrection took place is the *empty tomb.* "Now upon the first day of the week, very early in the morning, they came unto the sepulchre, bringing the spices which they had prepared, and certain others with them. And they found the stone rolled away from the sepul- chre. And they entered in, and found not the body of the Lord Jesus. And it came to pass, as they were much per- plexed thereabout, behold, two men stood by them in shining garments: And as they were afraid, and bowed down their faces to the earth, they said unto them, Why seek ye the liv- ing among the dead? He is not here, but is risen: remember how he spake unto you when he was yet in Galilee, Saying, the Son of man must be delivered into the hands of sinful men, and be crucified, and the third day rise again. And they remembered his words" (Luke 24:1-8). According to the angels Christ was among the living and not "among the dead."

Rationalistic Theories of the Empty Tomb

There are several rationalistic theories regarding the empty tomb.

1) The *unburied body theory* says that the body of Jesus was simply disposed of in some unknown place, as were the bodies of the two thieves.

2) Similar to that is the *unemptied tomb theory*, which contends that Jesus' body, now dust, is still in a tomb in some unknown location. These two views are obviously false. If Christ had not risen from the dead, it would mean that Satan had triumphed; and he certainly would have seen to it that the body of Jesus would have been found to prove his success.

3) The *mistaken woman theory*, or the *hallucination theory*, purports that Mary Magdalene was simply hallucinating at the tomb and thought she had encountered the risen Christ, but she was just emotionally overwrought and imagined that she had seen Him. This is shown to be wrong by the fact that Christ appeared to many others after the resurrection. Obviously, they were not all hallucinating.

4) Those who hold to the *resuscitation theory* believe that Jesus did not really die, but He merely fainted due to His pain and suffering on the Cross; then the cool air in the tomb and the stimulus of the embalming spices revived Him. There are obvious objections to this theory. In John 19:34 one of the soldiers "pierced his side, and forthwith came there out blood and water," which indicated that He was dead. Jesus'

own words to the Father prove His death, "Into thy hands I commend my spirit" (Luke 23:46). When the soldiers went to break the legs of the three, they saw that He was already dead (John 19:33).

5) The *fraud theory* supposes that the apostles purposely hid the body of Jesus in order to perpetuate their leader's memory and His ministry. In answer to this fallacy, all of the apostles except John were put to death for what they believed and taught about the resurrection of Jesus Christ. Which of them would have been willing to be crucified for some fraud?

6) The *spiritual resurrection* view erroneously says that Jesus did actually appear after His death, but it was only His spirit and not His body which appeared. This view is taught by the Jehovah's Witnesses and others, but is contradicted by the Word of God. For example, in Luke 24:36-39 the disciples were gathered together after the resurrection, "And as they thus spake, Jesus himself stood in the midst of them, and saith unto them, Peace be unto you. But they were terrified and affrighted, and supposed that they had seen a spirit [They thought they were looking at a spiritually resurrected Jesus]. And he said unto them, Why are ye troubled? and why do thoughts arise in your hearts? Behold my hands and my feet, that it is I myself: handle me, and see; for a spirit hath not flesh and bones, as ye see me have." He proceeded to eat some food which they gave Him and further proved that He had a resurrected body, not one of *blood* and flesh, but of *bone* and flesh—a glorified body. They were standing before their Lord and Savior who had been bodily raised, completely disproving the spiritual resurrection theory.

The Jewish View of the Empty Tomb

The *Jewish theory* or the *stolen body theory* originated with the Jewish leaders in Jerusalem after the resurrection of Jesus. In Matthew 28:11-15, after the disciples learned that Jesus' body was missing from the tomb, they went back to tell the others. "Now when they were going, behold, some of the watch [the soldiers guarding the tomb] came into the city, and shewed unto the chief priests all the things that were done. And when they were assembled with the elders, and had taken counsel, they gave large money unto the soldiers, Saying, Say ye, His disciples came by night, and stole him away while we slept. And if this come to the governor's ears, we will persuade him, and secure you. So they took the money, and did as they were taught: and this saying is commonly reported among the Jews until this day." The theory that Jesus' body was stolen away is still believed by modern Jews.

The Scriptural Proof of the Resurrection

Evidence of the resurrection of Jesus is found throughout the New Testament.

1) The supernatural experience of the guards at the tomb is a testimony to the resurrection of Jesus, as was the fact that the authorities offered them money so they would not tell what actually happened.

2) The *undisturbed grave clothing* is a witness to the resurrection in the sense that had the body been stolen or never put in the tomb, then why would someone have neatly

arranged the grave clothing in the empty tomb? In John 20:2-10, when the women came to the tomb, they found the body missing and went back and told the disciples. Peter and John "went into the sepulchre, and seeth the linen clothes lie, And the napkin, that was about his head, not lying with the linen clothes, but wrapped together in a place by itself."

3) The numerous *appearances* of Christ give evidence of His resurrection. He appeared to Mary in John 20:16; to the two disciples on the road to Emmaeus in Luke 24; to the other women in Matthew 28:9-10; to Peter in Luke 24:34-35; to the disciples with Thomas absent in Luke 24; to the eleven the following Sunday in John 20; and to the seven disciples beside the Sea of Galilee in John 21:2. Paul said that Jesus appeared to over five hundred at one time in Galilee (Matthew 28:16-17 with I Corinthians 15:6). He appeared to James, according to I Corinthians 15:7. His last appearance and ascension were recorded in Luke 24:51 and Acts 1:9-12. His appearance to Paul in Acts 9 was post-ascension. Stephen saw Him in a vision in Acts 7:55. Since the completion of the biblical record, Jesus has appeared many times, and it is still happening in this present age. Generally He appears in vision, but sometimes He has appeared bodily for His own purposes.

4) The fact that the disciples after Pentecost went out preaching the *gospel of the resurrection*, risking their lives and dying for that message, is further proof that it did occur. Earlier, they had fled and forsaken Christ at His crucifixion and fearfully met behind closed doors and windows. For example, compare Peter when he denied the Lord with Peter after he received the baptism in the Holy Spirit.

5) The sudden conversion of Saul, the archenemy and persecutor of the church, is one of the greatest proofs of the resurrection according to Philippians 3 and Acts 9, because it was the risen Christ who appeared to Him.

6) The events of Pentecost, when three thousand of the murderers of Jesus Christ were converted, and the church was established there in Jerusalem, give evidence of Jesus' resurrection, since that was the message to which the multitudes responded.

7) Another evidence is the change in the *day of rest and worship* from Saturday to Sunday (Acts 20:7; I Corinthians 16:2). There was no formal decree given to change the day, but the universal consent on the part of Christians was to dedicate Sunday to the commemoration of the resurrection of Christ.

8) Finally, the Christian's *personal experience of faith* assures him of Christ's resurrection. It is the faith that believers have concerning the deity of Christ, His substitutionary blood atonement, and His bodily resurrection from the dead, which is the gospel by which they are saved. Without the resurrection there would be no gospel. Paul said in I Corinthians 15:17, "And if Christ be not raised, your faith is vain; ye are yet in your sins"; but He was raised from the dead. Praise God!

The Ascension of Christ

The necessary sequel to Christ's resurrection was His *ascension* as recorded in Luke 24:51 and Acts 1:9-12. He was raised from the dead so that He might be exalted to the right hand of God, where He was before His incarnation. There are many prophecies in both the Old and New Testaments which predict His ascension and exaltation, such as Psalm 16:10-11, 68:18, and 110:4-5. In John 6:62 Jesus said, "What and if ye shall see the Son of man ascend up where he was before?" He later revealed, "I came forth from the Father, and am come into the world: again, I leave the world, and go to the Father" (John 16:28). There it is clear that He had been with the Father, and He would ascend back to the Father after His resurrection.

The Purposes for Christ's Ascension and Exaltation

What were the purposes of Christ's ascension and exaltation? In *relation* to *Himself*, it was to enthrone Him at God's right hand and to restore Him to His former glory. This may be seen in John 17:5, where He prayed, "And now, O Father, glorify thou me with thine own self with the glory which I had with thee before the world was." His exalted position at the right hand of God, making intercession for the elect, is seen in Hebrews 1:3, 7:26, 8:1.

In *relation* to His *church* Christ was exalted to be the Savior and the head of the church (Ephesians 1:20,22; Acts 5:31). He ascended so He could send the Holy Spirit to empower the church's witness, as shown in Acts 1:8. "Therefore being at the right hand of God exalted, and having received of the Father the promise of the Holy Spirit, he hath shed forth this, which ye now see and hear" (Acts 2:33). He is there to intercede on behalf of the saints, according to Hebrews 4:14,16; 7:1-28. His purpose there is also to prepare a place for His body, the church (John 14:1-3; Ephesians 2:6). When He ascended on high He gave gifts to men, including such ministries as apostle, prophet, evangelist, pastor, and teacher (Ephesians 4:7-11), as well as the charismatic gifts (Romans 12; I Corinthians 12). Finally, He is at God's right hand to provide a way for the Christian's ascension (I Thessalonians 4:16-17).

Christ has ascended and is exalted in *relation* to the *universe* so that he might reign and rule over it. "By the resurrection of Jesus Christ: Who is gone into heaven, and is on the right hand of God; angels and authorities and powers being made subject unto him" (I Peter 3:21-22). Another purpose of Christ's exaltation may be found in I Corinthians 15:24-28. He will reign and rule at the right hand of God until God makes all of His enemies His footstool. This is also seen in Acts 2:34-35 and Hebrews 10:12-13. He is there, finally, to sustain the very universe which He created. In Colossians 1:16-17 Paul said that Jesus made all things, and sustains all of His creation.

The Restitution of All Things

Another aspect of the exaltation of Christ is His work of the *restitution* (restoration) of all things, which is spoken of in Acts 3:19-21. Peter said to the Jews, "Repent ye therefore, and be converted, that your sins may be blotted out, when the times of refreshing shall come from the presence of the Lord; And he shall send Jesus Christ, which before was preached unto you: Whom the heaven must receive until the times of restitution of all things, which God hath spoken by the mouth of all his holy prophets since the world began."

145

This passage refers to Christ's work of restoration of all things to their original purity, holiness, blessedness, and happiness, as they were before sin entered the universe. Paul said in Romans 8:18-23 that this restoration would include the restoration of man and nature to the happiness, holiness, health, and prosperity that were lost in the fall into sin. For a detailed study of this subject, see the author's book, *Deeper Life in the Spirit*.

The Climax of Christ's Exaltation: His Second Coming

Another aspect of His exaltation will be the *Second Advent*—the return of Jesus to the earth. This topic is covered thoroughly under the study of Eschatology later in this text, but it is mentioned here for the sake of completeness. The exaltation will reach its climax when Jesus returns with His saints to establish His kingdom on this earth for a thousand years (Revelation 19-20). His return will be bodily and visible, according to Acts 1:11. Immediately after Jesus' ascension, the angels asked the apostles, "Ye men of Galilee, why stand ye gazing up into heaven? this same Jesus, which is taken up from you into heaven, shall so come in like manner as you have seen him go into heaven."

There are several *purposes* for the Second Advent, the first being *judgment*. Jesus said in John 5:22 that the Father "hath committed all judgment unto the Son." In II Thessalonians 1:8 Paul stated that Jesus would return to earth with His angels, "In flaming fire taking vengeance on them that know not God, and that obey not the gospel of our Lord Jesus Christ." Another purpose is for salvation, in the sense that

146

God's people will know *full redemption* (I Thessalonians 4:13-17; I Corinthians 15). His purpose will also be for *Israel's restoration* according to many prophecies in the Old Testament; the whole Book of Zechariah; Amos 9:15; also Acts 1:6-7; Romans 11.

The Doctrine of the Holy Spirit

The doctrine of the Holy Spirit is usually studied under three headings: His personality, deity, and work. Teaching on the personality of the Holy Spirit is significant because the cults and the liberals, contrary to the Bible, contend that the Holy Spirit is not a personality, but He is merely to be equated with a *power*. To support their view they quote Acts 1:8, where Jesus said He would send the Holy Spirit to empower man's witness. Others say the Holy Spirit is only an *influence* that God exercises in people's minds. They quote John 14:26 where Jesus said He would send the Holy Spirit to teach the disciples.

The Personality of the Holy Spirit

The Scriptures show that the Holy Spirit is a *personality*—not a mere power, or influence, or an impersonal attribute of God. This is obvious because *personal pronouns*, which indicate personality, are used in reference to Him. Although the Greek term "pneuma," meaning "spirit," is a neuter noun, whenever the Scriptures speak of the Holy Spirit, *masculine* pronouns (He, Him, Himself) are used. The Greek language is quite complex, and if the Holy Spirit were simply a neuter power or influence, the writers would have used neuter pronouns; but instead, whenever the Holy Spirit

147

is spoken of, masculine pronouns are used of Him, indicating that He is a personality. The term "paraclete," which is used in John 14:26 of the Holy Spirit, is the same one used in I John 2:1 of Christ, the man.

The Holy Spirit has *attributes of personality* such as wisdom and knowledge (I Corinthians 2:10-12; 12:8). In Romans 8:26-27 Paul spoke of the "mind of the Spirit." I Corinthians 12:11 shows that He wills to do things. He teaches (John 14:26); He can be grieved, indicating that He has emotion (Ephesians 4:30); He reproves the world of sin (John 16:8); and He appoints, commissions, and commands (Acts 13:2; 20:28). Paul was forbidden by the Holy Spirit in Acts 16:6-7 from going into certain areas to preach, but was sent instead to other places. The Holy Spirit was active in creation (Genesis 1:2; Job 33:4). A mere influence or power could not speak, but He spoke in John 16:13 and Acts 13:2. In Revelation 3:22 Jesus said, "Let him hear what the Spirit saith unto the churches."

The Scriptures lend no support to the error that the Holy Spirit is just a power or influence. If they did, it would result in tautology, that is, needless repetition in many passages. For example, Acts 10:38 reads, "God anointed Jesus of Nazareth with the Holy Spirit and with power." Substitute the word "power" for the Holy Spirit, then it would read, "God anointed Jesus of Nazareth with power and with power." The matter is settled in Zechariah 4:6 where spirit and power are contrasted. "Not by might, nor by power, but by my spirit, saith the Lord of hosts."

The Deity of the Holy Spirit

The deity of the Holy Spirit is a truth which is denied by the cults and the liberals, but is seen throughout the Word of God. First, in the triune passages the Holy Spirit's deity is shown in that He is *equated with God*. The Great Commission given to the church by Jesus in Matthew 28:19 says, "Go ye therefore, and teach all nations, baptizing them in the name of the Father, and of the Son, and of the Holy Spirit." Also see II Corinthians 13:14; I Peter 1:2.

Secondly, the Holy Spirit is *called God* in certain passages. For instance, in Acts 5:3-4 Ananias and Sapphira sold their property and brought a certain part of the money to the church. They said they were giving all they had received, but they were only giving part. Peter said to Ananias, "Why hath Satan filled thine heart to lie to the Holy Spirit, and to keep back part of the price of the land? Whiles it remained, was it not thine own? and after it was sold, was it not in thine own power? why hast thou conceived this thing in thine heart? thou hast not lied unto men, but unto God." In verse 3 Peter said they lied to the Holy Spirit, but in verse 4 he said they lied to God; so obviously, the *Holy Spirit is God*. Other passages in the New Testament where the Holy Spirit is equated with God are: I Corinthians 3:16; 12:4-6; Ephesians 2:22.

Thirdly, the Holy Spirit is revealed to be God by the fact that He possesses *divine attributes*. He is said to be *omnipresent* in Psalm 139:7. "Whither shall I go from thy spirit? or whither shall I flee from thy presence?" The Holy Spirit is also *omniscient*, all-wise (I Corinthians 2:10). His *omnipotence* is shown in that He created the heavens and earth

149

(Genesis 1:2), and He is the agent of the new birth (John 3:7-8).

The Work of the Holy Spirit

When speaking of the work of the Holy Spirit, one should avoid the error of dividing God's activity into dispensations to such an extreme that it borders on Sabellianism or the "oneness" error. This heresy, which confronted the early church and is still present today, teaches that God existed in three successive modes. Those who believe this say that in the Old Testament was the ministry of the Father; in the New Testament was the ministry of the Son; and in the present church age is the ministry of the Holy Spirit. Stated another way, this would mean that God is not one divine Spirit who eternally exists as Father, Son, and Holy Spirit; but He has existed in three successive modes: first, the Father; then, the Son; and now, the Holy Spirit.

On the contrary, in every work and activity of God, the eternal, triune God is personally and actively present. While it is true that each personality or manifestation of the triune God occupies certain offices or has specific functions within the unity in the Godhead, the Godhead cannot be divided. One never works without the entire Godhead acting. In John 14:16 Christ promised to send the Holy Spirit; in verse 18 He said, "I will come"; then in verse 23 He said, "We [the Father and I] will come unto him, and make our abode with him." In this passage it is clearly shown that Jesus promised to send the Holy Spirit, which He did on the day of Pentecost; but it would be He, Himself, who would be coming back, and not only He, but the Father also. Jesus was saying that when the Spirit is present, then the Father and Son are present. This may be difficult to comprehend; nevertheless, it is true. God is what He reveals Himself to be in His Word; He is one divine Spirit who eternally manifests Himself as Father, Son, and Holy Spirit.

The Holy Spirit's work *in relation* to the *Old Testament* is threefold. The Holy Spirit was the *agent* in *creation* (Genesis 1:2; Psalm 104:24,30; Job 33:4). In Colossians 1:16 Paul revealed that Jesus Christ was the creator of all things, which is confirmed in John 1:1-3. How did He do it? He created *by the Spirit of God*; therefore, there is no contradiction. The Holy Spirit, as the agent in creation, actually did the forming.

Secondly, the Holy Spirit *empowered* men *by anointing* them for special functions or work, as seen all through the Book of Judges. The Holy Spirit fell upon Samson, for example, and he was supernaturally empowered to do mighty works on behalf of God. It is interesting to note that there is a distinction between the work of the Holy Spirit with respect to believers in the old dispensation and in the New Testament. There are numerous cases in the Old Testament where He would anoint individuals for a certain task; He would be with them, and then He would leave after the work or function was finished. In the New Testament, however, when a believer received the baptism of the Holy Spirit, the Spirit would indwell him permanently. Jesus said in John 14:17 that the Holy Spirit "dwelleth with you, and shall be in you," referring, of course, to the initial outpouring of the Spirit on the day of Pentecost, and also to those in later times who would receive this experience.

151

In the Old Testament the Holy Spirit *inspired men* with *wisdom, knowledge,* and *skills.* This empowering enabled the men to implement the plans that God gave Moses for the tabernacle and the later temple and its furnishings. God gave skills by His Spirit to those He had chosen to perform these works (Exodus 31:3). He also *inspired* the *prophets* to *speak* (Zechariah 7:12). In Nehemiah 9:30, for example, God spoke to the Israelites through the prophets by His Spirit.

It was the Holy Spirit who *inspired* the *Old Testament Scriptures.* David was inspired to write the Psalms, for he said, "The Spirit of the Lord spake by me, and his word was in my tongue" (II Samuel 23:1-2). The apostle said in II Peter 1:21 that "holy men of God spake as they were moved by the Holy Spirit." According to II Timothy 3:16-17 all Scripture is inspired by God—both Old and New Testaments.

The Holy Spirit's work *in relation* to the *New Testament* dispensation is fourfold. First, with respect to *Scripture,* it was He who inspired the writer. In John 16:13 Jesus was even more specific. He said, "When he, the Spirit of truth is come, he will guide you into all truth: for he shall not speak of himself; but whatsoever he shall hear, that shall he speak: and he will shew you things to come." This is a direct statement of the fact that the Scriptures are inspired. In other words, "I will show you things to come by my Spirit. I will teach you all things by my Spirit."

Secondly, the work of the Holy Spirit was inseparably *related to Jesus* from His birth. According to Luke 1:35, Jesus' birth was to be a virgin birth by the Holy Spirit. Luke 3:22 says that after Jesus was baptized, "the Holy Spirit descended in a bodily shape like a dove upon him." When Jesus began His ministry as teacher, He said, "The Spirit of the Lord is upon me, because he hath anointed me to preach" (Luke 4:18). In Matthew 12:28 Jesus said He cast out devils by the Spirit of God. Further, He warned that if someone spoke against His works, he would be blaspheming the Holy Spirit, because Jesus did the works by the Spirit of God. The Bible also speaks of the Spirit's work with respect to the resurrection of Christ; it was the Spirit of God who raised Him from the dead (Romans 8:11).

Thirdly, the Spirit of God has a ministry in *relation* to the *church*. He is seen to be the creator of the church, which had its beginning when the believers were baptized by the Holy Spirit on the day of Pentecost (Acts 2:1-4). Paul said in I Corinthians 12:13 that all believers are baptized by one Spirit into one body, speaking there of the Spirit's work of regeneration, not of the baptism in the Holy Spirit. Ephesians 2:22 says that Christians "are builded together for an habitation of God through the Spirit." The Holy Spirit directs the church's ministry, as seen, for example, in Acts 13,16,20, as well as throughout the New Testament. It is evident in those passages that He is the sovereign agent in evangelism, for He told Paul to go one place and not to go to another. The Holy Spirit was not only empowering the church's witness, but He was also directing where they were to witness, just as He will today if Christians will look to Him for guidance.

Fourthly, the Holy Spirit's ministry in *relation* to the *individual Christian* is quite extensive. He convicts of sin, according to John 16:8; then, upon belief of the gospel, He gives regeneration—the new birth. He then enables the new convert to make a saving confession of Christ. "No man can say that Jesus is the Lord, but by the Holy Spirit" (I Corinthians 12:3). As stated earlier in this text, that does not mean man cannot say those words, but he cannot make a saving confession from the heart except by the Spirit. The Holy Spirit is also the one who sanctifies; that is, He sets believers apart unto service in God's kingdom (II Thessalonians 2:13; I Peter 1:2). Further, He educates and illumines the minds of His children (John 14:26; Mark 13:11; I Corinthians 12:8).

The Holy Spirit also empowers the Christian with respect to his ministry, witness, and walk with Christ. In I Corinthians 12 and 14 Paul shows that the Holy Spirit empowers the believer's ministry through the gifts of the Spirit. In Acts 1:8 Jesus said the Holy Spirit would empower the church's witness. In Galatians 5:16,22-23 the fruit of the Spirit is manifest through the saints. Paul taught that disciples of Jesus are to walk in the Spirit, and he listed the fruits of the Spirit which should be evident in their lives. The Holy Spirit intercedes for Christ's followers, according to Romans 8:26. Finally, He preserves the elect, according to Ephesians 4:30; and will resurrect them as He did Christ (Romans 8:11).

Clarification of Terms Regarding the Holy Spirit

In the study of the doctrine of the Holy Spirit, there are a number of terms and concepts which are sometimes confused or misunderstood. These include the gift of the Spirit contrasted with the gifts of the Spirit, as well as the earnest, sealing, anointing, baptism, infilling, fulness, and indwelling of the Spirit. Some of these terms are used synony-mously—being baptized in the Spirit (Acts 1) is being filled with the Spirit (Acts 2:4).

The first term to be discussed is the *gift* of the Holy Spirit which is the *"baptism of the Holy Spirit."* In Acts 2:12 the Jews were amazed when they heard the disciples speaking in tongues or other languages, and they inquired of Peter, "What meaneth this?" Peter replied that what they were ob-serving was that which had been spoken by the prophet in Joel 2:28, and that they could also "receive the gift of the Holy Spirit." This topic is covered thoroughly in Dr. Freeman's book, *Why Speak in Tongues?*

Many people confuse regeneration with the baptism of the Holy Spirit. They think a person automatically receives the baptism of the Holy Spirit when he is saved; however, they are not the same. In Acts 1:4,5,8 Jesus' promise was not "Wait to be born again," but was in essence, "Wait to be empowered; wait for the Holy Spirit."

In regeneration the Holy Spirit imparts life or the new birth, as seen in John 1:12, "But as many as received him, to them gave he power [the authority or right] to become the sons of God." The Greek term, translated "power," is "exousia." The term used in Acts, however, is "dunamis," from which the word "dynamite" is derived. In Scripture it is the enabling to do mighty works. Jesus said, "Ye shall receive power [dunamis]" in Acts 1:8. In the one case the promise is for the authority and right to become a son of God; in the other case, it is for empowering.

Just as the *gift* of the Holy Spirit is not to be confused with regeneration, neither is the *gift* of the Spirit to be confused with the gifts of the Spirit. The *gifts* (plural) are supernatural manifestations of the Spirit through the body of Christ, and are described in I Corinthians 12; 14; and Romans 12. The *gift* of the Spirit, as it is called in Acts 2:38, is the baptism of the Holy Spirit. Acts 10:45 and 11:15-17 speak of the gift of the Holy Spirit being poured out upon the Gentiles.

Another term used regarding the Holy Spirit is the *earnest* of the Spirit, which occurs in II Corinthians 1:22. Paul said, God "hath also sealed us, and given the earnest of the Spirit in our hearts." This signifies that God has given a downpayment, an earnest or a part, as a pledge or guarantee that the remainder will be given. There are two aspects of the earnest of the Spirit. The baptism of the Holy Spirit is God's pledge of full redemption; and it is also the prospect of the fulness of the Spirit, which will be mentioned later.

A third expression is the *sealing* of the Holy Spirit which occurs in II Corinthians 1:22, as well as in Ephesians 1:13-14 and 4:30. The earnest of the Spirit is God's pledge of full redemption, and the sealing is God's assurance of this. It is like an envelope—God put the promise inside and then sealed it.

Another term is the *anointing* of the Spirit, which is also called the *unction* of the Spirit in the King James Version. I John 2:20 says, "But ye have an unction from the Holy One, and ye know all things," and verse 27 continues, "But the anointing which ye have received of him abideth in you." Paul also spoke of the anointing in II Corinthians 1:21.

156

What is the *meaning* of *anointing*? In the Old Testament the prophets, priests, and kings were anointed with oil to signify that they were being set apart for service unto God, a ritual which depicted the Holy Spirit being put upon them. In the New Testament the anointing is said to be within the believer (John 14:17).

What is the *purpose* of the *anointing*? It brings illumination to the essential truths of Scripture (I Corinthians 2:14; I John 2:20,27; John 16:13). The anointing enables Christians to witness effectively (Acts 1:8 with 2:37-47). The anointing is the enablement to minister the gifts (I Corinthians 12; 14; Romans 12). The anointing is an empowering to preach and teach the Word, as in Luke 4:18 where Jesus was anointed to preach. The anointing gives believers the power needed to walk and live a consecrated life. Those who are baptized in the Spirit will experience the anointing in these various ways.

The Bible shows that being baptized in the Spirit is to be *filled* with the Spirit. These two terms are used interchangeably in the Book of Acts. However, the *fulness* of the Spirit is manifested in the Christian's life to the extent he yields himself to the Spirit after he is baptized in the Spirit. The baptism is an instantaneous experience received with the asking (Luke 11:13), but the *fulness is a growth* (Ephesians 4:11-16). The fulness is not a once-for-all experience, but is a gradual maturing unto the likeness of Jesus Christ. The command in Ephesians 5:18, "Be filled with the Spirit," was given to saints who had already received the infilling of the Spirit; but Paul knew that they needed to go on to the fulness. Since Acts 1:5 and 2:4 equate the baptism of the Spirit with being filled with the Spirit, obviously a deeper meaning is implied by Paul's exhortation to be filled with the Spirit in Ephesians 5:18. For an in-depth study on the subject, see the author's book entitled, *Deeper Life in the Spirit*, which shows how to receive the baptism of the Holy Spirit, as well as how to grow into the fulness of the Spirit.

Chapter Four

The Doctrine of Sin

The Scriptures clearly show that *sin* is a disease afflicting the whole human race. Because this worldwide epidemic is gaining in potency, Christians need to recognize its symptoms, discover its cause, determine its extent, and proclaim its cure. What is the origin of sin in the universe? Most people would immediately reply, "It was through the temptation of Adam by Satan. Adam was the first to sin." Actually, according to Scripture, the origin of sin was before the creation of man; it was not through him, but *through Satan*. I John 3:8 reveals that Satan committed sin from the beginning; and according to John 8:44, he was a murderer and a liar from the beginning. Sin was found in him.

The writings of the prophets offer much insight concerning Satan's origin and the entrance of sin into the world. Although Isaiah 14:12-14 speaks directly about the *king of Babylon*, it actually moves beyond him and refers to *Satan*. The language in verse 12, which is addressed to the king of Babylon, is also used of Satan in the New Testament in Luke 10:18 and in Revelation 12:7-10, where Satan is cast down from his exalted position. Satan said in Isaiah 14:13-14, "I will ascend into heaven, I will exalt my throne above the stars of

God: I will sit also upon the mount of the congregation, . . . I will ascend above the heights of the clouds; I will be like the most High." Of course the prophecy cannot be limited to a mere human being, the king of Babylon.

Isaiah 14 portrays Satan's fall and ultimate destruction; but a similar passage in Ezekiel 28:11-19 also refers to *Satan*, goes beyond the historical *king of Tyre* and describes the original, unfallen state of Satan. ". . . full of wisdom, and perfect in beauty. Thou hast been in the garden of God; every precious stone was thy covering, . . . in the day that thou wast created. Thou art the anointed cherub . . . . thou wast perfect in thy ways from the day that thou wast created, till iniquity was found in thee" (Ezekiel 28:12-15). Obviously, none of this could have been said of a mere human being. The king of Tyre was neither originally perfect nor created, nor did he later fall from his previous condition of righteousness. However, this is an accurate description of the career of Satan. See Colossians 1:16; Ephesians 6:12; John 1:3 with 8:44.

Why are these two prophecies addressed to the historical kings of Babylon and Tyre if they are descriptive of Satan? This type of dual fulfillment is one of the unique aspects of prophecy. For example, David apparently had reference to himself in many of the Psalms, but in reality he was describing Christ. "Thou wilt not leave my soul in hell [sheol]" (Psalm 16:10). In Acts 2:27 Peter was speaking of Jesus and quoting from Psalm 16, "Thou wilt not leave my soul in hell [hades], neither wilt thou suffer thine Holy One to see corruption."

In the characters and careers of these two kings the wicked character and career of Satan himself is seen. Satan fulfills himself and his evil administration in and through earthly kings. These rulers, like Satan, arrogated to themselves divine honors and prerogatives and called themselves gods.

There are other Scriptures where *Satan* was *addressed indirectly*. In Genesis 3 God addressed the *serpent*, but He was actually talking to *Satan*. In Matthew 16:23 Jesus addressed *Peter*, but He spoke beyond him to *Satan* and said, "Get thee behind me, Satan." Jesus also addressed *Satan* when He said, "That thou doest, do quickly," because Satan had entered *Judas* (John 13:27).

One might raise the question, "How could a perfect being sin?" The Scriptures reveal that only God is infinite; He cannot be tempted to sin (James 1). Finiteness is inherent in creation; all finite creatures are subject to temptation and sin. Satan fell because of pride in his great wisdom and beauty (I Timothy 3:6 with Ezekiel 28).

The *origin* of *sin* in the *human race* came through *man*. "Wherefore, as by one man sin entered into the world, and death by sin; and so death passed upon all men, for that all have sinned" (Romans 5:12).

For a detailed study of these questions, see the author's book, *An Introduction to the Old Testament Prophets*.

The Nature of Sin

In both the Old and New Testaments, *sin* is described under various concepts depicting its many sided *nature*. 1) Sin is basically *rebellion* against God, His laws, His Word, and His will. One of the terms used in the Old Testament for sin is the Hebrew "pasha," which means "to rebel." In Isaiah 1:2 God said, "I have nourished and brought up children, and they have rebelled against me." This rebellion stems from selfishness. Man rejects God's will and makes self-will the supreme goal of his life. Jesus stressed the absolute necessity for man to reverse this process if he is to be saved. Jesus said, "If any man will come after me, let him deny himself, and take up his cross, and follow me" (Matthew 16:24; Mark 8:34).

In Matthew 7:21-22 Jesus said that no one can enter the Kingdom of God unless he does the will of God, and in the Sermon on the Mount (Matthew 5-7) He sets forth God's will about many matters of life and conduct. God will not receive anyone into His presence if they refuse to surrender self-will to Him.

2) Sin is *disobedience* to the law of God (I Timothy 1:8-10); to the revealed will of God (Deuteronomy 28); and to one's own conscience—the voice of God within (Romans 2:15).

3) Sin is *unrighteousness*. "All unrighteousness is sin" (I John 5:17). Righteousness is measuring up to a perfect standard or norm which the Scriptures describe as God Himself. Therefore, He is the standard by which believers are to

measure their lives and conduct. Unrighteousness does not meet God's standard.

4) Sin is *falling short of* or *missing the mark*. In Psalm 51:4 the term used for sin is "chata," which means "missing the mark," in the sense of an arrow missing the target or just falling short.

5) Sin is *wickedness* or a *perversion* of what is right, which stems from the fact that man, outside of Christ, has a perverted, crooked, twisted inner nature. Sometimes a giant oak tree can be seen growing straight into the air, and beside it is a deformed, twisted tree. This term implies that man's nature is like the deformed tree; it is bent, twisted, and perverted.

6) Sin also means to *commit iniquity* or to do wrong. This is a term which includes the guilt of all men. In Romans 3:10 Paul wrote that none is righteous. All have sinned. No one does what is right all of the time. This does not imply only gross sins, like robbing a bank or committing fornication; but it can be telling a half truth or a white lie, not treating others properly, cheating on income tax, driving above the speed limit, not putting money in the parking meter—the whole realm of wrong doing. It is doing wrong when one knows to do right.

The Object of Sin

Who is the *object of sin*; that is, against whom does man sin? 1) Sin is an offense *against God*. In Psalm 51 David confessed to God, "Against thee, thee only, have I sinned." In

Acts 5:4 Peter said to Ananias, "Thou hast not lied unto men, but unto God." 2) Sin is committed *against man* or *against one's neighbor*. In the Ten Commandments God said, "Thou shalt not kill. Thou shalt not commit adultery. Thou shalt not steal. Thou shalt not bear false witness against thy neighbour. Thou shalt not covet . . ." (Exodus 20:13-17). These are sins against one's neighbor.

3) Sin is *against one's self*. Most people would admit that sin would be against God or perhaps against one's fellow man; but the Bible says that when a person sins, he is destroying himself or sinning against himself. "But he that sinneth against me," God said, "wrongeth his own soul: all they that hate me love death" (Proverbs 8:36). Proverbs 6:32, speaking of adultery, says, "He that doeth it destroyeth his own soul." The new morality says that it is all right to smoke marijuana as long as it does not harm anyone else; that an individual can get intoxicated in the privacy of his home. It also says that consenting adults can commit fornication, whether male with male, female with female, or man with woman; that they are not harming anyone to do that in private. On the contrary, according to the Word of God fornication is sin against the physical body (I Corinthians 6:15-18).

The Universality of Sin

The entrance of sin into the cosmos had universal consequence affecting both *heaven* and *earth*. Sin caused the downfall of the *non-elect angels* (II Peter 2:4; Matthew 25:41). Its effect was upon the whole *human race*. "By one man sin entered into the world, and death by sin; and so death passed upon all men" (Romans 5:12). "If we say that we have not sinned, we make him a liar" (I John 1:10). "All we like sheep have gone astray" (Isaiah 53:6). "There is none righteous, no, not one" (Romans 3:10). Sin's effect is also seen upon *nature*. In Genesis 3:17-19 God said that the creation itself would be a curse unto man's labors. Romans 8:19-22 shows that creation participated in man's fall; that is, it came under the bondage of corruption, but one day will also be delivered with the matured sons of God.

The Consequences of Sin

One of the *consequences* of *sin* is *alienation from God* (Genesis 3). Adam and Eve were put out of the Garden of Eden to keep them from eating of the tree of life; they were cut off spiritually from God. He said to them, "Dust thou art, and unto dust shalt thou return." Both *physical death* and *spiritual alienation* were the consequences of their disobedience.

Moral and *spiritual defilement* are also consequences of sin. Romans 1:18-32 shows the condition of man both in the time of Paul and in this present day. Paul painted a gruesome picture of man's defiled nature. Man is sinful—morally and spiritually defiled. The *works of the flesh* are also described in Galatians 5:19-21 as being totally evil. Corrupt trees produce evil fruit (Matthew 7:17). Man is corrupt; so his actions, his deeds, and his thoughts are corrupt.

According to Romans 6, another consequence of sin is man's *bondage to sin and to Satan*. I John 5:18-19 portrays the whole world as lying in the grip of the wicked one, Satan. A further consequence of sin is that *man is under the curse of the law*, which brings eternal death (Galatians 3:10; Deuteronomy 28). Outside of Christ, man is subject to sickness, misery, poverty, death, warfare, crime—all of the troubles that are so prevalent in the world today—which prove that man is under the curse.

The Extent of Sin's Effect Upon Man

What is the *extent* of *sin's effect* upon man? "The wicked are estranged from the womb: they go astray as soon as they are born, speaking lies" (Psalm 58:3). David said in Psalm 51:5, "Behold, I was shapen in iniquity; and in sin did my mother conceive me." The prophet said in Jeremiah 17:9, "The heart is deceitful above all things, and desperately wicked: who can know it?" Romans 3 shows that man is *totally depraved* until he has been redeemed by Jesus Christ. Is man as sinful at birth as he can become? No. The Scriptures do not imply that sinners are born as wicked as they can become, but there is a progression in their depravity. "But evil men and seducers shall wax worse and worse, deceiving, and being deceived" (II Timothy 3:13).

Are there degrees of sin and punishment? While it is true that all men are born with a sinful nature, it is also a fact that some individuals submit themselves to temptation and sin more than others. God, in His righteousness, bases the severity of judgment of the unsaved on the degree of their sin (Luke 12:47-48). For example, the punishment exacted upon a tyrant like Hitler will be more severe than that placed upon an unsaved Sunday school teacher. Although both are

166

doomed to the torments of hell, there are degrees of punishment based on the person's guilt.

Does man think only of sin and evil? The Bible does not suggest that a sinner has no knowledge or concern about right and wrong. Paul said in Romans 2:15 that all men "shew the work of the law written in their hearts, their conscience also bearing witness, and their thoughts the mean while accusing or else excusing one another." Even Judas knew he had sinned when he betrayed Jesus, because he later felt regret and said, "I have betrayed the innocent blood" (Matthew 27:4). Obviously his regret was not repentance, because verse 5 says, he "went and hanged himself."

Is man incapable of doing anything good? The Word of God does not say that the unsaved never do anything good with reference to others. The rich young ruler was living a good moral life, but he was not saved (Mark 10:17-22). In Matthew 7:22-23 Jesus said, "Many will say unto me in that day, Lord, Lord, have we not prophesied in thy name? and in thy name have cast out devils? and in thy name done many wonderful works? And then will I profess unto them, I never knew you."

Man's Spiritual State Before God

The Scriptures teach man's *total depravity*. 1) All men are sinners by nature and by choice (Ephesians 2:3; Romans 5:12; Isaiah 53:6). 2) In God's sight all men are unholy, unrighteous, and spiritually corrupt (Romans 3:10; Jeremiah 17:9; Isaiah 1:4-6). 3) All man's righteousness and good works are unclean and unacceptable to God (Isaiah 64:6). Man's works outside of God are tainted. Paul said in Hebrews 11:6, "Without faith it is impossible to please him [God]." Even religious works are sin if they are not in God's will and for His glory. 4) All men are guilty before God as violators of His holy commandments (John 3:36; Romans 3:10,23; Galatians 3:10).

Chapter Five

Doctrine of Redemption

Let Israel hope in the Lord: for with the Lord there is mercy, and with him is plenteous redemption. And he shall redeem Israel from all his iniquities (Psalm 130:7-8).

At the heart of Biblical Theology is the *Doctrine of Redemption*. It is the central issue of the Bible, and without it there would be no forgiveness of sin, no salvation, no gospel, and no hope for mankind. While the study of the sin, depravity, guilt, and misery which have plagued humanity has been necessary, it has not been a joyful matter. However, the topic of redemption is cause for rejoicing, because Jesus has purchased deliverance for His people.

The doctrine of redemption is inseparably related to the doctrine of sin, for without sin's entrance into this world, redemption would have been unnecessary. Redemption has been in the heart of God from the very beginning—from before the foundation of the world. Even in the Garden of Eden, God provided garments of animal skins for Adam and Eve when they sinned. By the death of the animal, He was not only covering their nakedness, but was also providing a blood sacrifice for their guilt, typical of what He would later provide through His Son, the Lamb of God. The necessity of a blood sacrifice was also seen when God accepted the offering of Abel, but rejected Cain's offering which was merely the work of his own hands. The institution of blood sacrifice under the law of Moses typified the final and perfect sacrifice, Jesus Christ, which validated the millions of sacrifices offered during the Old Testament dispensation.

The purpose for the study of the doctrine of sin was to learn of man's total depravity and his complete inability to save himself. Only a loving and sovereign God, who would give of Himself, could procure man's salvation from his helpless condition. The many aspects of *redemption* will be covered in this section, as well as the wonderful results that this redemption has purchased for the believer as his inheritance in Christ Jesus.

The study of redemption is quite extensive, including such subjects as atonement, grace, predestination, election, calling, faith, repentance, regeneration, conversion, justification, imputation, sanctification, adoption, and glorification.

A few fundamental truths of redemption are: 1) Salvation and redemption are the work of the total Godhead because the Father never works independently of the Son and the Holy Spirit (I Peter 1:2; Titus 3:4-6). 2) Salvation encompasses the total man—body, soul, and spirit (I Thessalonians 5:23; I Corinthians 15). 3) Salvation deals with the whole question of sin and guilt (I John 1:7; Psalm 103:3). 4) Salvation spans the totality of time and eternity (Ephesians 1:3-5; 2:6-7; I Peter 1:5; Romans 8:28f.). 5) Salvation includes the totality of blessings (Ephesians 1:3; II Peter 1:3; I Corinthians 3:21-22). 6) Salvation is promised all believers alike; not just New Testament saints, but all who have received salvation by faith throughout history (Romans 4:13-16).

Jesus Christ came to deliver the Christian 1) from God's punishment for sin, 2) from the power of sin, and 3) from the curse of the law. Man's response is 1) to exercise faith and repentance, which are both gifts from God (Ephesians 2:8; Romans 2:4; II Timothy 2:25), and 2) to be obedient to the will of God (Philippians 2:12). "It is God which worketh in you both to will and to do of his good pleasure" (verse 13). Thus, the redemption of man is God's work from beginning to end.

The Extent of Redemption

The *extent* of *salvation* or *redemption* of man is seen in the Bible to be the complete restoration of right relationship with God—as if man had never sinned. Those who are in Christ are born of God (John 1:13), are called "sons of God" (I John 3:1), receive eternal life (John 3:16), and are joint-heirs with Christ (Romans 8:17; Galatians 4:7). They are washed, sanctified, justified (I Corinthians 6:11), have peace with God (Romans 5:1), and are reconciled to God (Romans 5:10). They are the temples of the Holy Spirit (I Corinthians 6:19 with Acts 2). They receive forgiveness of sins (Colossians 1:14), are dead to sin (Romans 6:11), and are redeemed from all iniquity (Titus 2:14).

Theories Regarding Methods of Salvation

The study of church history reveals that men have taught various *methods* of salvation which are not in line with the Word of God. The *legal view* says that man can be saved by good works and by living a clean moral life. Some of the philosophers, moralists, unsaved Jews, and cults, such as Unitarians, teach salvation by works—that God accepts a man on the basis of what he does or does not do. The entire New Testament, particularly the Book of Galatians, refutes this view. In Romans 3 Paul clearly stresses that no man will be justified by the works of the law, but only by the faith that is in Jesus Christ. The *semi-legal view* is similar to the legal view except it says man must be saved by faith in Christ plus good works. Likewise, Paul refuted that view in the Book of Galatians. The most obvious example of this view is Roman Catholicism, which says that a person is saved by believing in Jesus, participating in the sacraments, and doing good works.

Socrates and many of the philosophers held an *intellectual view*, which purports that a man is good if he is a wise man, and that only the wise are in favor with the gods. Of course, that is contradicted by all of Scripture. The Jews believed the *biological view*, erroneously supposing that they would inherit salvation by birth; that they were automatically in the Kingdom of God because they were Israelites. However, John the Baptist said, "God is able of these stones to raise up children unto Abraham," indicating what small value their genealogy alone was in God's sight. The Jews also had to believe on the Messiah and receive Him to obtain salvation.

The *denominational view* of salvation is held by certain church members who believe that a person has to be in their particular denomination or church. The official position of the Roman Catholic Church is that one must be in their church to be saved; that all other Christian groups are heretical. In fact, their version of the Bible teaches that it is heresy to say that a man is saved by faith alone.

The Biblical View of Salvation

The *spiritual* or *biblical view* says that salvation is received by faith alone (Ephesians 2:8-9). "Not by works of righteousness which we have done, but according to his mercy he saved us" (Titus 3:5). Faith will produce good works. They will be works that *result* from saving faith, but will never be the *basis* for salvation.

The Doctrine of Atonement

What is the meaning of the word "*atonement*"? Some people have wrongly thought that the root word "atone" was derived from the phrase "at one." They say "atonement" signifies the restoration of the broken relationship between God and man; the sinner needs to be made "at one" with God or reconciled to God. However, this reasoning is incorrect because the Bible was not revealed in English, but in Hebrew and in Greek; therefore, the true meaning of atonement must be taken from the biblical languages, not from an English term.

The writers of the Hebrew Old Testament and the Greek New Testament used certain terms to express the

173

concept of "atonement." These terms are "covering," "reconciliation," and "propitiation." The Hebrew word literally means "to cover." God said the blood would *cover* man's sin for the purpose of *propitiating* (appeasing) His wrath against sin; it would restore the Israelite to a right relationship with God. The term used by the older theologians and the reformers was "satisfaction," which means that Christ's sacrifice satisfied God's demands against sin. Leviticus 4:33-35 shows that the priest sprinkled the animal's blood on the altar; then the sinning Israelite was forgiven and his relationship to God in the covenant community of Israel was restored. The English term "atonement" is abstract, but the Hebrew term is not—it describes what the sacrifice accomplished. The blood of the animal, which was a type of Christ's blood, covered over man's sin.

The word "atonement" occurs only one time in the King James Version, and that is in Romans 5:11. The Greek term which is used here speaks of *"reconciliation,"* to restore to right relationship two parties which have been alienated. Admittedly, it is difficult to express the full idea of Christ's sacrifice on man's behalf with one word—atonement—but these three aspects aptly describe His work on the Cross: *reconciliation, covering,* and *propitiation.*

The Necessity for the Atonement

Christ's ministry as priest was fulfilled in the atonement He made when He offered Himself as the sacrifice for sinners. Not only is the atonement the central theme of the Scriptures, it is the motivation for all preaching and teaching, and is the reason for the existence of the church. The atonement was *necessary* because of the biblical charge that *all men are sinners.* "All have sinned and come short of the glory of God" (Romans 3:23). Paul said that not even one person is righteous. "There is none righteous, no, not one" (Romans 3:10). God's attitude toward men who are outside of Christ is also revealed in Isaiah 53:6, which reads, "All we like sheep have gone astray; we have turned every one to his own way."

The atonement is also necessary because the divine sentence of *death* is *upon all men,* for all men are sinners. This sentence was passed upon Adam, the father of the human race, because of his sin. "Dust thou art," God said, "and unto dust shalt thou return" (Genesis 3:19). How does that relate to the rest of the human race? "Wherefore, as by one man [Adam] sin entered into the world, and death by sin; and so death passed upon all men, for that all have sinned" (Romans 5:12). There is no such thing as a person not being under the condemnation and sentence of death, because all have sinned. In Romans 6:23 Paul said, "The wages of sin is death."

The atonement is also necessary because of the *holiness of God.* His holiness requires Him to treat sin seriously, and His reaction to sin is His holy wrath. "The wrath of God is revealed from heaven against all ungodliness and unrighteousness" (Romans 1:18). God is too holy to look upon sin, or to allow sin to go unpunished in His universe. He must judge it! See Psalm 1:6; Isaiah 13:9; Hosea 5:10. The holy God will judge all unholiness.

Finally, the necessity of the atonement is seen in the fact that God is a just God, and His *justice* requires that every sin be judged. God is holy, so He must punish sin. Because of God's eternal love for His elect, He ordained that He would place the punishment for man's guilt upon His sinless Son, Jesus Christ, and would then impute the merits of Jesus' sacrifice for sin to the believer. Only by this means could God's justice be satisfied, man's sins be forgiven, and fellowship between God and man be restored.

Views of the Atonement

There have been several *views* of the *atonement* in the four periods of church history. The *Patristic Period* covered the first four centuries and was the period of the early church fathers. Some prevalent theories which they initiated were:

1) The *Recapitulation Theory*, proposed by Irenaeus in the second century A.D., was essentially an emphasis on the incarnation. Christ is said to have gone through (or recapitulated) the successive stages of human life and emerged victorious. He became what man is, and man becomes what Christ is.

2) An early *Substitutionary View* was advocated by Athanasius (295-373 A.D.). Behind all of his doctrinal writings is the central conviction that "God Himself has entered into humanity." This teaching says Christ did away with death for all who were like Him by offering Himself as their substitute.

3) The *Ransom Theory* was propagated by Origen (185-251 A.D.), as well as Justin Martyr and Augustine. They believed that God and Satan were in eternal conflict for

man's soul. Satan had captured man; and as captor, he had the right to be bought off with a ransom. The Scriptures, however, do not suggest that God paid a ransom to the devil to secure man's release. Matthew 20:28 signifies that Christ gave His life as a ransom which redeemed mankind from the bondage and power of sin and death. The term "ransom" is a figurative description of the *effect* of Christ's substitution or sacrifice. God was not paying Satan anything on the Cross.

The Medieval Period or "middle ages" was that period which followed the period of the early church fathers and continued until the Reformation (1517 A.D.). Several theories arose during that period: 1) The *Satisfaction Theory* (or *Commercial Theory*) was held by Anselm, 1033-1109 A.D., who placed the emphasis on sin as a violation of God's *honor*. However, the Bible teaches that it is God's *holiness* which has been violated. Anselm agreed with Tertullian that divine justice requires satisfaction for sin. He said man could do nothing to repay the debt to God's honor; therefore, the death of the God-man was necessary.

2) The *Moral Influence Theory* was held by Abelard (1079-1142 A.D.). This was the beginning of the modern view which says that the birth and death of Christ are God's greatest expressions of love for man. This is supposed to awaken in man a love for God. Allegedly, a sinner looks at the Cross and loves God; in reality, this never happens.

3) The *Merit Theory* was taught by Aquinas, a Roman Catholic theologian (1224-1274 A.D.), who combined the views of Anselm and Abelard. He said the atonement was a satisfaction; but it was also an expression of God's love,

which was intended to move man to a responsive love toward God. He believed that Christ's atonement super-abounded man's sin (that is, the payment far exceeded the debt); and the reward (or excess payment), which Christ cannot personally receive, comes to the advantage of the human race. This superabundant merit is placed in a treasury in heaven and is disbursed by the Roman Catholic Church. Man's good works or works of "supererogation" are supposedly added to this treasury also. However, Jesus said, "So likewise ye, when ye shall have done all those things which are commanded you, say, We are unprofitable servants: we have done that which was our duty to do" (Luke 17:10). God requires total obedience twenty-four hours a day, allowing no accumulation of rewards which could be withdrawn in case of a bad day or sin on the part of the believer.

The *Reformation Period*, which was initiated by Martin Luther in 1517 A.D., was that period in history when reforms were attempted in the Catholic church that led to the establishment of Protestant churches. Some views which arose were: 1) The *Socinian* or *Example Theory* which was propagated by Faustus Socinus in the sixteenth century. He said the only way for man to be reconciled to God was by improving himself. He taught that Christ's death was only the death of a martyr—only an example for other men. He also denied the trinity.

2) The *Government Theory* was taught by Hugo Grotius (1583-1645 A.D.). He was a Dutch jurist who believed the atonement or death of Christ was to satisfy God's divine law (or government), and it was not the payment for man's sin.

3) The *Penal Substitutionary View* or *biblical view* came forth in its strongest emphasis during the Reformation Period. "Penal" means "punishment." "Penal substitution" means that the punishment which was due the sinner was placed on Christ. As man's substitute, Christ suffered vicariously. This was the view of the reformers, Anselm, Athanasius, the prophets, the apostles, etc.

The Bible clearly teaches the penal substitutionary atonement. Christ died for the ungodly (Romans 5:6-21; Galatians 3:13; John 1:29; Isaiah 53). In his *Systematic Theology,* A. H. Strong said the atonement is a satisfaction of the ethical demand of the divine nature by the substitution of Christ's penal sufferings for the punishment of the guilty.

The *Modern Period* is that time in church history which followed the period of the reformation and has continued to the present day. All the modern theories reflect liberal theology. 1) Friedrich Schleirmacher (1768-1834 A.D.), the father of *modernism,* rejected the penal substitutionary atonement. He said all men have God in them and are God-conscious. He taught that Christ awakens the God consciousness in man; and when he recognizes who he is, then he is saved. This is also the theory of the cults, which contend that man is reborn as he becomes aware of God.

2) The *Vicarious Repentance Theory* was propagated by J. M. Campbell (1800-1872 A.D.). He taught that man's repentance as well as punishment for sin are necessary to satisfy divine justice. He said Christ did not take man's punishment, but He repented for man. In answer to that, Christ's repentance would not change man—man must repent for

himself (Acts 16:30; Mark 1:14-15). Jesus Christ "did no sin, neither was guile found in his mouth" (I Peter 2:22).

3) The *Example or Moral Influence Theory* of the liberals calls the penal substitutionary view barbaric. They say Christ's death was an example and should have a moral influence on man.

4) The *Neo-Orthodox View* does not have a clear statement on the atonement; however, this view equates the atonement with the incarnation, and says that Christ redeemed man by identifying with him in humanity.

5) The *Atonement in Hell Theory* teaches that Christ became, as man was, unregenerate. He was subject to Satan for three days, and redeemed mankind through His sufferings in hell. He is said to be a "substitute sinner" instead of the sinner's Substitute. This heresy is thoroughly exposed in the author's book, *Did Jesus Die Spiritually?*

The Doctrine of Grace

The *doctrine* of *grace* is a part of the study of redemption. Apart from grace, the world would perish because of divine judgment against sin. The origin of the term is the Greek "charis" which literally means "favor." When applied to salvation it means "unmerited favor." God's grace is the bestowal of God's love and blessings upon undeserving sinners. "For by grace are ye saved through faith; and that not of yourselves: it is the gift of God: Not of works, lest any man should boast" (Ephesians 2:8-9).

There are several *characteristics* of grace which should be examined. First, grace is *sovereign*. If grace were not sovereign, it would not be grace; it would just be cooperation with God, and He would be rewarding or paying man for his good works. Salvation is by grace alone without man's works; it is all God's work from beginning to end. When Adam sinned he became aware of his nakedness, so he hid from God and was ashamed that he had disobeyed. It was while Adam was hiding from God that the Lord went into the Garden searching for Adam. "And the Lord God called unto Adam, and said unto him, Where art thou?" (Genesis 3:9.)

God always seeks man. Christianity is not a religion of *discovery*, but of *revelation*. Grace is sovereign because it flows in one direction only—from heaven to earth. Apart from the presence of lost sinners, grace would have no meaning, because there would be no objects to receive it. Grace is the bestowal of God's favor to *undeserving* people. "Even when we were dead in sins, [God] hath quickened us together with Christ, (by grace ye are saved;) And hath raised us up together, and made us sit together in heavenly places in Christ Jesus" (Ephesians 2:5-6).

Secondly, grace is the very *antithesis of good works*. The concept of salvation by grace is boldly opposed to any attempt of man to be saved by works (Ephesians 2:8-10). Romans 4 says the same thing of Abraham—that he was justified, not by works, but by faith. "For if Abraham were justified by works, he hath whereof to glory; but not before God. For what saith the scripture? Abraham believed God, and it was counted unto him for righteousness. Now to him that worketh is the reward not reckoned of grace, but of debt.

181

But to him that worketh not, but believeth on him that justifieth the ungodly, his faith is counted for righteousness" (Romans 4:2-5). Grace is the very opposite of good works.

Grace is also an *attribute* of God (Exodus 34:6; 22:27; Joel 2:13; Jonah 4:2). David testified of God's graciousness in Psalm 103:8. God said of Himself in Exodus 34:6 that He is gracious. Grace has provided a *full redemption* for man. Christians are *called* by grace (Galatians 1:15); *saved* by grace (Ephesians 2:8); *forgiven* by grace (Ephesians 1:7); *justified* by grace (Titus 3:7); and granted *eternal consolation* by grace (II Thessalonians 2:16).

Is Grace Dispensational?

Often people speak of the "*dispensation of the law*" as contrasted with the "*dispensation of grace*," and that believers are not under law, but are under grace. "This is the dispensation of grace," some say, "and the Old Testament was the dispensation of law." Furthermore, they quote John 1:17, "For the law was given by Moses, but grace and truth came by Jesus Christ." So the question is this: "Is grace limited only to the New Testament dispensation?" No. Remember the definition of grace, that it is the bestowal of God's love and blessing upon undeserving sinners. Whenever God dealt in love and mercy toward sinful men, it was a demonstration of His grace.

Grace was bestowed upon Adam and Eve when God provided skins to cover them, which implies the slaying of animals and blood sacrifice. Through grace Noah and his family were saved from the flood. God's grace is evident in the call and salvation of Abraham in Genesis 12. God could have selected anyone, but He chose Abraham. This same unmerited favor is seen in the election of Israel. In Deuteronomy 7:6-8 God said to Israel, "For thou art an holy people unto the Lord thy God: the Lord thy God hath chosen thee to be a special people unto himself, above all people that are upon the face of the earth. The Lord did not set his love upon you, nor choose you, because ye were more in number than any people; for ye were the fewest of all people: But because the Lord loved you, and because he would keep the oath which he had sworn unto your fathers." God said later in chapter 9 that He did not choose the Israelites because they were a righteous people, for they were a stiffnecked and stubborn people; but God said He bestowed His love and grace upon them because of His own purpose.

When David sinned with Bathsheba and caused the death of her husband, he was required by the law of Moses to pay the penalty of death; but in II Samuel 12:13 God sent Nathan, the prophet, to say, "The Lord hath put away thy sin." David was not executed, but he was severely chastened, showing God's mercy and grace.

Even in this present day, God still bestows His grace upon undeserving humanity. In Matthew 5:44-45 Jesus said that God is gracious to all people because He sends His rain and sun upon His enemies, as well as upon those who follow Him. His grace is still being poured out upon sinners who turn to Him and receive salvation in Jesus Christ. It is proof of grace that God sustains man's life and allows this world to exist, and that He gives sinners the breath to say no to Him or to blaspheme Him. According to II Peter 3, God's longsuffering and grace are giving man an opportunity to turn to Him and to be saved.

The Difference Between the Dispensations of Law and Grace

The *difference* between the Old Testament *dispensation* of *law* and the New Testament *dispensation* of *grace* is not that grace was absent in the Old Testament dispensation, but that the Old Testament *emphasis* was upon *obedience* to the law. Why? Paul showed in Galatians 3:24 that the law acted as a teacher or a tutor to bring Israel to the time of Christ. He also said in Romans 5:20-21, "Moreover the law entered, that the offense might abound." Sin would be recognized as evil—would be recognized *as sin.* "Where sin abounded, grace did much more abound: That as sin hath reigned unto death, even so might grace reign through righteousness." Paul showed that grace is now reigning. The difference between law and grace is in emphasis. The more that the law and its inadequacy to save were stressed in the Old Testament period, the more that grace would be magnified now in this church dispensation, the dispensation of grace.

Unscriptural Attitudes Toward Law and Grace

There is a popular misconception in the church today that under grace the Christian has more freedom to live as he pleases than the Jew had under the restrictions of the law. The reply to that should be obvious! It is unthinkable for a true Christian to suppose that he can sin simply because grace abounds. Remember, Paul said that where sin abounds, grace much more abounds to forgive that sin; but he also said in the following chapter, Romans 6:1-2, "What shall we say then? Shall we continue in sin, that grace may abound?" or so that God can have His grace magnified in forgiving man's sins? "God forbid. How shall we, that are dead to sin, live any longer therein?" Paul further wrote that if a man sins, he is still a slave to sin; but if he has been born again, he is a servant of righteousness.

In Galatians 5:1 the apostle taught that believers are not to be brought again under the bondage of the law. Then in verse 13 he said that even though Christians are free, nevertheless, they are not to use their liberty under grace as an occasion to the flesh. In other words, "Do not sin just because you are under grace and can be forgiven." A true Christian would never raise the question, "Can I sin so that grace may abound?" Titus 2:11-12 gives the answer, "For the grace of God that bringeth salvation hath appeared to all men, Teaching us that, denying ungodliness and worldly lusts, we should live soberly, righteously, and godly, in this present world."

The Cross of Calvary represents God's attitude toward sin. It was there that He gave the life of His Son, laying upon Jesus the penalty and punishment for man's sins (John 3:16). Having paid such a price to deliver His elect from the curse and penalty of the law, He would not just turn them loose in the world and allow them to live like the world. It is true that grace sets man free, but not free to do as he pleases. In I Corinthians 6:12 Paul said, "All things are lawful unto me, but all things are not expedient." He does not mean sin is lawful, but that he is no longer under the law.

Another misconception concerning grace is that sin under the law resulted in punishment or death unless atoned for by a sacrifice; but under the dispensation of grace the once-for-all atoning blood of Jesus *automatically* cleanses the believer from sin. Those who believe this cite Hebrews 10:10-14 where Paul spoke of the once-for-all sacrifice made by Jesus Christ. While it is valid that the Christian under grace can obtain forgiveness without making an animal sacrifice, he is not *automatically* forgiven. He must meet certain conditions. He must repent and confess his sins, and then Jesus is faithful to forgive his sins (I John 1:9; 2:1). Under the dispensation of grace, instead of offering a sacrifice for sin, the Christian can claim the merits of the blood sacrifice of Jesus Christ.

Sins Against God's Grace

There are four kinds of *sin against God's grace*. First, there are sins which reveal a *careless attitude* toward grace: indifference, lukewarmness, and sins of the flesh, such as anger, gossip, overeating, lust, and disobedience. God deals with these sins by chastening (I Corinthians 11:27-32; Hebrews 12:5-11), and by withholding present blessings and future rewards. Moses was not allowed to go into the promised land because he sinned with his lips, and David was sorely chastened for his sin. Sometimes God even removes the one who has sinned (I Corinthians 5:5; 11:30).

Secondly, there is the sin of *legalism*. Grace is made ineffective in the lives of some believers because of their substitution of religious works, legalism, and the teachings of man instead of their obedience to the principles found in the

Word of God. For example, Paul said, "Christ is become of no effect unto you, whosoever of you are justified by the law; ye are fallen from grace" (Galatians 5:4).

Thirdly, there is the sin of the *perversion of grace.* "For there are certain men crept in unawares, who were before of old ordained to this condemnation, ungodly men, turning the grace of our God into lasciviousness, and denying the only Lord God, and our Lord Jesus Christ" (Jude 4). Also see Galatians 5:13; II Peter 2:9-22.

Fourthly, there is the sin of *apostasy,* the contempt for grace, as seen in Hebrews 6 and 10. This sin is committed, not by a new convert to Christianity, but by one who has understood and embraced the faith. This would not include a person who, in a time of temptation and with a careless attitude, says, "I don't want to have anything to do with religion or Christianity," but later repents. This willful rejection of Christ is final and unforgivable. Another example of apostasy is blasphemy against the Holy Spirit, which the Scriptures say can never be forgiven (Mark 3:29).

Predestination and Election in Relation to Redemption

It should be noted that *predestination* and *election* are related to redemption. These subjects have already been covered in detail, so the following will only be a summary.

Predestination is God's eternal plan encompassing all events, including the establishment of a kingdom made up of His redeemed children, and ruled over by the Lord Jesus

Christ. Election is God's choice of those who will inhabit that kingdom. This distinction between the two terms is seen, for example, in Ephesians 1:4-5. Paul spoke of *election* or choice in verse 4, "According as he hath chosen us in him [Christ] before the foundation of the world," and in verse 5 he set forth the more comprehensive concept of *predestination*, the plan of God, "Having predestinated us unto the adoption of children by Christ Jesus." The plan is set forth in verse 11. "In whom also we have obtained an inheritance [speaking of Christ], being predestinated according to the purpose of him who worketh all things after the counsel of his own will."

Predestination and election cannot be lifted out of their context or they seem harsh. Man is dead in trespasses and sin and if left to himself he could never rise above these circumstances; however, it has been in God's eternal plan to take the initiative and redeem those He has chosen or elected. Predestination and election are not harsh if presented Scripturally because God in His mercy has freely offered the gospel to all men; but not all men "will" to receive it. It is not so much they "cannot," but they "will not." Jesus and Paul presented the truth of election to a person only after he had accepted or rejected the grace which was offered him (John 6:41-44; Romans 9-11). The Bible does not suggest that all people will be saved (universalism), but it teaches just the opposite—that some will reject the gospel and be lost. Revelation 13:8 shows that there are those "whose names are not written in the book of life of the Lamb slain from the foundation of the world."

Calvinism and Arminianism

The study of predestination and election as they relate to redemption would not be complete without some understanding of *Arminianism* and *Calvinism*, since they are definitely a part of modern theology.

John Calvin (1509-1564 A.D.) moved to Geneva, Switzerland, in 1536 to guide the Reformation that had already begun there. His system of theology is based on the absolute sovereignty of God, and is essentially in line with Scripture. He taught that man through the fall became totally depraved and lost his freedom of will and his power to choose what is right. He said Christ died for the ones He effectually calls and saves, leaving the rest of mankind under condemnation, which man justly deserves because of willful sin and rejection of the truth. Since all men are under the just condemnation of God because of sin, he taught that God cannot be charged with unjust action in choosing some by His grace from among those who are dead in sins and trespasses, and predestinating them to eternal life.

The five points of Calvinism are as follows: 1) Total Depravity. Man is entirely lost and dead in sin, and thus, cannot choose salvation apart from grace. 2) Unconditional Election. God chooses whom He will. 3) Limited Atonement. Christ died savingly for the elect. 4) Irresistible (effective) Grace. God's grace produces the effect which He intended. 5) Perseverance of the Saints. All those God calls and saves will endure to the end. These five principles may be best remembered by the acrostic T-U-L-I-P, formed by the first letter of each point.

Arminianism arose in the Reformed Church in the Netherlands in protest to Calvinism. Jacobus Arminius (1560-1609 A.D.) and his followers basically rejected: 1) limited atonement to the elect, 2) unconditional election where God alone chooses who will be saved, and 3) irresistible grace. He also tried to refute the doctrine of the absolute sovereignty of God. His teachings were later adopted by Wesley.

The essential points of Arminianism are: 1) Election or condemnation is dependent upon man's free choice of God's grace. 2) Christ's atonement was for the whole world, not just the elect. 3) Saving grace is not irresistible; it can be rejected. 4) Man can fall away from grace and lose his salvation.

Arminianism emphasizes that man *accepts* Christ. Nowhere in the Bible are sinners ever said to have accepted Jesus, and they are never invited to accept Him. On the contrary, the Word of God says He must accept man, and man receives Him. Ephesians 1:4-6 says that God has accepted the Christian in Christ Jesus when he believes. John 1:12 says that as many as receive Him, to them He gives the power or authority to become the children of God. Men receive Him; He accepts them.

An extreme to avoid is *Hyper-Calvinism*, which results in a fatalistic attitude toward one's destiny. As one man said, "If I'm elected, I'll learn of it before I die, and I'll be saved. If not, then it's hopeless, and there is nothing I can or should do about it." Calvin did not teach Hyper-Calvinism, but some of his followers did.

The Calling

The Bible speaks of a *calling* that God gives to sinners through the preaching of the gospel to believe, repent, and be saved. Mark 1:14-15 says, "Jesus came into Galilee, preaching the gospel of the kingdom of God, And saying, The time is fulfilled, and the kingdom of God is at hand: repent ye, and believe the gospel."

The General Calling

There is one gospel call with two aspects: a general call and a special or effectual call. The *general call* is an outward call to all men through the gospel, to which they may or may not respond. It is heard by the ear but not necessarily by the heart (Mark 1:14-15). This general call is a warning—repent or be eternally lost! The one who responds to the warning is saved. There is nothing to prevent a man from responding; each person makes his own choice. "Whosoever will may come" (John 3:16; Isaiah 55:1; Revelation 22:17). "Come unto me, all ye that labour and are heavy laden, and I will give you rest" (Matthew 11:28).

The Special Calling

Within this one call is the *special* or *effectual call*. This inner call is the Spirit's work in a man which effects the necessary response to the gospel. The sinner believes, repents, acts on what he hears, and he is saved. The Holy Spirit's ministry here is not only to convict, but also to influence and lead the sinner to exercise faith and to repent of his sins (I Peter 1:2). This call makes effective what God

191

predestinated (I Thessalonians 5:23-24; Romans 8:28-30; Ephesians 1:3-11).

The effectual call is distinguished from the general call in certain passages in the New Testament. "For many are called, but few are chosen" (Matthew 22:14). Also Matthew 20:16; I Corinthians 1:23-31; Matthew 11:27. This effectual call is a holy calling, according to II Timothy 1:9, "Who hath saved us, and called us with an holy calling, not according to our works, but according to his own purpose and grace, which was given us in Christ Jesus before the world began." In the Parable of the Sower in Matthew 13 there were several responses to the call. There was no response; external, superficial, conditional responses; and an inward response.

How is the teaching on *calling* related to the doctrine of *redemption*? The Christian was predestinated and elected to salvation before the foundation of the world. This is clearly taught in Ephesians 1:4-5, "According as he hath chosen us in him before the foundation of the world, . . . Having predestinated us unto the adoption of children." God did not choose someone who would later refuse to believe; but he that is chosen must *hear* the gospel, believe the gospel, and exercise faith in the Lord Jesus Christ. He will see, after he has done all this, that God had chosen him before the foundation of the world. This is seen in II Thessalonians 2:13-14 where Paul said, "We are bound to give thanks alway to God for you, brethren beloved of the Lord, because God hath from the beginning chosen you to salvation." Before the world began, He chose believers to salvation. How? "Through sanctification of the Spirit and belief of the truth: Whereunto he called you by our gospel." The elect are *called* by the gospel at a specific time in history for the purpose of obtaining the salvation to which they have been *predestinated*.

Predestination is God's eternal plan to save a people and to prepare a kingdom for His own name's sake. Election is the eternal choice of those people who are to be in His family and who are to be the citizens of His kingdom. The call is God putting that plan into operation.

Some people who object to the truth of predestination and election would argue, "If predestination and election are true, God would be making an arbitrary choice and the person chosen to be saved would not have to do anything—he would be saved anyway." However, that is not what the Bible teaches about election, predestination, and calling. Remember, Paul said in II Thessalonians 2:13-14 that sinners have to hear the gospel and respond to it. They have to believe! From the beginning God has chosen some to salvation through the belief of the truth. The elect are those who will believe the truth when it is preached to them.

Why does God give a call to all men if all men will not be saved? It will make them responsible. There is nothing hindering them from responding to the gospel, except their own unwillingness. They do not want to give up an evil heart of unbelief. From God's side, He chooses those whom He will call effectually to salvation. From man's side, he hears the gospel call, and it is his responsibility to respond. The decision is entirely left in the hands of the one who hears. In John 5:40 Jesus said to the Jews, "You will not to come to me." He said that it was by an act of their will that they chose not to believe Him and receive salvation.

193

The denominational church today is largely Arminian. They deny the sovereignty of God in salvation. They deny the truths of predestination, foreknowledge, and election, or they twist and pervert their meanings so much that they end up with a salvation-by-works theology. They say, "God foresaw who would believe and He elected them." However, that would not be salvation by grace; it would be God foreseeing something man would do—his works. The precious truths of election and predestination do not minister pride in those who understand their purpose; rather, they are humbled, knowing that God has chosen them by His grace before the foundation of the world.

The Doctrine of Faith

Another aspect of redemption is the *doctrine of faith*. Faith and the Christian religion are really synonymous. All that man receives from God is by faith, whether salvation or the healing of every disease. Hebrews 11:6 says that without faith it is impossible to please God; therefore, faith is the key to everything in the Christian's life. It is very important for the believer to have a thorough understanding of the subject because the principles of faith apply to all the promises of God.

The Nature of Faith

In reference to the *nature of faith*, its *general usage* in the New Testament refers to the whole body of Christian truth. Jude 3 exhorts, "Earnestly contend for *the faith* which was once delivered unto the saints." In Galatians 1:23 Paul said he was preaching *the faith* which he once destroyed.

In *personal application* faith is an *attitude* of the heart (John 3:16). "For with the heart man believeth unto righteousness; and with the mouth confession is made unto salvation" (Romans 10:10). Faith is also an *act*. Peter was acting his faith when he walked on the water to Jesus (Matthew 14:27-31). Faith is also a *confession* (Matthew 8:7-8; 9:21-22; Mark 9:23-24; 11:23-24; Romans 10:10). Faith is *trust* in God. "Trust in the Lord with all thine heart; and lean not unto thine own understanding. In all thy ways acknowledge him and he shall direct thy paths" (Proverbs 3:5-6; also Job 13:15; Mark 11:22; Hebrews 10:23).

The Definition of Faith

The *definition of faith* is given in only one place in the Bible—Hebrews 11:1. "Now faith is the substance of things hoped for, the evidence of things not seen." Faith consists of two elements. It is the *substance* of whatever a Christian is believing or hoping for, and it is the very *evidence* of things yet invisible. Faith is the material used by God to provide His children with what He has promised them. When the child of God exercises faith, he is giving God the substance out of which He will provide the answer. Faith is not seeing or feeling, but is evidence of the *invisible*. When God manifests the answer visibly, exercising faith for it is no longer necessary. Faith is present when the believer knows he has received the answer to his prayer before it is manifested in the visible realm, and he believes in his heart that God has heard and answered his petition. Evidence of anything is absolute proof of its existence. God's Word is to be believed by faith, and this faith in the heart is the evidence that God has supplied the answer. The author's book, *Faith for Healing*, gives a detailed study of the subject of faith.

In Galatians 5:22 faith is listed as one of the *fruits* of the Spirit, and it is one of the *gifts* of the Holy Spirit according to I Corinthians 12.

Saving Faith

Salvation by faith means that faith, not works, is the ordained means of obtaining salvation from sin. The Scriptures state that all have sinned; there are none righteous; all have violated God's laws and commandments. If forgiveness comes to a man, it has to be on God's terms—by faith in the sacrificial blood atonement of Jesus Christ. Nothing is more clearly stated in the New Testament than the truth of salvation by faith. "For by grace are ye saved through faith; . . . Not of works" (Ephesians 2:8-9). No one can be saved by religious works, nor by personal merits or goodness, but solely by the grace of God and by believing the gospel. While the believer's works are not the means to obtain salvation, they are not to be absent in his life either. Paul also said in Ephesians 2:10 that Christians have been ordained to the producing of good works. "For we are his workmanship, created in Christ Jesus unto good works."

Saving Faith Versus Intellectual Assent

It is very important to see that genuine *saving faith* is to be *distinguished from intellectual assent*. Many people in the churches believe with their heads and not their hearts, but that is not saving faith. They do not have a living faith in Jesus Christ; they only have an intellectual belief in the historical facts about Him. They have faith *about* Jesus, and they think that is faith *in* Jesus. Some join a church and delude themselves into thinking that they have saving faith because they believe in the historical account about Jesus. They believe what the Bible says about Him, His works, and His deity, and they have adopted Christianity as their religion; but they have not really repented of their sins. Many who regularly attend church services have not been born again. Proof of this is that they do not have changed lives; they do not believe His promises; and they often oppose anyone who exercises faith in those promises. Only those who have a living faith in Jesus can believe for the things He has provided.

Some will say, "Well, I believe Jesus was the Son of God." They may even believe in the fact of the resurrection, in the facts of the incarnation and virgin birth; yet they still lack a personal relationship with the Lord Jesus Christ. A man can believe these truths with his intellect and still be lost, which is often the reason he may fall away in time of trial and testing.

The Parable of the Sower clearly presents a form of belief that is not a saving faith. This explains why some resist the move of the Holy Spirit today, and why some support denominational, institutional religion and reject the clear teaching of the Word of God concerning the nature and pattern of the church in the New Testament. The conclusion is that some have given intellectual assent to John 3:16, but they do not have a personal relationship with the Lord Jesus

Christ. To these He will one day say, "I never knew you: depart from me, ye that work iniquity." See Matthew 7:21-23.

Ministers need to put the emphasis on salvation where the Bible puts it: on a new birth, a changed life, and obedience to all of God's commandments. Then their hearers will not be deluded into thinking that they have a saving faith because they believe certain facts in the Bible about Jesus and some of the things He said. Jesus said in Matthew 7:21, "Not every one that saith unto me, Lord, Lord, shall enter into the kingdom of heaven; but he that doeth the will of my Father which is in heaven." It is impossible for men to enter the Kingdom of God by merely confessing Jesus and calling Him Lord; they must also do the will of God.

Saving Faith Versus Believism

Some teach that all the sinner has to do is believe; "Just come and make a confession, and you will be saved." This is not biblical—it is *believism*. The one in need of forgiveness must exercise faith in the Lord Jesus Christ, and this will result in a changed life. "Therefore if any man be in Christ, he is a new creation" (II Corinthians 5:17). Believing in Jesus is a fact of Scripture; "For God so loved the world, that he gave his only begotten Son, that whosoever believeth in him should not perish, but have everlasting life" (John 3:16); but if a man has a saving belief, it will change him. A person is not saved, according to the Bible, just because he says he believes in Jesus. That is the basis, to be sure; but if he truly believes in Jesus savingly, he will walk in His steps. Jesus said, "And whosoever doth not bear his cross, and come after me, cannot be my disciple" (Luke 14:27). Not to be His disciple is not to be saved.

How can someone test if he has head faith or heart faith? If there is a radical, godly change in his life, it is evidence of genuine faith. If his belief about Jesus has been translated into actions and deeds, he has been born again. If not, it is just mental assent.

The Relationship Between Faith and Reason

Faith is not intellectual knowledge, wisdom, or reasoning (I Corinthians 1:18-29; 2:1-5). One cannot reason himself into faith. Figuratively, Christians believe with the heart and not with the head. In the Old Testament the "heart" was the inner man, the person, the ego, in contrast to the educated intellect. On the basis of that usage, Jesus and Paul used the term "heart" in reference to the inner man. Jesus said that out of the heart come murders and other evils. Paul said that with the heart man believes unto righteousness. Such faith is born, not of the mind or intellect, but of the inner man.

The Scriptures do not obscure the fact that man was created with a mind, with senses, with powers of reason, wisdom, knowledge, and understanding, which can glorify God if rightly motivated. God gave man a mind capable of believing and exercising faith, and God reaches man's spirit by speaking to his mind. There is nothing wrong with reason, intellect, and the mind when a person is sanctified, born again, and a new creation in Christ.

The disciples were eye witnesses of *sense evidence facts,* which formed the basis of their gospel (John 2:11; 10:37-38; 20:30-31; II Peter 1:16-18; I John 1:1-3). All of these Scriptures present factual evidence, and are written that the reader might believe. When the disciples *saw* Jesus turn water to wine, they believed He was the Messiah on the basis of sense evidence. The disciples had *seen* Jesus, had *heard* Him, and had *touched* Him, so they could say, "That which we have seen and heard declare we unto you" (I John 1:3). Peter said in II Peter 1:16-18, we "were *eyewitnesses* of his majesty." In John 10:37-38 Jesus appealed to His *works* so the people would believe on Him.

The significance of these things is this: Paul said in Romans 10:17 that faith comes through hearing the Word. The Word comes through the ear or the eye, and not by some mystical impartation of faith apart from hearing the Word. This does not mean spiritual comprehension is with the mind, because faith is a gift of God; but it does not come apart from hearing or reading the Word. The only basis for faith is the Word of God. As one hears or reads the Word, it enters the mind, and can be picked up by the spirit.

There is no contradiction between faith and the intellect if the proper distinction is kept between them, and if one is not substituted for the other; however, the powers of reason and sense knowledge cannot be used in the faith realm. The disciples saw and reported sense evidence facts, which men may hear with the physical ear and brain. God has given man a mind, intellect, and reason to enable him to live his physical life on this earth—to exist in the *sense realm.* He could not understand God's Word if he were not a rational creature with adequate senses to comprehend the Word of God.

Saving faith is a gift, and redemption is by grace; but man has the responsibility to believe. If he will heed the Word when he hears it, the gift of faith will be given him. The gospel is based on eyewitness reports, and is received by the intellect; yet the mind is not the source of faith—it is but the doorway to the inner man. The gospel is to be believed with the heart and not the head. God contacts man through the ear, the eye, and the mind; but it is only the spirit which is capable of discerning and responding to the hidden wisdom of God which resides in the outward letter of the Word.

The Doctrine of Repentance

Faith and *repentance* are always found together when a person becomes a Christian. Faith precedes and is the basis for repentance. Why? No one repents of his sins until he has heard the gospel concerning God's judgment against sin, and His offer of pardon and forgiveness in Jesus Christ. If he believes this, it becomes the basis or the motivation for genuine repentance.

The term for repentance in the Old Testament means "to turn," that is, to turn from walking in one direction and to begin walking in an opposite direction. In this case it would be from the world toward God. In the New Testament, the term "repent" means to change or turn the mind. In regard to redemption, it means to turn away from sin unto righteousness, to change the mind about sin, Jesus Christ, and God.

Sometimes a form of this word is translated "to feel regret." A man does feel regret for his sins when he truly repents; but regret for sin is not the same as the idea of true repentance, which is changing the mind about sin and turning to God. After a murderer has been sent to prison, he may be sorry he killed someone; but if he does it again after he has been freed, it proves that his regret was not repentance. The idea of regret is used of Judas in Matthew 27:3. After he betrayed Jesus, he had remorse; but he did not change his ways. He went out and committed suicide.

Repentance is seen in Scripture to be a gift. It is God who gives repentance, just as He gives faith. God gave repentance to Israel (Acts 5:31). He gives repentance to the Gentiles (Acts 11:18). Even though repentance is a gift, it is man's responsibility to do the repenting. In Mark 1:14-15 Jesus preached that men were to believe the gospel and repent of their sins. In Acts 17:30 Paul said that God "commandeth all men every where to repent." This means that man repents under the influence of the Holy Spirit and responds in faith to the message of the gospel.

A man who has genuinely repented of his sins cannot remain in those sins—he has been "born again" to a new life in Christ. This term, "born again," is used loosely today by many people who give no evidence that they have changed their ways. Celebrities, movie stars, and sports figures talk about being born again; but they continue living and talking like the world. Their interests are in the world; but evidence of genuine repentance is a changed mind toward God, sin, and Jesus Christ. The truly repentant person recognizes that he is guilty before God, and acknowledges it. He abandons all of his resistance and rebellion against truth, God, and His commandments. He accepts God's rule in his life. He changes his mind toward everything, and this changing of his mind changes his ways, so he no longer walks in sin.

True repentance will result in works of righteousness in the Christian's life. In Matthew 3:8 John the Baptist said to the religious leaders who came to his baptism, "Bring forth therefore fruits meet for repentance." In other words, *"Prove that you have repented by your good works*, and then come to my baptism." Faith and repentance are inseparably related. If a man has saving faith in Christ, it will result in repentance from sin, and these together will result in a changed way of life, a changed mind about sin.

The Doctrine of Regeneration

Regeneration and conversion are really two sides of the same coin. From God's side the salvation experience is regeneration, and from man's side it is conversion. According to God's Word, man is in a desperate state; he is *dead spiritually* and in need of being regenerated or converted. Paul said, "And you hath he quickened, who were dead in trespasses and sins;" *alienated from God spiritually*, "and were by nature the children of wrath" (Ephesians 2:1-3). Also see Romans 3:9-23; 5:12-21. While man was yet a sinner, God showed His love toward him and sent His Son into the world to die for him (Romans 5:8). All men are sinners, alienated from God, and are totally *unable to change* their spiritual condition. "Can the Ethiopian change his skin, or the leopard his spots? then may ye also do good, that are accustomed to do evil" (Jeremiah 13:23). Paul said in I Corinthians 2:14,

"The natural man receiveth not the things of the Spirit of God: for they are foolishness unto him: neither can he know them, because they are spiritually discerned." In Romans 1 Paul said that God gave the ungodly up to uncleanness, gave them up to vile affections, and gave them over to a reprobate mind. These are not just assumptions, but they are truths set forth in the Word of God. Man's need is nowhere more clearly taught than in Jesus' own words in John 3 where He said that a man must be born again or he will never see the Kingdom of God.

Evidences of Regeneration

There are certain *evidences* which would indicate that a person has truly been born of God. Regeneration is known by its effects on the internal man as well as on the outward man. Belief in Christ is an *internal evidence* of regeneration (I John 5:1). John 8:42 says if God is a man's Father, that man will love Christ; and in Romans 8:16 Paul said that the Spirit within the Christian will bear witness within his own spirit that he is a child of God.

There are certain *external evidences* of regeneration. For example, I John 2:29 says, "Every one that doeth righteousness is born of him." The Christian will not live in sin and in the habits of the old life. I John 4:7 says, "Every one that loveth is born of God, and knoweth God." If a person is born of God, he will overcome this world (I John 5:4). "We know that whosoever is born of God sinneth not" (I John 5:18), and will do works of righteousness (Ephesians 2:10).

The Doctrine of Conversion

The other side of regeneration is *conversion*. Regeneration speaks of God's work; conversion speaks of what happens to man. Regeneration is described as the new birth, and it results in a new way of life. "If any man be in Christ [that is, if he is converted], he is a new creation: old things are passed away; behold, all things are become new" (II Corinthians 5:17). Paul further stated in Romans 8 that a person who has been born again will be walking in the Spirit.

Regeneration or conversion is not a process or a growth; it is an instantaneous experience. It is called a birth. Some individuals are trying to live righteous lives and are doing religious works in substitution for the new birth; but the new birth "converts" a man into a new creation, and the good works follow.

Regeneration is an instantaneous, supernatural work of God wrought in the heart or life of the new believer. If a man has been born again, a new power in his life takes over and enables him to overcome sin. The Spirit of Christ and the new life within are more powerful than that old life, Satan, and the world. The Apostle Paul, in Galatians 5:16-25, contrasted the works of the flesh with the fruit of the Spirit. If a professing Christian is still performing the works of the flesh, he is not in Christ and has not become a new creation. Without the evidence of the fruit of the Spirit in his life, there is nothing to convince others that he has been born again.

205

The Doctrine of Justification

Justification is a vitally important aspect of *the doctrine of redemption*. In fact, justification is one of the central issues of the Bible because it deals with the complex question, "How can a righteous, holy God forgive sinners and accept them as if they had never sinned?" The answer will indicate why justification and atonement, which are given by grace, are inseparably related.

The doctrine of justification is taught in both the Old and New Testaments. In Isaiah 53:11 the prophet foretold that Messiah by His death would "justify many." Hebrews 11:4 speaks of justifying sinners. Romans 4:3 and other passages show that justification is by faith. It was the restoration of the truth of man's justification by faith that brought on the Protestant Reformation under Luther. For a detailed study of the truth of justification by faith, see Romans and Galatians.

The term for justification never means "to make one righteous." In reference to man it means "to count, impute, or declare one righteous," and in reference to God it means "to be righteous" or "declare to be righteous." See Luke 7:29; I Timothy 3:16; Deuteronomy 25:1. The Bible does not teach that a man *is righteous* because he believes in Christ, but he is *counted as righteous*. To be sure, if a man is born again, he has a new nature which is righteous; but God at some point had to deal with man's sins. He cannot overlook sin. Because man is guilty before the law, God, in His love, has provided an atonement. He does not ignore sin; but He, through Christ, has satisfied the demands that His law has against sinners. Since all men are sinners, all are guilty; all

206

must die. God's plan to justify man does not suggest that the believer has never sinned, or that he is not guilty; but by the repentant sinner's faith in the atonement of Jesus, God will treat him as if he had fulfilled His law and as if he were not guilty. The righteousness of the law is fulfilled in the Christian's heart by faith (Romans 8:4).

The Moral Basis for Justification

The *moral basis* for justification could not be through man's obedience to God's commandments (Romans 3:20; Galatians 3:10,21), or through the observance of religious rites. Romans 4:9-11 shows that Abraham was justified before the religious rite of circumcision was given. The *moral basis* for justification could not be man's moral nature or character, because men are by nature children of wrath (Ephesians 2:3; Psalm 130:3).

The moral basis for justification was the satisfaction fully rendered by Jesus Christ, the innocent, for the demands the law held against the guilty. "Whom God hath set forth to be a propitiation through faith in his blood, to declare his righteousness for the remission of sins that are past, through the forbearance of God; To declare, I say, at this time his righteousness: that he might be just, and the justifier of him which believeth in Jesus" (Romans 3:25-26).

God sent His Son to declare His righteousness for the remission of sins that were past, those committed prior to His coming. All of the sins that were atoned for by animal sacrifices were not remitted. God's wrath was appeased by those sacrifices on the basis that His Son would eventually satisfy

His wrath through the shedding of His own blood. If Christ had not come, all the Old Testament saints would have perished even with their sins forgiven. His ultimate sacrifice made all the others valid.

These verses reveal God's patience in waiting for Christ to be offered, so that those who believed could be justified. God cannot arbitrarily justify a sinner; that is, He cannot forgive sins without a basis. He could not arbitrarily justify Jesus if He became a sinner. These verses show that the Cross itself proves Jesus could not have become a sinner, because God was demanding righteous payment for the sins of man—all those sins He forgave in the past and those He is going to forgive that will be committed in the future. God put Christ on the Cross to prove He was righteous. God did not arbitrarily forgive, but He came Himself in the person of Himself.

Remember, the Godhead cannot be divided. God was in Christ reconciling the world unto Himself. How could Jesus be a sinner if the Father was in Christ while He was reconciling the world unto Himself? It proves Jesus could not literally become sin on the Cross. Man's sins were imputed to Him, charged to Him. He bore the guilt and punishment for sins as the lamb did. The lamb could not become a sinner. Sinfulness is what a person does. When did Jesus ever sin? Never! At Calvary Jesus was saying He was in the perfect will of God. On the Cross Jesus was righteous and remained righteous, and God accepted Him.

Moses and Elijah were concerned about the soon death of Jesus because they came and talked to Him about it on the Mount of Transfiguration. Their sins were forgiven, but the curse had to be lifted by the death of their sinless substitute, Jesus Christ.

The Doctrine of Imputation

The term for *imputation* in the Hebrew means "to think, to account, to reckon, to impute." The Greek term is "to reckon, to account, to impute." See Psalm 106:30-31; Romans 4; Leviticus 7:18; 17:4. It does not imply a transfer of moral qualities but of legal guilt and punishment, or legal righteousness.

The Scriptures teach that Christians are *counted as righteous*. In imputation God considers the believer no longer guilty, as if he had fulfilled His law. For example, Genesis 15:6 says that Abraham believed God and it was counted or imputed to him for righteousness. He was not righteous in himself, but his faith was counted as righteousness. This may be seen again in Romans 4 where Paul said that God counts His children as righteous because of their faith in the atoning sacrifice of Jesus Christ. God said, in effect, "I will not impute man's guilt to him. I will impute his punishment to an innocent substitute, Jesus Christ. I will impute to him righteousness; that is, I will credit it to his account. I will count him as righteous." Man is neither guiltless nor righteous in himself; but by his faith in the guiltless, righteous Son of God, who suffered in his place and paid the punishment for the guilt of his sins, the Father God treats him, counts him, as guiltless and righteous.

The subject here is not specifically the new birth, but is the method God has ordained to deal with man's guilt so that he can become a new creation. God cannot say that man is righteous simply because he believes in Christ. Actually, man is guilty and is alienated from God. He is a sinner; but through his faith in Christ, the righteousness of the law is imputed unto him.

To impute something to someone is to enter it to his account. The Bible speaks of the books that God keeps in which men's works are recorded. When a sinner turns to Christ, the blood of Jesus covers over the pages, figuratively speaking, and erases them. Then God takes His pen and writes on the other side of the ledger, "Not guilty—because he trusted in My Son, Jesus Christ. Because of his faith, I now impute righteousness unto him."

The following hypothetical story illustrates the principle of imputation: A man violated the speed law, but had no money to pay the fine. However, his friend stood in his place before the judge and paid it. The judge accepted the payment and released the offender. The judge did not say that the man was not guilty, that he had not violated the law of the land, but he acknowledged that payment for his guilt had been imputed to his record. The innocent suffered the penalty of the guilty, and the offender was set free. In the context of justification, it may be said that Jesus paid the fine on man's behalf. The punishment for man's guilt was imputed to Him, as an innocent substitute. As a result, His righteousness, His fulfillment of the law, and His payment of the debt were imputed or credited to man's account.

With this in mind, the greatest work of God in this universe from the beginning to the end of time was neither the creation of the world, nor the resurrection of the dead, nor the performing of miracles, nor the parting of the Red Sea; but it was God's justification of the ungodly. He has great power, but the only way for Him to justify the ungodly was to come into the world and do the work Himself. Moral, spiritual righteousness is *ascribed* to God as one of His attributes, but it must be *imputed* to man. In God's sight "there is none righteous" (Romans 3:10). It is an abomination to God to justify the wicked (Proverbs 17:15). This is not speaking of the one who receives forgiveness on God's terms.

Aspects of Imputation

There are three major *aspects* of *imputation*: First, the imputation of Adam's guilt to the entire human race (I Corinthians 15:22; Romans 5:12-21). Next, the imputation of the guilt and punishment of man's sins to Christ (Isaiah 53:5-6; II Corinthians 5:21; I Peter 2:24). Jesus Christ was not made literal sin; but sin was imputed to Him, and He became a most holy sin offering. Finally, the imputation of the righteousness of God to believers (Genesis 15:6; Psalm 106:31; Romans 3:22; 4:22; 8:32-33; Philippians 3:8-9).

The Doctrine of Sanctification

Another area of study related to redemption is the *doctrine of sanctification*. The term "sanctify" in English, Hebrew, and Greek literally means to be "set apart," "consecrated," "dedicated," and "separated" for some special function or use. There is a derived meaning in religion which means to be

211

holy and pure, but basically the term does not speak of those concepts. In fact, in the Old Testament the word sanctify was used in reference to sodomites and prostitutes who were set apart for an evil purpose.

The Scriptures refer to the Levites and priests as being sanctified, but literally they were set apart for God's service. The altar was said to be sanctified (Exodus 40:10); it was set apart for God's sacrifice. The nation of Israel (Exodus 19:14) and the firstborn were sanctified or set apart (Exodus 13:2). In John 17:19 Jesus said, "I sanctify myself." He could have said, "I set myself apart or consecrate myself for this task."

Sanctification in the Scriptures is equated with holiness in the sense of moral purity and piety, because whatever is sanctified partakes of that to which it is set apart. For example, if someone is sanctified to God, it means that he is partaking of the moral qualities of God. It means that person is to be like Him. "But as he which hath called you is holy, so be ye holy in all manner of living; Because it is written, Be ye holy; for I am holy" (I Peter 1:15-16; I Thessalonians 4:7; Ephesians 1:4).

There are three views of sanctification. 1) The *Roman Catholic view* teaches that water baptism of infants washes away all sin, as well as the depravity of the human nature. This error, which is also found in some Protestant denominations, is referred to as baptismal regeneration and baptismal sanctification. 2) *Protestants* developed the view of progressive sanctification which they say begins at conversion. *Past tense* sanctification is by the blood of Christ; *present tense* sanctification is by the Word; *future tense* sanctification is the belief that Christians will be perfect only when Christ returns. 3) The *biblical view* of sanctification is based on the literal meaning of the term and not the derived meaning. The Christian has been set apart unto God, and He expects him to be distinctly different from the world. The Scriptures say that the believer is free from sin (Romans 6:18), he is a new creation (II Corinthians 5:17), he is dead to sin (Romans 6:2; I Peter 2:24), and he has ceased from sin (I Peter 4:1). Sanctified is what the believer is; perfected is what he is to be.

When the Scriptures speak of sanctification, they always speak of it in the past tense, already completed. "And such were some of you: but ye are washed, but ye are sanctified, but ye are justified in the name of the Lord Jesus, and by the Spirit of our God" (I Corinthians 6:11). See Acts 20:32; Romans 15:16; I Corinthians 1:2; Jude 1. "For by one offering he hath perfected for ever them that are sanctified" (Hebrews 10:14). Paul said in Ephesians 5:25-26 that Christ sanctified and cleansed the church "with the washing of water by the word." Further, "God hath from the beginning chosen you to salvation through sanctification of the Spirit and belief of the truth" (II Thessalonians 2:13).

There are two erroneous theories prevalent in most denominations which serve only to encourage defeat and indifference in the life of a Christian. These are the "two natures" theory and "the progressive sanctification" error. Because of such wrong teaching many Christians are convinced that they cannot be sanctified fully in this life, and they believe they have two natures—one good and one bad. As a result they resign themselves to half-hearted Christianity. The Scriptures reveal that the Christian had one nature

213

before salvation, which was sinful, corrupt, and alienated from God. After salvation, however, that one nature is renewed by faith in Jesus Christ, and replaces the old. All men were by nature children of wrath, according to Ephesians 2:3. Man does not merely *possess* a sinful nature before salvation; he *is* sinful. After salvation, Paul said, "If any man be in Christ, he is a new creation: old things are passed away; behold, all things are become new" (II Corinthians 5:17). This would include his nature.

To argue that the believer cannot be perfect in this life confuses perfection with sanctification and contradicts the Word which commands it; "Be ye therefore perfect, even as your Father which is in heaven is perfect" (Matthew 5:48). It also ignores the fact that the Scriptures say certain men in biblical history were perfect, for example, Job (Job 1:8), Noah (Genesis 6:9), Enoch (Hebrews 11:5; Genesis 5:22), and Moses (Numbers 12:7). II Timothy 3:16-17 declares that all Scripture is given "that the man of God may be perfect, throughly furnished unto all good works." This perfection is not to be confused with "sinless perfection," an erroneous concept which states that it would be impossible to sin. Nor is it freedom from temptation or perfection of doctrine. It is the perfection of character and conduct in a Christian. Some do not walk in a perfection of consecration; but in regard to their standing, they are sanctified. There is a perfection of holiness (Ephesians 1:4; Titus 2:12-14); and there is a perfection of the maturing of the fruit of the Spirit in a Christian's life, such as love, joy, peace, and longsuffering (Galatians 5:22-23).

The Doctrine of Union With Christ

Regeneration places the believer in *union with Christ*, or, as expressed in the New Testament, "in Christ." All of the promises of God are applied to those who are "in Christ." "There is therefore now no condemnation to them which are in Christ Jesus, who walk not after the flesh, but after the Spirit" (Romans 8:1). When God looks at the one who is "in Christ," He sees that person covered with the righteousness of Christ. Paul said in Colossians 3:17, "And whatsoever ye do in word or deed, do all in the name of the Lord Jesus." That includes praying in His name, baptizing in His name, casting out demons in His name, healing the sick in His name, receiving the Holy Spirit in His name, etc. (John 14:13-14; Mark 16:17-18).

In some cults, such as Hinduism and Buddhism, the worshiper's so-called salvation consists of union with his deity. Supposedly, this union is achieved by absorption into the deity, and in this state the worshiper loses his own identity; he becomes one with the world or universal soul. Only in Christianity is the believer brought into union with a personal God—into a true oneness in Spirit. The Christian does not lose his personal identity, but he is restored to the image of God in all its fulness through this union (II Corinthians 5:17).

The union of the Christian with his God is a mystery and is compared with that of husband and wife as one flesh (Ephesians 5:21-32). Since the saint partakes of the divine nature (II Peter 1:4), this union is not a mere figure of speech;

215

but it is an actual union with God Himself. The believer has been bought with a price, has become one with Christ, and is called a temple of the Holy Spirit (I Corinthians 6:17-20). The believer is in Him, and He is in the believer (John 14:20-23). According to Romans 8:38-39 this union is inseparable.

There are several analogies in Scripture which describe this union with Christ. By man's human nature he is *in Adam*, but *in Christ* he partakes of His divine nature. "For as in Adam all die, even so in Christ shall all be made alive" (I Corinthians 15:22). The Christian's spiritual nature is from God. "Whosoever believeth that Jesus is the Christ is born of God" (I John 5:1). That spiritual seed of God makes him pure (I John 3:9).

Another analogy which describes the union with Christ is the relationship of a vine and its branches (John 15:1-5). God is the *Creator* of all men, but He is the *Father* of only those who are redeemed. Jesus Christ has given life to all men, but spiritual rebirth is only granted to His elect. Only those who are "in Him" are sustained by the life of the vine (John 15:1-8).

In Ephesians 2:20-22 Paul gave the analogy of the Christian being like a building or temple which is built as a habitation for God. Also see I Corinthians 6:17-20. In John 6:48-63 Jesus used the analogy of partaking of the bread in Communion as His life-giving presence in His followers. By their faith in His sacrificial offering, He dwells in them. He said that eating His flesh would profit nothing, but His words would give life.

The mystery of the union with Christ is symbolized by the Christian's baptism, which shows his death to sin and his resurrection to a new life (Romans 6:1-5). The Communion of the bread and cup witnesses to the truth that Christ is in the believer, and that he is in Him (I Corinthians 10:16-17). Washing of the saints' feet also symbolizes being one with Christ (John 13:6-8).

What are the benefits of being in union with Christ? 1) The Christian possesses the divine, eternal life of God. "This life is in his Son" (I John 5:11-12). 2) He becomes a partaker of the divine nature (II Peter 1:4). 3) He becomes a new creation by the new birth (John 3; II Corinthians 5:17). 4) He literally becomes a child and son of God (Galatians 4; Romans 8; I John 3). 5) He becomes a joint-heir with Christ (Galatians 4; Romans 8). 6) Union with Christ secures all spiritual and temporal blessings (Ephesians 1:3; Romans 8:31-32; I Corinthians 3:20-21). 7) It secures completeness in Him (Colossians 2:10). 8) It secures for the believer a participation in Christ's total redemptive experience. That which happened to Christ is paralleled in the life of the believer. For example, Paul related that he had to experience a crucifixion similar to Christ's. "I am crucified with Christ: nevertheless I live; yet not I, but Christ liveth in me: and the life which I now live in the flesh I live by the faith of the Son of God, who loved me, and gave himself for me" (Galatians 2:20).

The Doctrine of Crucifixion With Christ

What does it mean to be *"crucified with Christ"*? "Knowing this, that our old man is crucified with him, that the body of sin might be destroyed, that henceforth we should not serve sin" (Romans 6:6). Paul said in Romans 6:3,8, "Know ye not, that so many of us as were baptized into Jesus Christ were baptized into his death? . . . Now if we be dead with Christ, we believe that we shall also live with him." He further said in II Corinthians 5:14, "If one died for all, then were all dead." The Scriptures speak of these aspects of redemption in a legal sense. As soon as a sinner repents, God immediately imputes to him the righteousness of His Son, Jesus Christ. This is a legal transaction. God sees the new Christian as if he had obeyed the law and had been righteous, even though righteousness has only been imputed to him. In a sense, when Jesus died, God saw every elect person dead, as if that person had paid the penalty for his own sins. If God counts the Christian as righteous, He sees him as righteous. The righteousness of the law has been fulfilled by the Christian's faith (Romans 8:4). The Christian is buried with Christ in baptism (Romans 6:4), is made alive with Him (Romans 6:4-5), is raised with Him (Colossians 3:1), is exalted with Him (Ephesians 2:6), and is glorified with Him (Romans 8:17,30).

The Doctrine of Adoption

Redemption makes a man a child of God; *adoption* makes him a son of God and gives him the rights of sonship. Every child is a son; but not every child recognizes, realizes, or walks in his sonship. The Christian needs to be taught what adoption has obtained so he can live like a son and not just a child.

The word "adoption" is not the best translation of the biblical term because God does not adopt His children in the modern sense. The term should have been translated "to place as a son." In the Greek, Roman, and Jewish cultures, when a boy became a certain age he was "placed as a son" and given all the legal rights, powers, and authority of sonship. Paul's use of adoption referred to the legal act of God's grace by which a believer may be considered a son of God. He is a "child" by the new birth; but his adoption grants him the position of an adult son, and permits him to call the One who adopted him, "Father."

In the current concept of the term, a son by adoption is not a child by birth; but in Scripture a son of God by adoption is always first His child by birth—the new birth. A parent never adopts his own children, but God never adopts any other. Being a son of God is the Christian's legal relationship to God, affording him his inheritance, position, authority, rights, and power over the enemy. See Romans 8:14-18; Ephesians 1:3-5; Galatians 4:1-6.

The Doctrine of Eternal Security

Another study in the area of redemption is the *doctrine of the eternal security* of the believer. Reformation theologians (Calvinists) called it the doctrine of perseverance. Actually, it could be better thought of as the *doctrine of preservation and perseverance*. From God's side, it is preservation; from man's side it is perseverance. If one is absent, they are both absent. God clearly promises to preserve His sheep (Psalm 121), but He also admonishes them to make sure they persevere (Hebrews 10:23).

Can a saved person ever be lost? There are different views. 1) The Roman Catholics say salvation may be forfeited by a mortal sin, such as murder and blasphemy. 2) The Calvinists say that a saved person will persevere to the end and not be lost. 3) The Pentecostals believe any saved person may be lost by sin. 4) The Methodists teach that a person may be lost by sin or apostasy. 5) The biblical view shows that the elect will persevere because God will preserve them.

There is a distinction between a *mere believer*, one who has simply embraced Christianity as his religion, and an *elect believer*. There are people who make professions and endure for a time, as illustrated in the Parable of the Sower. Some received the Word and acted on it, but did not endure (Matthew 13). Jesus said, "Every branch in me that beareth not fruit he [the Father] taketh away" (John 15:2). He said they were *in Him*. Paul said in I Timothy 4:1, "Now the Spirit speaketh expressly, that in the latter times some shall depart from the faith, giving heed to seducing spirits, and doctrines of demons." Notice that they were in "the faith." But there are some who *profess* the Christian faith who do not endure to the end. See II Timothy 2:20-22; Hebrews 6:4-8; 10:26-31.

The Scriptures show there is an elect group who will endure: a remnant according to the election of grace (Romans

11:5). Paul said in Romans 11:7, "The election hath obtained it, and the rest were blinded." According to I Peter 1:2-5 the elect will be preserved. He spoke of those "who are kept by the power of God through faith unto salvation ready to be revealed in the last time" (verse 5). Jesus said the days of the great tribulation would be shortened for the elect's sake (Matthew 24:22). Paul said, "I endure all things for the elect's sakes, that they may also obtain the salvation which is in Christ Jesus with eternal glory" (II Timothy 2:10).

The elect will persevere because they are preserved by God. "To them that are sanctified by God the Father, and preserved in Jesus Christ" (Jude 1). The Christian has been predestinated and "sealed unto the day of redemption" (Ephesians 4:30; 1:5). Jesus said, "My sheep hear my voice, and I know them, and they follow me: And I give unto them eternal life; and they shall never perish, neither shall any man pluck them out of my hand. My Father, which gave them me, is greater than all; and no man is able to pluck them out of my Father's hand" (John 10:27-29). The elect will not fall away or be lost (John 6:39; 17:2; Romans 8:29-30; I Corinthians 1:7-9; Philippians 1:6; I Thessalonians 5:23-24; II Thessalonians 3:3; Hebrews 6:9; I Peter 1:2-5).

Why do the Scriptures warn against the dangers of sin if the elect will be saved anyway? The admonitions and warnings are the means by which God secures the true believer's perseverance. "Wherefore the rather, brethren, give diligence to make your calling and election sure: for if ye do these things, ye shall never fall" (II Peter 1:10). Jesus said in Revelation 3:11, "Behold, I come quickly: hold that fast which thou hast, that no man take thy crown." Paul told the Philippians to "work out your own salvation with fear and trembling" (2:12). Even the Apostle Paul said, "I keep under my body, and bring it into subjection: lest that by any means, when I have preached to others, I myself should be a castaway" (I Corinthians 9:27).

Chapter Six
The Doctrine of the Church

Christ, in this hour, through the latter day outpouring of the Holy Spirit, is desiring to restore the pattern of the church as it is revealed in the New Testament; but this cannot happen until believers have a biblical understanding of what the church is supposed to be. Most people think the church is a *building* used for religious services, but some believe it is a *denomination* or a *local assembly* of believers. Others think of the church as *Christendom* as a whole—the universal body of Christ throughout the world. Some say the *universal invisible church*, the so-called mystical body of Christ, is the true church. Members of the Roman Catholic Church say their church is the *universal visible church*. The fact that there are over 250 denominations is proof of the confusion which prevails in Christendom regarding the nature, function, and organization of the church.

Some of the discord stems from the fact that the term "church" comes from the German word "kirche," which means "house" or "building." As a result, most people, when they say, "Let us go to church," are thinking of a building located on some street corner, not realizing that *they, the Christians, are the church*.

When speaking of the church, the New Testament does not use a word which means building or house; instead, "ekklesia" is used, which is a Greek term meaning "an assembly of called out ones." This term occurs 112 times in the New Testament.

The New Testament views the church as an organism—something with life—an assembly of living people. It is not just an organization which meets periodically, nor is it a building or a house. In Matthew 16:13-19, when Jesus asked, "Whom do men say that I the Son of man am? . . . Peter answered and said, Thou art the Christ, the Son of the living God." Jesus said to Peter, "Upon this rock I will build my church." In other words, "Upon this revelation that I am the Christ, the Son of God, I will establish my assembly." When Jesus used the term "ekklesia," He was not inventing a new concept, because the term "assembly" was used in Old Testament times, speaking of the whole congregation of Israel assembled together. The Hebrew word for assembly was "qahal." The term "assembly" was not unique to Jesus; but the uniqueness of its use here lies in the fact that He said, "Upon this rock I will build *my* assembly." He called it *His* assembly.

The church in the New Testament and in early Christian history would never refer to the church as a building or a meeting place because *the church* met in the homes of believers (Acts 2:46; 12:12; Colossians 4:15). In Romans 16:3-5 Paul extended greetings to several saints; then he said, "Likewise greet the church that is in their house."

The Nature of the New Testament Church

The *nature* of the *church*, as it is set forth in the New Testament, is that of a living *organism*—not of an organization. In I Corinthians 12 the Apostle Paul compared the church to a human body with numerous essential members. There is a vast difference between an organism—something with life—and a dead corporation or organization with its impersonalness, complexity, and lifelessness. An organism, on the other hand, is like the human body with each of its members in vital relationship to the others, all partaking of a common life. Whatever happens to one part of the body affects the entire body. It has unity (I Corinthians 12:12) and diversity (verse 4); it has one source of life (verse 13); it is interdependent (verses 21-27); and it is visible (verse 27).

Views Regarding the Nature of the Church

In regard to the *nature* of the church, there are basically three views: the Roman Catholic view, the Protestant view, and the view of all other churches. The Roman Catholics formulated the *universal visible church theory*, which alleges that the Kingdom of God is universal, and all who are saved are in the Kingdom of God. They equate the church with the Kingdom of God and say there is no salvation outside of the true church, which to them is the visible Roman Catholic Church.

In 1520 Martin Luther was excommunicated from the Roman Catholic Church because of his stand on justification by faith. Since he was no longer a member of the *visible* church, he invented the theory of the *universal invisible church*. He said, "Jesus taught us the Kingdom of God is within you; that means it is invisible. The Kingdom of God is also universal; therefore, the true church is universal and invisible." He taught that alongside the local visible churches was also a *universal invisible mystical body of Christ* to which all Christians belong. Most Protestants today agree with that teaching, although there is not one word in the Bible to support their view. Because of this conception of the church as a mystical, invisible body, many have a shallow attitude toward the local assembly and their responsibility to it.

Luther and his followers in the Protestant Reformation attempted to explain this view by saying that a believer may or may not be a member of a local visible church; but that every believer, whether in the past, present, or future ages of Christianity, whether living or dead, does belong to the universal invisible church or the mystical body of Christ. To support this supposition, they cite I Corinthians 12:27, where the term "body of Christ" is used. However, their use of this text is invalid because it is a metaphor showing *relationship within* the church, not the *nature of* the church.

Another text they use is Hebrews 12:23, where Paul said, "To the general assembly and church of the firstborn, which are written in heaven, and to God the Judge of all, and to the spirits of just men made perfect." They contend that this verse says all the saints living or dead are registered in heaven; thus, they all belong to an invisible universal church.

Obviously, Paul was not just speaking of the church of his day, but of all the saints who have their names registered in heaven. Therefore, the use of "assembly" and "church" in this passage speaks of the completed church as a thing in prospect, and not of the church then in actual existence. He was saying, in effect, that one day there will be a general assembly composed of Old and New Testament saints, all whose names are written in the Lamb's book of life, and with myriads of angels.

All born again believers are citizens of the kingdom; but by no means have all been, nor are they now, members of true New Testament churches. The Kingdom of God in its present expression is universal, spiritual, and invisible; and it is broader in concept than the church, which is always local and visible, consisting of the various assemblies in specific locations. It is significant that Christ's last message to His body in the Book of Revelation was not to a vague universal mystical church, but to certain specific local churches of Asia. In I Corinthians 1:2 Paul wrote, "Unto the church of God which is at Corinth," and in Galatians 1:2, "Unto the churches of Galatia." In I Corinthians 12:12-13,27 Paul used a metaphor to teach about the many-membered body of Christ which he applied to the local church in Corinth. Paul made no suggestion of an invisible mystical universal body or universal church somewhere. In I Corinthians 1:2 Paul addressed himself to the church at Corinth; then in chapter 12, verse 27 he said, "Now ye are the body of Christ, and members in particular." Thus, Paul forever disproved the false invisible mystical body theory of the reformers, who would have believers belonging to two churches.

Advocates of the universal invisible mystical church theory frequently cite the "one body" concept of Paul. In I Corinthians 12:13 Paul said that all Christians are baptized by one Spirit into one body, obviously speaking of regeneration. In I Corinthians 12:12-31 Paul used the body as a metaphor to show the spiritual relationship between Christ and His church. Again, in Ephesians 2:16 and 4:4 he showed that there is one body. Paul had reference to the church being one—one body. He was not teaching the universal invisible mystical theory, but was illustrating that the church is made up of all races, all kinds of people, and all social classes of people. Jesus said in John 10 that there is one Shepherd and one fold; that is, that one day both Jews and Gentiles will belong to the same body. Whenever a literal, geographical church is referred to, it is always spoken of as a local, visible assembly.

A metaphor is a figure of speech containing an implied comparison, such as the phrase, "a mighty fortress is our God." God is not an actual fortress, but use of this metaphor shows the nature of His power to deliver and protect those who trust Him (Psalm 91:2). In I Corinthians 12 Paul used the terms "hand," "feet," "eyes," and "ears" to portray the many parts of the body. The metaphor shows a spiritual relationship. Christ is the head; the church is the body. To insist that the body of Christ means a literal invisible mystical body somewhere is to absolutize what the Holy Spirit intended as a metaphor. Care must be exercised when interpreting the Bible not to literalize or absolutize the many metaphors found in the Word of God; or God's eyes, for example, would be running to and fro throughout the earth (II Chronicles 16:9).

The Revelation of the Church

Few people realize that the church was a mystery until it was revealed in the New Testament (Ephesians 3:5-6; Romans 16:25-26; Colossians 1:25-27). Although the Old Testament saints were given occasional glimpses of a future age in which even the Gentiles would worship their God, it was a mystery to them how this would be fulfilled. No wonder—for the promises were made only to Israel (Romans 9:4)! The mystery was not that God would have an assembly; He had the assembly of Israel in the Old Testament. But the truth had not been clearly revealed that He would make *one body* out of every tribe and nation, and He would call it His assembly.

The mystery of the church was first revealed by prophecy in the transitional period between the Old and New Testaments, according to historians. Matthew 16:18-19 is also a prophetic reference to the church. The church in action is recorded in the entire Book of Acts, and its doctrines are disclosed throughout the Epistles.

The Beginning of the Church

There is little agreement among Bible scholars as to when the church actually began. There are four basic views: 1) Some say it began with the call of the twelve apostles who were sent forth to preach and to baptize. 2) Others believe it began at the time of Peter's confession in Matthew 16. 3) Another group believes the church had its beginning at the time of the Last Supper when they say the new covenant was instituted; however, the new covenant was not effective until

Jesus went to the Cross. 4) The Scriptural view is that the church began on the day of Pentecost (Acts 2).

There are several reasons the church did not begin before Pentecost. There was no death, no shedding of blood, no sacrifice made, and no resurrection before Calvary. In other words, there was no gospel to preach. When Jesus sent forth the disciples in Matthew 10, He told them to proclaim the Kingdom of Heaven so that the Jews would have a foretaste of what was going to take place in the subsequent dispensation of God's kingdom. They preached a partial gospel which pointed to the Cross. This was intended to get the Jews ready to receive the Messiah; but their rejection of Him resulted in His death and resurrection, and brought about the birth of the full gospel. Paul clearly showed in I Corinthians 15 that the resurrection is the gospel, and that without the shedding of blood, there is no remission of sins (Hebrews 9:22).

The Purpose of the Church

There are four essential *purposes* for the church. 1) The church was established for *ministry*. Jesus commissioned the disciples to make citizens for the kingdom through the proclamation of the gospel (Matthew 28:19-20; Mark 16:15-18). 2) The church is for the *manifestation* of the glory of Christ (John 17:10,22-23; I Peter 2:9; John 9:5 with Philippians 2:15; Matthew 5:14-16). 3) The church is for *demonstration*. It is to exhibit to the universe the wisdom and grace of God in saving sinners (Ephesians 3:8-11; 2:6-7). 4) The church exists for *fellowship* with other Christians at the present time (Acts

2:42; I John 1:3,7), and with Jesus at the Second Advent and throughout eternity (John 14:1-3; 17:24).

Views of the Organization of the Church

There are three principle *views* of the *organization* of the *church*: the ecclesiastical theory of the Roman Catholics and most Protestants, the mystical theory of the reformers, and the biblical view. Those who support the *ecclesiastical theory* believe that the church is an ecclesiastical institution which is led by a priesthood under the headship of a Pope, whom they deem to be Christ's Vicar on earth. Its organization was laid down, they say, by the apostles and their successors. Protestants, of course, do not follow the Roman Catholic Pope, but their hierarchy is conformed to some extent to that of Rome. There are two extremes among *Protestants*. The *Anglican* view is essentially that of the Roman Catholics; however, instead of the Pope, they substitute the Archbishop as head of the church. The *reformers* and their successors stated that there was no definite pattern of organization laid down by Christ and the apostles, and that each church in every age should be left free to adopt whatever organization is best suited to its situation. For example, some churches would be episcopal in form with bishops and archbishops, and other churches would have democratic or congregational forms of government ruled by boards and trustees.

Those who hold to the *mystical theory* in its extreme form say that the church is not a visible, formal organization or institution, but that the body of Christ is a universal

231

invisible mystical body in which all believers are bound together in spiritual union. They say Christ never intended for His body to be organized into a formal institution, meeting every Sunday, observing ordinances, and hearing sermons. Followers of this extreme view are convinced that there is no formal organization, no place established to worship the Lord, no ordinances or sermons; but that the church is simply those who believe in Christ and are bound together in a mystical union in some invisible, universal body concept. As previously discussed, this belief is unscriptural.

The *biblical view* regarding the nature of the organization of the church is set forth clearly in the Book of Acts and in the New Testament Epistles, and is well expressed by the following definition: A New Testament church is a local, visible, autonomous body with Christ as its head, consisting of born again, properly baptized believers, gathered together by the Holy Spirit for the purpose of spiritual worship, observance of the ordinances, propagation of a full gospel, and the teaching of the Word of God, all in accordance with biblical revelation alone.

Reasons for the Rapid Spread of the Church

There were several *reasons* for the *rapid spread* of the local *church* in the first three centuries. 1) The church was *empowered* and *led by* the *Holy Spirit*, as seen in the Book of Acts. 2) The early church conceived of itself as an organism, a body in which *every member functioned*. They believed it was their responsibility and privilege to witness to the gospel. 3) Another reason was the *zeal* of the Christians in their witness for

Christ. Judaism and other religions make very little attempt to convert others to their beliefs, but Christianity is different in that true born again Christians are eager to win others to the truth of salvation in Jesus Christ. 4) The great *unity* of the *faith* which the Christians experienced also contributed to the rapid spread of the church. 5) The *transformation* in the lives of the Christians was an effective witness to the world.

The Rise of the Formal Church Organization

The *formal church organization* developed, essentially, because of a departure from the biblical pattern of the church. There was the loss of regenerate church membership, followed by the loss of the experience of the baptism in the Holy Spirit, the loss of the supernatural offices and ministries in the church, and the loss of the exercise of the charismatic gifts. The fourth century witnessed the rise of a religious organization, religious activity, and institutionalism as substitutes for the power and work of the Holy Spirit.

A progression of events led to the rise of the organized church. In the third century certain men began to set themselves up as alleged successors to the apostles, making claims regarding their authority, and teaching unscriptural doctrines. One of these was Cyprian of North Africa, who was a man of great influence. Propelled by his dogma, errors began to creep into the church before the beginning of a formal organization. He taught that the Bishop is a Priest who stands between men and God, that the church resides in the priesthood, and that the people are the wards of the church. He taught baptism of infants as an antidote for original sin, and that the Communion was a sacrifice to be offered repeatedly by a priest. The Roman Catholic Church accepted these doctrines, claiming much of their authority from the teachings of these early men. Later, since Rome was the leading city of the empire, it assumed the status of the headquarters of the church.

Christianity was illegal, and Christians were severely persecuted until the Edict of 311 A.D. when the Roman Emperor Galerius made Christianity a *tolerated religion*. Persecution ceased, the members of the church were accepted by the world, and their beliefs or practices were no longer important.

The church moved from *toleration* to *organization* under Emperor Constantine, a heathen who embraced Christianity. By the Edict of Milan in 312 A.D., Christianity was placed on an equal basis with other religions of the empire. Constantine allowed freedom of worship, restored property to the Christians which the State had confiscated, made the clergy exempt from taxation and civil duty, licensed the churches which made them legal, and allowed wills to be made which left property to the church. Laws were passed by the State favoring Christianity. Sunday was made the official day of worship in 321 A.D., and all work was forbidden on that day. Christians had already been worshiping on Sunday since the resurrection of Christ, but Constantine legalized what was already taking place. He also gave State protection to the Christians, and aided in building churches by donating lands and money to them. The State began to differentiate between so-called orthodox churches and those that did not follow the Roman system.

The end of persecution and the beginning of State recognition resulted in the church becoming an unregenerate body. 1) It was no longer a stigma to be a Christian. The world and the church were in fellowship. 2) By calling himself a Christian, the pagan could secure many advantages, such as political, social, military, and religious promotion. Constantine Christianized the Roman Empire; however, *Christian* and *Christianized* are not the same. Citizens who were not "Christians" were persecuted and discriminated against. Twenty pieces of silver and a white robe were given to every heathen who would join the church.

The scope of the church's experience moved from persecution to toleration and from toleration to organization. Down through the Middle Ages the church controlled the State and appointed kings and princes. No king or prince dared defy the authority of the Pope. Even in the present day, many countries, such as England and Italy, continue to have State churches. The United States is one of the few countries that does not have a State church.

There were several factors that contributed to the rise of the Roman church and its dominance in the world. Rome, as the capital of the empire, was the center of commerce, industry, travel, politics, etc. Just as in denominationalism today where the large city churches seem to have more influence and are more important, smaller assemblies began to look to the Roman church for decisions. The Eastern Church (Greek Orthodox) did not agree with Rome, so it established its own hierarchy.

The Roman Catholic Papacy began with Gregory the Great, who literally ruled over the Roman Catholic Church from 590-604 A.D. He claimed that the Popes were successors of Peter, who supposedly founded the Roman Catholic Church, although there is no Scriptural evidence that Peter was ever in Rome.

Gregory the Great was trained for civil office, but he became a monk and established six monasteries. He was appointed Bishop of Rome in 590 A.D.; later he called himself Pope Gregory I. His rule is considered to be the beginning of the Papacy for several reasons: 1) He claimed to be successor to Peter. 2) He emphasized the temporal power of his religious office over all secular authority and governments. 3) He taught strange doctrines which the Roman church now considers to be of equal authority as the Bible. For example, (1) Salvation is by grace *and* works, (2) Grace comes through the sacraments, (3) Baptism washes away sins, (4) Communion is a perpetual sacrifice giving perpetual grace, (5) Purgatory is a condition of temporal punishment after death and provides satisfaction for sin, (6) Penance is a means of obtaining forgiveness for sins, and (7) Prayer to the "saints" is a means of receiving their help.

The Government of the Church

There are various forms or systems of church government. 1) In the *Papal* system the authority is centered in the Pope and an ecclesiastical hierarchy of archbishops, bishops, and priests. 2) The *Episcopal* system is governed by bishops. 3) The *Presbyterian* system's authority is centered in the elders. 4) The *Congregational* system of government is called the *democratic* system, which is majority rule by the church membership. 5) In *Theocratic* government, which is the Scriptural pattern, the authority is in the local assembly under Christ.

Theocratic Government in the Church

In the theocratic government of the church as seen in the New Testament, there is no ecclesiastical domination or rule. Each local church, under the Holy Spirit's leadership, has authority in its own affairs, and cannot be dominated or interfered with by any other authority, whether civil or religious. It is a sad fact that organizational churches will frequently submit to civil authority even when it contradicts the Word of God. They conform to the unscriptural principles of expediency and compromise in order to maintain a good standing in the community. The church in the New Testament, however, never submitted to any authority except the Holy Spirit in religious matters. It should be emphasized that Christians are to obey civil authorities (Romans 13:1-7), except when such obedience interferes with their allegiance to Christ. In such cases the believer, out of his loyalty to Christ and His Word, would decline to submit to the secular authority, but would accept the consequences.

The Authority of the New Testament Church

There are several examples in the Scriptures where the church has been exhorted to exercise authority.

1) The local church has authority to discipline its own membership (I Corinthians 5:1-13). Even though Christ has given the highest authority on earth to the apostle, and that office is more closely related to the authority of heaven than any of the other five-fold ministries, the Apostle Paul did not get involved in that situation of fornication in the Corinthian church. Instead, he told the local body to deal with it. Each church is responsible to Christ alone, not to any other church or higher authority.

2) The local church has authority to select men to help meet the temporal needs of that body. In Acts 6:1-6 the Apostles did the appointing, but the church did the selecting.

3) The local church also has the authority to observe and perpetuate the ordinances (I Corinthians 11:23). Paul said he had received instructions concerning Communion of the bread and cup from the Lord, then he delivered those instructions to the church—the people—not to the clergy, hierarchy, or bishops. The New Testament gives no evidence that the clergy has the exclusive right, privilege, or responsibility to administer the ordinances.

4) The local church has authority to settle its own internal difficulties. The Jews to this hour have rabbinical courts, and the Catholics have their religious courts where they judge matters. Protestants, however, utilize the secular or civil courts, not even considering the Scriptural admonitions given in I Corinthians 6:1-5 where Paul said the local body even has power to settle civil disputes among its members. This passage, with Matthew 18:15-19, shows that the authority of the local church under Christ is final, as far as its

own affairs are concerned. The secular authorities have no jurisdiction over the church in issues of conscience and obedience to Christ, although the believer is not to have a defiant and rebellious attitude toward them if they attempt to impose such authority.

The Practice of the New Testament Church

How should the local church deal with matters concerning its doctrine, practice, business, and the conduct of its members? That will be answered in two ways: with the application of theocratic principles of government and with church discipline.

The Application of Theocratic Principles of Government

All matters of faith, doctrine, practice, and business that are subjects for the church body to consider should be acted upon according to the principle that the church is a theocracy under Christ. Experience has proven that when the church uses the form of secular democratic government, in which each member is given the right to vote as he pleases, it tends to promote discord, division, and the formation of opposing groups and factions within the body, rather than unity. As often as not, this expression of human will results in a spiritual stalemate and not in a true harmony of mind and spirit. Believing that no Christian has or really wants the right to vote whether or not he will or will not obey God and His Word concerning any matter under consideration, the church should follow the New Testament instructions and example, seeking only to express the mind and will of Christ. After prayer, discussion, and soul-searching, the church members should be confident that the Holy Spirit, who dwells in every believer alike and is not the author of confusion and disunity, will reveal the same mind to each of them. It is, therefore, the responsibility of the leaders of the church to seek such a harmony of mind by this spiritual method.

There are two key concepts in the New Testament regarding how to decide all religious matters. The members must be of the same mind; and they must seek the will of God in the matter, believing the Holy Spirit will reveal it. "Now I beseech you, brethren, by the name of our Lord Jesus Christ, that ye all speak the same thing, and that there be no divisions among you; but that ye be perfectly joined together in the same mind and in the same judgment" (I Corinthians 1:10). In Acts 1:24 the disciples prayed, asking God to show them which one He had chosen to succeed Judas, and in Acts 13:1-4 the disciples fasted and prayed as they sought the will of God. When Paul and Barnabas were dealing with the question of whether or not the Gentiles should keep the law and be circumcised, the apostles, elders, and the whole church agreed to send chosen men to Antioch with the decision (Acts 15:22-23). In writing to the church at Philippi, Paul told them to "be like-minded, having the same love, being of one accord, of one mind" (Philippians 2:2-3). The church of Jesus Christ is to be a theocracy, with all members seeking unity of mind and the leadership of the Holy Spirit in determining the will of God.

Paul said in Philippians 4:6-7 that believers are to submit everything to God by prayer and supplication with thanksgiving. Romans 8:26-27 also shows the ministry of the Holy Spirit on behalf of the saints if they will seek it. Other Scriptures which express the two ideas of oneness of mind and guidance of the Holy Spirit concerning the will of God are Romans 12:16; II Corinthians 13:11; I Peter 3:8. If the body of Christ is not of one mind, someone is wrong. The church should be seeking the ideal of perfect harmony.

What should be done in the event that such harmony and unity of mind is not apparent after these methods have been applied? If possible, the matter under consideration should be deferred temporarily. Each one involved should reexamine his position in the light of Scripture, with prayer and further soul-searching, and the readiness of mind and willingness of spirit to change his position if it can be shown that he is wrong in the view of biblical teachings or principles. The Holy Spirit is not the author of confusion and division; He will lead the body to one mind and one spirit.

There can be a rare instance where the church cannot come to a unity of mind. If that is the case, the church must follow that course which it believes to be the mind of the Spirit and the teaching of God's Word, proceeding prayerfully and cautiously in a humble spirit of love.

The entire biblical revelation argues for the view that the church is a theocracy under Christ, its head, and that He has never delegated His headship or authority to any board, institution, or even to a majority group within the church. The church is to ascertain and perform His will, and should not obey the will of the majority, which may or may not be the will of God. If a church cannot, by the spiritual means revealed, ascertain the same mind of the Holy Spirit on all matters of faith and practice, it is not the fault of the Spirit or the method; but it is a clear indication that some or all of the body are spiritually immature, deficient in knowledge of the Word, self-willed, or yet carnal.

Church Discipline

The second aspect of how the local body is to deal with matters concerning the conduct of its members is through *church discipline.* One of the reasons the church is in such a poor spiritual state is that a member can do almost anything, within limits, yet continue to be a part of the church. The popular attitude toward a sinning member is always Matthew 7:1, "Judge not, that ye be not judged." But Jesus also said, "Judge righteous judgment" (John 7:24).

There are very clear procedures in the Scriptures for correcting those who are in sin or error; and if a church is to maintain its integrity, it *must* exercise discipline. The major texts for church discipline are: Matthew 18:15-17; Romans 16:17; I Corinthians 5:1-13; 6:1-8; II Corinthians 2:1-11; 7:8-13; Galatians 6:1; II Thessalonians 3:6-15; I Timothy 1:19-20 with II Timothy 2:17-18; Titus 3:10-11; I and II John.

The first purpose for discipline is for the spiritual welfare of the entire body, which is a living organism, with its members in vital relationship to one another. According to Jesus, sin or error on the part of one will affect or infect the entire body if it is ignored. The responsibility of discipline by the church is clearly commanded because its neglect would weaken the church's testimony and would encourage spiritual carelessness and sin. Without discipline the church's spiritual life would ultimately be destroyed and the presence of sin and error would eradicate its distinctiveness as the salt of the earth and light of the world. People in the world should not be able to point a finger at the church and say that the members are not paying their bills, or that there is an alcoholic in the church, or that one of the members is living in adultery. The Word of God commends the proper exercise of discipline (II Corinthians 7:8-13; Revelation 2:2), and threatens and rebukes a church that neglects it (I Corinthians 5; Revelation 2:14-16,20-23).

A second purpose for discipline is to preserve the purity of the church's testimony, doctrine, and practice (Matthew 5:13-16; I Timothy 5:20; II Timothy 2:17-18 with I Timothy 1:19-20; I Peter 2:11-12). Christians must walk in such a way that even if they are called evildoers and are charged with things that are not true, yet by their good works people will have to glorify God in that day when He reveals the works and motives of all men.

A third purpose for discipline is so the sinning member will be led to repentance and restoration to fellowship in the body. Passages which show this are Matthew 18:15-17; II Thessalonians 3:14-15; I Corinthians 5:5; II Corinthians 2:1-11; 7:8-13.

There are four degrees of discipline. The first is private admonition (Matthew 18:15). Many times the problem can be solved in this way, but the warning must be given in love and

243

in a humble spirit. The second is public reprimand (Matthew 18:16; I Timothy 5:20). If the person will not hear the one confronting him in private, he should take with him one or two others. If he neglects to hear them, then they should tell the church, making it public. The third action is withdrawal of fellowship (II Thessalonians 3:6,14). This is a command and not a request. The last degree of seriousness would be excommunication of the member (I Corinthians 5:1-13; Matthew 18:17; Romans 16:17).

Causes and Procedure for Discipline

The method in which discipline is administered is based largely on the reason that it is needed.

1) The first cause for discipline would be personal difficulties between members, which are to be reconciled according to the procedure outlined in Matthew 18:15-17 and I Corinthians 6:1-8. If one refuses to be reconciled, he cannot fellowship or be part of the body, but "let him be unto thee as an heathen man and a publican."

2) Another cause for discipline is unchristian or immoral conduct. The procedure to be employed depends on the seriousness of the sin. Sins of weakness or temptation which result from pressures are dealt with in Galatians 6:1. This person may be restored, assuming he has repented.

If a member demonstrates persistent unchristian conduct or habits, he is to be dealt with in a different way. This could be a person who is irresponsible concerning his Christian obligations; he is indifferent, shallow, attends services only occasionally, does not support the work with prayers or financially, and manifests confirmed habits and conduct contrary to the Bible. The privileges of fellowship are to be withdrawn from this person. "Now we command you, brethren, in the name of our Lord Jesus Christ, that ye withdraw yourselves from every brother that walketh disorderly, and not after the tradition which he received of us. . . . Yet count him not as an enemy, but admonish him as a brother" (II Thessalonians 3:6,15). Paul was not talking about a person who fell into sin because of weakness, but about a person who is walking disorderly and is a disgrace to the body of Christ.

3) A third cause for discipline is gross immorality. Such sins are to be dealt with promptly by the excommunication of the offender. There is never any preliminary procedure prior to excommunication. Of course, if there is repentance, the individual may be restored to fellowship (I Corinthians 5:1-13).

4) Another reason for discipline is when a person causes division in the church. Paul said to mark those who cause divisions and avoid them (Romans 16:17). In Titus 3:10-11 he further said if a man is factious, continuing to cause division after the first and second admonition, he is to be rejected. Faction can be caused by a person with a critical spirit opposing the church or the God-appointed ministry. This term for factious is also found in II Peter 2:1, referring there to the heresies of false teachers. It is translated "heresy" in both passages but should be translated "factious."

The Discipline of Heretics and Deceivers

The Scriptures also deal with discipline regarding heretics and their heretical doctrines. Heretics are actually deceivers who, in the guise of being Christians or ministers of the gospel, intentionally deny or pervert the doctrine of Christ, especially with regard to His incarnation, His deity, or the substitutionary atonement. Paul treated denial of the resurrection with severity; in fact, the Bible treats *any* denial of such essential truths with the same severity. Whenever a person tampers with the doctrine of Christ, in ignorance or willingly, he is in grave danger. He is not to be dealt with in the same manner as someone who has been disfellowshipped or even excommunicated, but he is to be treated in an entirely different way because he is perverting the one thing that can save mankind—the doctrine of Christ.

The deceiver described in II John 7-11 is a false teacher, an apostate, and an antichrist by virtue of his denial or perversion of the doctrine of Christ. He is called a deceiver in this passage because he professes to be a Christian or a minister of the gospel. John's command to deny a normal greeting to a known deceiver, or admittance into a Christian home, should not be applied to unbelievers. It was not the apostle's intent for Christians to treat the lost in such a manner, or none would be reached with the gospel; but he was obviously speaking of one who would use the occasion to pervert the believer and lead him away from the truth. An unbeliever is dealt with in an entirely different way.

The form of treatment for a deceiver is clearly set forth in II John 10. He is to be denied any form of hospitality in a

Christian home or any conventional form of greeting. The force of the Greek shows that one should not even say hello because that would be partaking of his evil deeds. The separation of the Christian and the antichristian must be absolute because any hospitality or greeting is tantamount to recognition or endorsement of the heresy.

Church Discipline of Family Members

What is the procedure and attitude the saint should have when the heretic or person under church discipline is a member of his family or is a relative? The Scriptures make no exceptions to the requirements merely because the person under discipline is a relative. It is often the believer's family that will give him the most trouble (Matthew 10:34-38; Jeremiah 12:6; Luke 14:26-33). In this case the Christian must be willing not to side in with his family, if doing so would mean he must turn away from Christ. In Matthew 10, where Jesus said a man's foes would be those of his own household, He was speaking to Jews who had to make their decision to follow Jesus in opposition to their families who were heretics and enemies because they denied the doctrine of Christ.

In the context of a local church, the person under discipline usually has relatives in the assembly. A pastor will often hesitate to deal with the sinning member out of fear that he will lose the rest of the family. The family members still in the church must not sympathize with the person under discipline, nor should they act toward him as if nothing had happened. The whole church must act as one (I Corinthians 5:4-5; II Corinthians 2:6). Failure along these lines would generally permit the person under discipline to have a detrimental effect upon the rest of the family who are members of that church.

Fortunately, the Bible gives some guidelines for the Christian's attitude and procedure if the person disciplined is a member of the immediate family or a relative. There are no rules of conduct under grace, but the Bible does give principles by which the Holy Spirit can guide him.

1) Jesus warned that it was a basic test of love and loyalty to Him, as well as a mark of genuine conversion, if a man would reject his family rather than the truth (Matthew 10). Jesus said that a person cannot be His disciple if he puts his family first (Luke 14:26). 2) While it may temporarily grieve a family when the conduct of a loved one requires Christian discipline; nevertheless, they will act willingly in harmony with the whole church and the Word of God. Their oneness of mind with the body is shown to the one being disciplined by their attitude and even by the public word if it were required. 3) They should in faith claim salvation and/or deliverance for the person and hold fast regardless of the circumstances. 4) They should feel it is their responsibility to go to the erring loved one and try to show him his error and lead him to repentance. If they cannot pray *with* the person, they can surely pray *for* him.

Of course, none of these actions should be expressed in either a self-righteous or in a sympathetic spirit. Having been lovingly confronted, if he refuses to change, repent, and be reconciled, the believing family should humbly inform the one under discipline that their loyalty in the matter is to Christ and His church, and that his own attitude and action has already severed spiritual fellowship with the local body of which they are a part. Further, they should inform him that their position is being made clear, so that he will see the seriousness of his present condition. His behavior has not only broken spiritual fellowship with the assembly but with the family. If they continued to act as though nothing had happened, and perpetuated the former fellowship—talking about the Bible and religion—he would never be challenged to examine his relationship with God. A person who is disfellowshipped from the body often has a detrimental influence on his family, even in ways they do not know. He may plant seeds of discord, faction, unbelief, opposition, and criticism. As a result the family must constantly be on guard to avoid being led astray by his unchristlike attitudes and speech.

It is necessary to point out the distinction between *spiritual* and *family* relationships when one member of a family has been disciplined or is in heresy. While *spiritual* fellowship has clearly been severed, it does not necessarily mean that *family* relationships must be severed, unless the sinning member so desires. I Corinthians 7:12-16 does not directly deal with church discipline; but it does show that if a wife is converted and her husband is not, she is not to leave him. Generally, when a person of Corinth was converted, it could be assumed that his spouse and family were unbelievers, probably worshiping and believing in the pagan gods of Greece. A wife who has an unregenerate husband is exhorted in Scripture to live her Christianity before him with the possibility of winning him to Christ (I Peter 3:1-2).

What course of action should be taken if the family member is a heretic—not just an unbeliever—but a deceiver?

What if he is posing as a Christian or as a Christian minister, but is perverting the doctrine of Christ? How should a relative be treated who is a Jehovah's Witness, a Christian Scientist, a Mormon, or who belongs to a cult which perverts the doctrine of Christ, denies the blood atonement, the eternal deity of Christ, or His incarnation? The teaching in I and II John should be followed. Also he should be warned that he has a deceiving spirit, a spirit of antichrist. He should be firmly advised that there can be no spiritual fellowship or even religious discussion unless he is willing to hear the truth and be delivered and saved. As unpleasant as this relationship may be, the situation is not hopeless. The family should assume the responsibility to pray for their erring loved one, and to claim his salvation and restoration by faith.

The Discipline of an Elder

The sin of an elder is treated separately in the New Testament. "Against an elder receive not an accusation, but before two or three witnesses. Them that sin rebuke before all, that others also may fear" (I Timothy 5:19-20). The Greek in this text for sin is in the continuing sense—one who is sinning. It does not imply someone who fell into temptation, who repents and is restored. It is one who is living in some form of habitual sin or is in gross error such as adultery, drunkenness, violence, political strife and agitation, or serious errors in doctrine.

Accusations against an elder should be received with caution for several reasons. 1) As a minister and spiritual leader, he is constantly exposed to malicious gossip and attack by those who resent his teaching or preaching. There has never been a man born who could please everybody. 2) His ministry and spiritual influence would soon be destroyed if every charge, rumor, and bit of gossip were sufficient grounds to rebuke him publicly. 3) The Holy Spirit has placed the leaders in authority, and their calling requires normal respect (I Thessalonians 5:12-13; I Timothy 5:20). They are to be esteemed highly for their work's sake, and respected for the Word which they preach.

If the elder is guilty of habitual or gross sin, or conduct which would lead others astray, he should be publicly rebuked (Galatians 2:9-14). An elder is to be shown deference; but if the accusation is true, the elder must be publicly rebuked because his conduct is an infectious example to others. This public rebuke will discourage others from following his example, and it would vindicate the church in the eyes of the world.

To conclude this whole subject of discipline, there are four principles to follow: 1) There should be a thorough investigation and clear unmistakable proof that the sin or charge is correct. Even if three witnesses say it, that does not make it true (Matthew 18; I Timothy 5:19). 2) Assuming the accusation is true, solemn action should be taken by the whole church (I Corinthians 5:4-5). 3) All discipline should be taken with firmness, tempered with a humble and loving spirit and concern for the sinning member that he may repent and be restored. 4) If there is evidence of genuine repentance, there should be restoration to fellowship (II Corinthians 2:6-11).

Receiving Members Into the Church

There are various ways members are received into a church. Basically, the denominational church is an *organization* which a person *joins*. New members must meet certain criteria; they are received into the church by vote (either by the members or the church board); then their names are added to the membership roll. In order to change churches, they transfer their membership by a church letter.

The New Testament picture of the church is entirely different. The revelation found in the Scriptures is not of an *organization*, but a *body*. Remember, each local church is an expression of the metaphor, the *body of Christ*, which is a living, spiritual organism. This expresses the relationship which members share with each other and with Christ; it is *fellowship*—not *membership*. Thus, identification with the body of Christ is established when the Holy Spirit baptizes a person into a local assembly (I Corinthians 12:13-27). This relationship is sustained because all partake of the same Spirit, and cannot be transferred by a mere letter. It is God who places His people where He wants them.

The Requirements for Participation in Fellowship

According to the New Testament, the *requirements for participation* in fellowship in the local assembly are as follows:

1) Saving faith in Jesus Christ and confession of such faith (John 3:16; Acts 16:31). This faith must be expressed by confession because there is no salvation apart from confessing that Jesus is Lord and Savior (Romans 10:10).

2) Repentance from sin (Acts 2:38). There must be a turning away from the life of sin and self interest. "If any man be in Christ, he is a new creation: old things are passed away; behold, all things are become new" (II Corinthians 5:17).

3) Scriptural water baptism in the name of Jesus (Acts 2:38; 8:16; 10:48; 19:5; Colossians 3:17). Details of this baptism are covered under the *Ordinances of the Church.*

4) Baptism of the Holy Spirit (Acts 2:1-4; 10:44-46; Mark 16:17). Acts 19:1-6 describes a situation in which Paul met "certain disciples" (verse 1) who had not yet heard of this experience. "And when Paul had laid his hands upon them, the Holy Ghost came on them; and they spake with tongues, and prophesied" (verse 6). Clearly, this baptism was the normal experience for a Christian in that day, and it was promised just as clearly to future generations and to "afar off" believers (Acts 2:39).

5) Regular participation in the church's worship, Bible study, and the ordinances (Hebrews 10:25; II Timothy 2:15; I Corinthians 11; John 13).

6) Support of the local assembly by prayers and offerings (Ephesians 6:18; Galatians 6:6; I Corinthians 9:1-14; II Corinthians 9:6-7).

7) Willingness to testify to the gospel message (Acts 8:3-4; Matthew 5:13-16; 10:27,32-33; 28:19-20; Colossians 3:16; Mark 16:15-20; Jude 3).

8) Loving submission to the God-appointed ministry which has been given responsibility of leadership (Hebrews 13:7,17,24; Ephesians 4:11-14; Acts 20:28).

9) Living a life consistent with the Christian faith and the message of the New Testament (Matthew 5-7; I Peter 1:16; Galatians 5:14-26; Titus 2:11-13).

10) Recognition that a New Testament assembly is a *theocracy* under Christ its head, not a democracy of the people; that it is a living *organism*, not a religious organization and institution; acceptance of one's responsibilities to the local assembly, and concurrence in its Scriptural discipline (I Corinthians 5; 12; Romans 16:17; II Thessalonians 3:6f.; Titus 3:10-11; Matthew 18:15-17).

11) Belief in *unity* and *oneness of mind* concerning the Word of God and its relation to all matters concerning the Christian life, as well as the refusal to engage in any criticism of the local assembly, its membership, or its ministry (I Corinthians 1:10; 10:1-12; Philippians 2:1-4; Titus 3:1-2,10-11; Proverbs 6:16-19; Romans 16:17; James 3).

The Church Offices

The *church offices* are set forth in Ephesians 4:11 as apostles, prophets, evangelists, pastors, and teachers; in I Corinthians 12:28 as apostles, prophets, and teachers; in

I Timothy 3 as elders and deacons; in Titus 1 and I Peter 5 as elders; and in Philippians 1:1 as elders and deacons. Thus, the only church office found in the Scriptures besides the five-fold ministers of Ephesians 4:11 is the office of deacon.

The *apostle* and *prophet* are essential offices in the New Testament church, which is "built upon the foundation of the apostles and prophets, Jesus Christ himself being the chief corner stone" (Ephesians 2:20). The Scriptures show that they establish churches, appoint men to offices in the church, and receive direct revelation on behalf of the body. This direct revelation is not new Scripture, but is in harmony with the written Word, and is for the benefit of the assembly. In I Corinthians 14:29-31 Paul said that the prophets received and gave revelation in the church. The Apostle Paul established churches and ordained or chose elders in those churches (Acts 14:23). Notice that they were not elected by the congregation nor appointed by a church board.

The ministry of the *evangelist* is to add members to the body and to extend the churches into new fields. Philip was an evangelist, and he "went down to the city of Samaria, and preached Christ unto them" (Acts 8:5). In II Timothy 4:5 Paul exhorted Timothy to "do the work of an evangelist."

The ministry of the *teacher* is to train and prepare the body for its ministry, to instruct it in obedience to the Word of God, and to develop its maturity in the faith and in its spiritual life (Ephesians 4:11-16). The teacher himself must have been trained in the doctrines of the faith and in the biblical languages so that he can competently expound the Scriptures to others. Christians need to be *taught* the truths of the Word,

255

rather than *evangelized* week after week, as they are in most churches. While some passages in the Bible are written for the purpose of saving sinners, most of it has been given to the church as a guidebook for its own instruction and edification. The teacher is gifted by the Holy Spirit in putting thoughts together from the Scriptures and in communicating them to the church.

The *pastor* leads, feeds, and teaches the flock as a shepherd (I Peter 5:1-4). The question could be asked, "If the pastor is exhorted in verse 2 to teach, why did God ordain the separate office of teacher?" The answer lies in the fact that the pastor cannot fulfill all the responsibilities of a teacher, nor vice versa. God has set the offices in the church according to His will. Occasionally God calls one man to both offices; but generally the pastor ministers to one *local* body, and the teacher may minister to all of Christendom, as the Holy Spirit directs.

In the New Testament the *deacons* were reliable and spiritual men, chosen to serve the body of Christ, especially to care for the needy. But today the deacons' function depends on what each denomination has established. In the high liturgical churches the office of deacon is a clerical office, close to that of priest. In some churches he is an appointed officer; in others he is elected and becomes a member of a deacon board which rules the affairs of the church, often having authority over the pastor. Obviously these were not the duties of the deacons in the New Testament church.

The Importance of the Pastor and Deacon

The Scriptures show the *importance* of the *pastor* and *deacon* by listing specific *qualifications* concerning their character and conduct. The reason for this is that they are related directly to the local church, and in their daily function they constantly influence other members in the body. Of necessity, their lives must be patterned after the life of Jesus. The apostle and prophet receive their calling directly from heaven, so the Bible does not give a list of their qualifications, although this does not mean they should be less qualified.

The Office of Elder

There are many misconceptions in the church in regard to the office of the *elder*. The progression from the literal meaning of "elder" (an "aged" or "mature" person) to an office in the church is an interesting study. In ancient times the older men who governed a community and made all major decisions were known as the "elders." Elders are often mentioned in Scripture during the time of Moses (Exodus 4:29; 12:21; 24:9; Numbers 11:25). After God established kings in Israel, elders were still functioning (I Kings 8:1; I Samuel 16:4; Ezekiel 8:1). In New Testament times the members of the Sanhedrin, which was the highest Jewish tribunal during the Greek and Roman periods, were drawn from the three classes—chief priests, scribes, and elders. The elders were the tribal and family heads of the people and priesthood, and were, for the most part, the secular nobility of Jerusalem. The elders are often mentioned in the Bible in close connection with the rulers, the chief priests, and scribes;

but the first reference to the elder as an *office* in the church is in Acts 14:23. "And when they had ordained them elders in every church, and had prayed with fasting, they commended them to the Lord, on whom they believed."

There are three terms used in Scripture for the elder: bishop, elder, and pastor. The basic term is elder, but all three terms speak of the same office. The terms for bishop and elder are synonymous in the New Testament. This is seen in Acts 20 when Paul was returning to Jerusalem, "And from Miletus he sent to Ephesus, and called the elders of the church" (verse 17). In verse 28 Paul said to the same men, "Take heed therefore unto yourselves, and to all the flock, over the which the Holy Ghost hath made you overseers [episkopos] to feed the church of God." In I Timothy 3:1 when Paul said, "If a man desire the office of a bishop [episkope], he literally said, "If a man seeketh overseership."

In Titus 1:5-7 Paul showed that elder and bishop are the same office when he said, "For this cause left I thee in Crete, that thou shouldest set in order the things that are wanting, and ordain elders in every city, as I had appointed thee: If any be blameless, the husband of one wife, having faithful children not accused of riot or unruly. For a bishop [episkopos] must be blameless, as the steward of God."

Peter said in I Peter 5:1-2, "The elders which are among you I exhort, who am also an elder. . . . Feed the flock of God which is among you, taking the oversight [episkopeo] thereof." Peter could have said, "Function in the office of bishop as you feed the flock."

Since the two terms are synonymous, why use two terms? They refer to two aspects of one office. The term *"elder"* refers to the *office* or five-fold ministry position in the church. The term *"bishop"* describes the nature of that office as an *overseer* or guardian. The other term for this office is *pastor* (Ephesians 4:11). The Greek term "poimen," translated "pastor," would have been better translated as *"shepherd."* In I Peter 5:4 Jesus is called the "archipoimen" or "chief Shepherd." A shepherd is one who herds, tends, and guards sheep. In the New Testament context the pastor or shepherd of the church is the one into whose care the members, as God's sheep, have been committed for feeding, care, protection, and for their growth to maturity.

The Qualifications for an Elder

The qualifications for an elder are found in I Timothy 3:1-7 and Titus 1. With respect to the *life* of an elder, he must be blameless, of good behavior, righteous, and holy. With respect to *temperament*, he is to be "no striker" and "not a brawler"; that is, he must not be one who gets involved in arguments or in physical violence or fighting; but he is to be patient and gentle, "not self-willed" and "not soon angry." He should be temperate or self-controlled. This does not imply that an elder is an angel in a man's clothing or that he would never lose his temper; but it should not be his way of life, his habit, or his walk. They are "earthen vessels" just like other men.

With respect to his *family relations*, he is to be the husband of only one wife if he is married. He is to rule his own house well, having his children in subjection. Titus 1:6 adds

259

that his children should be faithful and not accused of riot or unruliness. This does not mean the elder is responsible if a child is of age and has turned away from the Lord.

With respect to *character* and *reputation*, "he must have a good report of them which are without" (I Timothy 3:7). This qualification may be somewhat of a dilemma because the closer the elder is to the Word, the less likely it is that he will have a good report from those in the community. The actual requirement here is the necessity of an honest character and a good reputation, so nothing could *truthfully* be said against his character or reputation, even though he might be despised for his Christian faith. Other requirements are: he must "not be given to wine." He must be "given to hospitality," but "not greedy of filthy lucre," and "not covetous."

With respect to *faith*, he must hold "fast the faithful word as he hath been taught, that he may be able by sound doctrine both to exhort and to convince the gainsayers." With respect to *ability*, he must be "apt to teach." This means an elder must be prepared and skilled with a deep knowledge of the Word, so he can teach others. With respect to *experience*, he is "not [to be] a novice, lest being lifted up with pride he fall into the condemnation of the devil." This qualification speaks of spiritual maturity, not of age, although as a person grows older he should mature spiritually.

With respect to *gender*, to follow the biblical qualifications an elder must be a *man*. All of the nouns and pronouns concerning an elder are masculine; and he is to be a "husband," not a "wife." The Scriptural pattern for authority, in which the man stands in headship over the woman, is revealed in I Timothy 2:12; a woman is not "to teach, nor to usurp authority over the man." This is in reference to the specific office of elder, not "whether" or "how" God may use women in ministry. There are offices for women which do have Scriptural basis, such as the office of prophetess.

What about the qualifications for an apostle, a teacher, an evangelist, or a prophet? Very simply, they should not be any less qualified than elders and deacons. Paul, the apostle, was not dictating to the local churches a list of qualifications for local ministry offices that he was not fulfilling himself. The fact that elders and deacons are much more common, and function in the local body, shows the importance of their qualifications being set forth. Obviously the offices that are not as common should have the same or higher requirements.

The office of elder is to be respected because the Bible teaches that it should be. This is not to elevate men but to show respect for the office. Jesus was called an elder in I Peter 2:25. Peter and John were elders (I Peter 5:1; II John 1). I Thessalonians 5:12-13, I Timothy 5:17, and Hebrews 13:7,17,24 teach respect for those who rule, because they must give an account, and they desire to do it with joy and not with grief.

The Duties of the Elder

The *duties* of an *elder* are clearly set forth in the New Testament. 1) His duties are *administrative*. He is to be the overseer in the church (Acts 20:28). He is to rule the church

261

(I Timothy 5:17). He is called the "steward of God"; that is, God has appointed him as a steward over His flock (Titus 1:7). The aspect of ruling is not in an ecclesiastical sense, but as a shepherd rules over the sheep, leading and guiding the flock. 2) The duties of an elder are *pastoral*. He is to be a shepherd of God's flock (John 21:16; Acts 20:28; I Peter 5:2). 3) The elder's duties are *educational*; he teaches the church (I Timothy 3:2; 5:17; Titus 1:9). The concept of *feeding the flock* is in the sense of a shepherd and his relationship to sheep—feeding, protecting, guiding, correcting, and exhorting. 4) The elder's function is *representative*. He represents the body in situations where it is not necessary or convenient for the entire assembly to be involved. In Acts 20:17 Paul called the elders together as representatives of the body, and in James 5:14 the elders had the responsibility of praying for the sick. Although any Christian can pray for the sick, the elder takes that responsibility as a representative of the church, and is careful to ascertain that the Scriptural conditions have been met by the one needing prayer. 5) The elder's function is *spiritual*. He gives himself to the Word and to prayer (Acts 6:4; II Timothy 2:15).

The Authority of the Elder

The elder exercises his *authority* in several ways: 1) Unlike the prophet or apostle whose authority extends to wherever God sends him to minister, the authority of the elder in the New Testament did not extend beyond the local church. 2) His authority is *by divine appointment*, not from people who elect him to be a pastor of a church, or from a board which appoints him. In Acts 20:28 Paul said the Holy Spirit appoints overseers. Ephesians 4:7-11 includes shepherd or elder (translated "pastor") as one of the gifts Christ gave to men when He ascended. 3) His authority is *spiritual*, not ecclesiastical or authoritarian. He cannot pass laws and require the members of the church to abide by them; but when he preaches God's Word, he has the injunction to speak, exhort, and rebuke with all authority. He is to let no man in the assembly despise this responsibility (Titus 2:1,15; II Timothy 4:1-5; Hebrews 13:7,17). I Peter 5:1-3 likewise shows that his authority is as shepherd over the flock, one who leads the sheep. 4) His authority is *governmental*, or as previously stated, administrative. I Corinthians 12:28 makes reference to this, where the term "governments" refers to the elder's administrative role.

The Number of Elders

Some groups emphatically teach a plurality of elders, each having the same authority, based on the use of the plural form "elders" in some passages. They oppose the idea of one pastor who has the final responsibility or the final say in any matter. In Acts 14:23, 20:17, and Philippians 1:1, where the plural word "elders" was used, it is obvious that the writer was referring to the leaders of various bodies scattered throughout a geographical area. The "church" at Ephesus, for example, consisted of several congregations in the city and surrounding region, with a pastor over each one. For twenty centuries it was clear to Christendom that each flock had its own pastor. The idea of plurality of pastors is actually a very recent development, and cannot be established from the New Testament.

On the other hand, this does not rule out a plurality of elders functioning in one local body if the need would arise. God did not say, "You can only have one elder." But neither can anyone insist, based on Scripture, that there must be several elders in each congregation. A very large congregation may need more than one elder just to get the work done, and there may be other ministries functioning in deliverance, intercession, prayer for the sick, and so on. But these do not function "officially" as the pastor. There should still be one pastor to whom the rest look for final decisions—one who has the final responsibility. There may be more than one man in the church who has the gift or calling of elder, whom God will utilize in His time; but only one can function as the elder, the pastor. The very nature of leadership in the home, in the church, or in a nation is singular leadership, with a helper or helpers as needed. It is contrary to human nature for it to be otherwise.

I Timothy 3:1-13 suggests a single elder and plurality of deacons. In the first seven verses Paul was clearly speaking of one man, but beginning with verse 8 he was describing the deacons and used the plural. In Titus 1:5 he said, "Ordain elders in every city"; but when he listed the qualifications beginning in verse 7, he reverted to the singular.

Those who insist on plurality of elders sometimes use I Timothy 5:17 to support the idea of two classes of elders—"teaching" and "ruling" elders. "Let the elders that rule well be counted worthy of double honour, especially they who labour in the word and doctrine." But the use of the word "especially" clearly shows that the phrase following is selective from the same group defined at the beginning. In other words, "the elders that rule well" form a group, of which some, but not all, also "labour in the word and doctrine." Some denominations have developed a system where "teaching elders" are the "ordained" ministers, and "ruling elders" are the lay leaders of the congregation. Ruling elders may form an ecclesiastical order like a deacon board or an official board, but these are man-made and are not found in the New Testament.

The Permanence of the Office of Elder

The institutional church licenses, ordains, appoints, or elects a man to the office of pastor in a local congregation. In this system, an elder can likewise be removed for any one of many reasons. Sometimes the cause for his removal is valid, but often it is party strife among members or his lack of cooperation with the particular denomination. Any time a leader is selected by vote, there will be those who oppose the outcome. The very system of voting actually promotes a party spirit and division.

Some systems have an annual call, where they vote on the pastor every year. In order to keep his job the pastor is under continual pressure to please the congregation. But no matter how long the duration of the office, the denominational view is that the office of elder is *not permanent.*

In the New Testament the elder is not elected, licensed, appointed, nor controlled by men. His calling is a gift from heaven (Ephesians 4:7-11; Acts 20:28). A pastor who does not know that his call is from God alone preaches "the system's message" in place of God's Word. God's plan is for the elder and the other five-fold ministries to keep the office for life (Romans 11:29), but not necessarily without interruption. He cannot be removed from his office by the mere vote of a congregation for petty reasons, but he can be removed if there are Scriptural grounds where he no longer meets the requirements to be an elder.

There is also the possibility of being an elder in a *general* sense. Paul and Peter were elders, and Jesus is called an elder, although they did not pastor churches. In the author's book, *Charismatic Body Ministry*, he mentions that there are several elders in the church where he is pastor. They are not all pastors, but they do have the title and office of elder. A pastor could have another elder to help him in the ministry as an associate pastor. Even though there would be two men functioning as pastors, one would still take the final responsibility.

If for any reason an elder would cease to meet the qualifications found in I Timothy 3 and Titus 1, he can temporarily remove himself from functioning. It does not mean he is no longer an elder, but he should step down until he again meets the qualifications. Or, in an extreme situation, he may be asked to step down. This does not necessarily mean he is unfit to be a member of the body, but the requirements for being an elder go beyond the requirements for being a member of the body. The Holy Spirit may direct an elder to move into another ministry, perhaps as one who only travels and teaches, or as an evangelist. Then that would be his ministry, but he would still be an elder in a general sense, because the office is for life.

Although an elder may be led into broader fields of ministry, the office remains *local* in nature; that is, he cannot exercise his authority in any other local body unless he is asked to do so by that body, by the direction of the Holy Spirit. This applies to elders who are between pastorates, or to retired pastors who are in a local body.

The Ordination of Elders

Ordination, as a formal service or ceremony, is not taught in the New Testament. Ordination, in the biblical sense, comes from heaven, not from men. The word "ordain" occurs twenty-one times in the King James Version of the New Testament. Of these, it is used five times with respect to ordaining ministers, and in these five cases it is used to translate five different Greek words, none of which means ordain in the sense it is used today. None of these can possibly be construed to suggest any kind of formal service.

There are three passages which show the laying on of hands upon a man whom God had appointed to ministry. In Acts 6:6 there was an impartation of power and anointing with the laying on of hands. In I Timothy 4:14 a direct reference was made to a gift which had been imparted by "prophecy, with the laying on of the hands." In Acts 13:2-4 it was the Holy Spirit who separated Paul and Barnabas, who, after the laying on of hands, were "sent forth by the Holy Ghost."

267

The Office of Deacon

The origin of the word "deacon" is the Greek "diakonos," which means "one who serves." This term is used many times in the New Testament. It is translated as "minister" twenty times in the King James Version, as "servant" seven times, and as "deacon" three times. Those three times are Philippians 1:1 and I Timothy 3:8,12.

Most scholars believe that this office had its beginning in Acts 6:1-6, although this cannot be proven since the word "deacon" does not occur in this passage. However, most churches consider Acts 6 to be the origin of the office of deacon, as does this author.

The unusual dignity of the office of deacon is to be seen in the fact that the same term, "servant," is used of Jesus, of the Lord's ministers, of the angelic host, and of the apostles. "For they that have used the office of a deacon well purchase to themselves a good degree, and great boldness in the faith which is in Christ Jesus" (I Timothy 3:13). Their special reward is a good standing or position in the church, a place of respect and honor, as well as great boldness in their ministries.

The Duties of a Deacon

Assuming that Acts 6 is the appointment of the first deacons, these men were assigned to help the needy members of the body. In general the deacon serves the body in those capacities where he can relieve the elders. Although the deacons were first called upon to serve tables, this was a temporary aspect of their service, necessitated by the thousands of new converts to Christianity in Jerusalem. Multitudes were saved in the early months of the church, and they did not have homes to go back to, because in the context of Israel, anyone who confessed Jesus was put out of the synagogue and put out of his family. Even today, an orthodox Jewish family will hold a funeral for a family member who becomes a Christian.

The Selection, Appointment, and Number of Deacons

Paul said that men who are selected as deacons must "first be proved" (I Timothy 3:10). This may be accomplished by examination of their lives and their convictions about the Word. In Acts 6 the assembly in Jerusalem was instructed to look among themselves and find men that they already knew were honest and full of the Holy Spirit and wisdom. Once selected by the people, they were appointed by the apostles, with the laying on of hands. They were not voted in by the people, but were chosen out of the congregation.

How many deacons should there be? The New Testament does not specify their number; but the church in Jerusalem only needed seven deacons for a body of ten to fifteen thousand—and they had some real problems! In principle, there should be enough deacons to relieve the elder of temporal responsibility, allowing him to give himself continually to prayer and to the ministry of the Word (Acts 6:2,4). According to the need, they are appointed.

The length of a deacon's service is not given in Scripture. In the institutional church deacons are rotated in and out of office, but in the New Testament there is no time limit. A deacon would serve until his death, unless he became unqualified.

The Qualifications for a Deacon

What qualities should be present in the life of a deacon? This question is significant because there are many more elders and deacons than all the other offices put together. Since he ministers directly to Christ's own sheep, he should be highly qualified.

First, a deacon is to be serious and temperate. "Likewise must the deacons be grave, not double-tongued, not given to much wine, not greedy of filthy lucre" (I Timothy 3:8). With regard to his faith, he should be "holding the mystery of the faith in a pure conscience" (verse 9). A deacon must be thoroughly acquainted with the principles of the Christian faith, and hold to them in sincerity.

As to family relations, "Let the deacons be the husbands of one wife, ruling their children and their own houses well" (verse 12). Assuming that Acts 6:3 is speaking of the first deacons, there are other qualifications that could be noted here. "Wherefore, brethren, look ye out among you seven men of honest report, full of the Holy Ghost and wisdom, whom we may appoint over this business." Therefore, his reputation should be of honest report, his judgment full of wisdom; and he should have the fulness of the Spirit. What should his gender be? I Timothy 3:12 reads, "Let the deacons be the husbands of one wife, ruling their children and their own houses well." Obviously, the deacon is to be a *husband*—a *man*.

The Office of Deaconess: Scriptural or Unscriptural?

Some denominations argue that the office of *deaconess* is found in the New Testament, and is, allegedly, the female counterpart for deacon, based on I Timothy 3:11. Actually, in verses 8-10 Paul was talking about deacons, in verse 11 about their wives, and in verse 12 about deacons again. The word translated "wives" in verse 11 is "gunaikas," which simply means *woman*, either single or married; it does not say which it is. The contention is that it should not have been translated "wives," but "women." Thus, it would read, "Even so must the *women* be grave." Why, then, was it translated "wife" if it is the word for "woman"? Simply because it *can* be translated wife, and it *is* translated that way all through the New Testament, such as in I Corinthians 7:3. When Paul spoke about the wife in Ephesians 5:22, the same word is used. The translators knew that the bishop is to be the husband of one wife, just as the deacon is, and his wife is to be grave.

The only other verse which is appealed to in support of the deaconess is Romans 16:1, "I commend unto you Phoebe our sister, which is a servant of the church which is at Cenchrea." The word here is "diakonos," from which "deacon" is derived. However, keep in mind that "diakonos" means *servant*. Some denominations make an office out of it, but Phoebe was not called a deaconess. The Greek says she was a servant, and she served the body of Christ faithfully.

271

That is all it says. The term is used all through the New Testament. Jesus is called a servant. The apostles are sometimes called servants. Why are they not called deacons? If that type of logic were to be forced upon Colossians 1:23, Paul would have said, "I am a deacon" (diakonos), but he did not. Actually, he said, "I am a servant," as it was translated. Accordingly, the Roman rulers would have been called deacons in Romans 13:4, as would Jesus in Matthew 20:28.

If God did, in fact, establish the office of deaconess, it seems strange that for a function so important there is no mention of it in the New Testament. There is no suggestion of the office of deaconess in Philippians 1:1 where Paul spoke about deacons. The most logical place for the office of deaconess to have been introduced was in Acts 6, where the first deacons were selected; however, they were all men.

The Ordinances of the Church

There is a wide diversity of opinion concerning the nature and number of church ordinances, ranging all the way from seven, as held by some Brethren groups, two or three, as held by Baptists, to none, as the Quakers contend. However, there is no reason for such confusion because there are definite New Testament principles or standards for identifying an ordinance.

To be classified as an ordinance, 1) it must have been instituted by Christ Himself; 2) it must symbolize a spiritual reality; and 3) its perpetuation must have been specifically commanded by Christ. In view of this, it is obvious that only three practices can be properly classified as ordinances: Baptism, Communion of the Bread and Cup, and Washing of the Saints' Feet. Some churches observe these three together, calling the practice the "Three-fold Communion."

Water Baptism

Not only is there confusion over the number of ordinances, there are various opinions regarding how each should be administered. Most Christians agree that water baptism is an established rite in the New Testament, yet they find it difficult to agree on the method. Is it to be done by immersion? Or sprinkling? Or pouring? Is it to be done in the name of Jesus? Or in the name of Christ? Or in the name of the Father, Son, and Holy Spirit? Or in the name of "the Lord"? Should it be accomplished shortly after a child's birth into a Christian family? Or after his salvation? Or when he becomes a member of his denomination at a predetermined age? The assortment of answers is almost as vast as the number of different denominations.

The answers to these questions can only be found in the Scriptures where God initially set forth the principles which were to guide His church. How did the early church interpret the New Testament writings which pertain to baptism? Early church history should not be ignored, for it is a record of how the church in its beginning fulfilled what was written. Generally speaking, later church history cannot be considered, due to the adoption of diverse opinions and methods of men, especially after denominations began to be established.

"And whatsoever ye do in word or deed, do all in the name of the Lord Jesus, giving thanks to God and the Father by him" (Colossians 3:17). In John 16:23-24 Jesus instructed His disciples to pray in His name. Salvation is in His name (Acts 4:12). Jesus Himself said that repentance was to be preached in His name (Luke 24:47). Mark 16 says that healing, the baptism in the Spirit, deliverance, and protection are in His name. For some strange reason, most Christians do everything in that name *except baptize.*

Jesus said to the disciples in Matthew 28:19, "Go ye therefore, and teach all nations, baptizing them in the name of the Father, and of the Son, and of the Holy Ghost." In most churches the words of this Scripture are used in baptism as a formula, but do they actually fulfill Jesus' command? What do they do with the fact that, always and without exception, the apostles baptized in the name of Jesus? The question is not to be answered from the commission alone in Matthew 28:19, but by observing how the apostles who received that commission interpreted it. What did they do? How did they obey it? How did they carry it out?

The disciples had just received the baptism of the Holy Spirit when Peter began to preach to the people; some were pricked in their hearts and asked, "What shall we do? Then Peter said unto them, Repent, and be baptized every one of you in the name of Jesus Christ" (Acts 2:37-38). Even though Peter had heard Jesus give the commission, he told them to be baptized "in the name of Jesus Christ." Matthew, the one who recorded the commission, was one of the twelve who heard Peter preaching. It is noteworthy that Matthew did not

274

interrupt him and say, "Wait a minute. You are not following the formula."

The New Testament records several instances where believers were baptized in water. The Samaritans "were baptized in the name of the Lord Jesus" (Acts 8:16). In Acts 10:48 after Peter had preached to Cornelius, his kinsmen, and friends, "he commanded them to be baptized in the name of the Lord." After Paul had preached to the Ephesians, "they were baptized in the name of the Lord Jesus" (Acts 19:5). The Romans were baptized into Jesus Christ (Romans 6:3-4). The Corinthians were apparently baptized in the name of Jesus (I Corinthians 1:12-15). The Galatians were baptized into Christ (Galatians 3:27). The Colossians were "buried with him in baptism" (Colossians 2:11-12). Every time, without exception, when there is a reference to baptism, it is always into Christ. There is no indication in church history of baptism by the Trinitarian formula (Father, Son, Holy Spirit) until the second century, and it was not popularized until the fourth century. It is significant that in the New Testament the apostles baptized only one way. Either they willfully disobeyed the words of Jesus, or they knew the way to obey His command in Matthew 28:19.

Why did the disciples not use the words of Matthew 28:19? The answer to that question lies in the symbolism of Christian baptism. The apostles who had just received the commission—baptize in the name of the Father, Son, and Holy Spirit—carried it out by baptizing in the name of Jesus. What does baptism signify? It is baptism into the death of Jesus (Romans 6:3). The Father did not die; the Holy Spirit did not die. Water baptism signifies the believer's death, burial, and resurrection with Christ.

There is only one method of baptism which depicts the Christian's burial with Christ, and that is immersion. No other form except a total burial in water could adequately witness that a believer is severing all connection with sin and his life in the world, and that he is dead to the old life. When he is raised out of the water, this depicts the fact that he is a new creation coming forth—raised to a newness of life (Romans 6:3-10; Colossians 2:12).

The way the apostles carried out the formula of Matthew 28:19 was by baptizing into the name of Him who was revealed as the only way to God. "For in him [Jesus] dwelleth all the fulness of the Godhead bodily" (Colossians 2:9). Father, Son, and Holy Spirit are not names; they are titles. God's saving name, God's baptizing name, God's healing name on earth is Jesus.

The Communion of the Bread and Cup

The ordinance of the *Communion of the bread and cup* is found in I Corinthians 10:16; 11:23-34; Matthew 26:26-30; Mark 14:22-26; Luke 22:17-20; Acts 2:42; 20:7. Communion is erroneously called the "Lord's Supper" by the majority of denominations, but church history and the Scriptures concur that these are not the same. They are related, but they are different. Communion is commanded; the Lord's Supper is not.

Many liturgical churches use the term "Eucharist," which comes from the Greek word "eucharisteo," meaning "to give thanks." "And when he had given thanks, he brake it, and said, Take, eat: this is my body, which is broken for you: this do in remembrance of me" (I Corinthians 11:24). Jesus did *thank* the Father as He broke the bread, but the meaning of the Communion is not "to give thanks."

The Greek term for this observance is "koinonia," which means "communion" or "fellowship." Paul said in I Corinthians 10:16-17, "The cup of blessing which we bless, is it not the communion [koinonia] of the blood of Christ? The bread which we break, is it not the communion [koinonia] of the body of Christ? For we being many are one bread, and one body: for we are all partakers of that one bread." The common translation of koinonia is "fellowship." In the New Testament it is a communion or fellowship in the body and blood of Jesus Christ.

What is the meaning and significance of the Communion? There are two basic ideas revealed in the Scriptures. The broken bread, which symbolizes Jesus' body broken in death, and the cup of wine, which symbolizes His spilled blood on the Cross, bear witness to the death of Christ on man's behalf until He returns. "This cup is the new testament in my blood: this do ye, as oft as ye drink it, in remembrance of me. For as often as ye eat this bread, and drink this cup, ye do shew the Lord's death till he come" (I Corinthians 11:25-26). The Communion of the bread and cup graphically reminds the Christian of Jesus' death on the Cross.

The Bible does not say how often the Communion should be observed; it just says that as often as it is practiced, it serves as a reminder of Christ's sacrificial death. Some churches and individuals partake of the bread and cup on a weekly basis, which is not too often, as long as it does not become a mere ritual and lose its meaning.

The other meaning of Communion is that it testifies to the new covenant Jesus has made with the believer through His blood. I Corinthians 11:25 reads, "After the same manner also he took the cup, when he had supped [literally "after supper"], saying, This cup is the new testament in my blood." Jesus actually said, "This cup is the new covenant in my blood." In all the passages in the Bible where it says new "testament," it should have been translated new "covenant."

A testament is an affirmation of beliefs or a testimonial about something, but a covenant is a contract or an agreement between two parties. Under God's old covenant with Israel, the blood of sacrificed animals atoned for sins; but under the new covenant, the blood of Jesus Christ provided this atonement. As believers participate together in the Communion, they signify that they are in covenant relationship with Jesus, and that all of the promises He has made are fulfilled or will be fulfilled in them.

The Lord's Supper

The Lord's Supper precedes the Communion. I Corinthians 11:20-34 shows that the Lord's Supper was an evening meal separate from the Communion, but should be celebrated in close connection with it. According to church history, for centuries the church continued to practice the Lord's Supper, calling it the "agape" or "feast of love." After the supper they would take some of the wine and bread, just as Jesus did, and observe the Communion. Today, most churches have forgotten the Lord's Supper, and equate it with the Communion. Peter referred to the love feast in II Peter 2:13, as did Jude in verse 12. "These are spots in your feasts of charity [love]."

When Jesus instituted the Communion of the bread and cup, it was in the context of the eating of a meal with His disciples—the Last Supper. "And as they were eating, Jesus took bread, and blessed it, and brake it, and gave it to the disciples, and said, Take, eat; this is my body" (Matthew 26:26). Mark 14:22 says, "As they did eat, Jesus took bread, and blessed, and brake it." Luke's account reads, "Likewise also the cup after supper, saying, This cup is the new testament in my blood, which is shed for you" (Luke 22:20). In I Corinthians 11:25 Paul said, "After the same manner also he took the cup, when he had supped," or after supper.

The word "supper," spoken of in I Corinthians 11:20, is the Greek term "deipnon," which means "a full evening meal." In that account Paul was dealing with the people because of the way some of them were eating that evening meal; they were being selfish and clannish. He said those who partook of the Communion should examine themselves, because they could become sick and die if they ate the bread and drank the cup in an unworthy manner. In verse 23 Paul continued and told how the Lord instituted the Communion of the bread and cup after supper. In all the Gospels there is no justification given to call the Communion the Lord's Supper.

Tertullian, the second century theologian, said, "Our supper [speaking of the Lord's Supper] shows its reason by its very name, for it is called *agape* because it signifies love among the Greeks." Religious historians agree that there is no reason to confuse the two, because they are totally different.

What is the significance of the Lord's Supper? Just as its name implies, it is a *love feast*—a feast of love and fellowship. While it is patterned after the Last Supper which Jesus shared with His disciples, a very somber occasion, it should no longer reflect the seriousness and solemnity of that gathering. After all, Jesus has been raised from the dead in great victory and joy! It is a time for Christians to fellowship around a meal in unity of heart and faith, and to show their love for each other and for their Lord.

The church has reduced the Lord's Supper to a social event: a church supper, a father and son banquet, or a spaghetti dinner, rather than a feast of love. Paul rebuked the people when they did not eat the supper properly, but ate with selfish, carnal attitudes, because it is supposed to signify love for one another, concern, and fellowship. When a person having a wrong spirit partook of the Communion of the bread and cup, he was not discerning the Lord's body. For this reason, some were sick, weak, and "asleep" in the grave. The Lord's Supper was not intended as a community social gathering, but gave opportunity for the disciples to enjoy a fellowship feast together.

Washing of the Saints' Feet

In John 13 Jesus initiated the washing of the saints' feet. "He [Jesus] riseth from supper, and laid aside his garments; and took a towel, and girded himself. After that he poureth water into a basin, and began to wash the disciples' feet, and to wipe them with the towel wherewith he was girded. Then cometh he to Simon Peter: and Peter saith unto him, Lord, dost thou wash my feet? Jesus answered and said unto him, What I do thou knowest not now; but thou shalt know hereafter. Peter saith unto him, Thou shalt never wash my feet. Jesus answered him, If I wash thee not, thou hast no part with me. Simon Peter saith unto him, Lord, not my feet only, but also my hands and my head" (John 13:4-9).

Most Christians believe that washing of the saints' feet was a customary act of hospitality for Jesus' day, but not an ordinance to be observed in this present time. There are several facts which prove that this practice was not simply an ancient custom or merely a show of hospitality.

1) The *time* of its observance was of utmost importance. Jesus knew that His hour had come to depart unto the Father. He was fully aware of His authority and deity; yet, in spite of these, He humbled Himself to wash His disciples' feet.

2) It was a customary act of hospitality to offer a person a basin of water to wash his feet when he entered a home, but the timing was very unusual for Jesus to wash the disciples' feet at the supper table unless He intended to teach them a spiritual lesson.

3) In Genesis 18:2-4 and 19:1-2 the angels and the Lord were invited to wash *their own* feet. Even when it was an act of hospitality, the guests washed their own feet.

4) Peter would have known what Jesus was doing if it had been a mere custom. "Jesus answered and said unto him, What I do thou knowest not now; but thou shalt know hereafter" (verse 7).

5) Jesus performed this act upon men whose feet were already clean. They could have said, "Our feet are already clean. Why are you washing us?" Obviously, it must have been a *symbolic washing* with a *spiritual meaning*.

6) Jesus replied that washing of their feet was essential for fellowship with Him. His stern rebuke in verse 8 caused Peter to plead, "Lord, not my feet only, but also my hands and my head." Peter was immediately moved to obedience, although he did not know what Jesus meant.

7) If this were just a custom of the day, why was it restricted only to believers? In verses 10-11 Jesus was speaking only to those who were "clean."

8) The crowning proof that this was not an act of hospitality or a custom can be seen in I Timothy 5:10 where Paul made it a requirement for a widow to practice washing of the saints' feet if she were to get help from the church. "Well reported of for good works; if she have brought up children, if she have lodged strangers, if she have washed the saints' feet." Paul contrasted her treatment of saints with that shown to strangers. He portrayed a godly widow as one who

showed hospitality to strangers, but in contrast extended her love to the saints by the washing of their feet.

9) In the entire passage where it was instituted, Jesus made no suggestion that feet washing was a custom or act of hospitality. In fact, the disciples were perplexed at what was happening to them. Obviously, that was the first time Jesus washed their feet, even though the disciples had experienced intimate contact with Him for three years.

What is the meaning of this rite? Jesus told the disciples that they did not know then, but that they would know as He explained it. Christ was teaching, by this lowly example, the self-abasing nature of godly humility and brotherly love. Furthermore, He stated clearly that this act was to be solemnly perpetuated by His disciples. "Ye call me Master and Lord: and ye say well; for so I am. If I then, your Lord and Master, have washed your feet; ye also ought to wash one another's feet. For I have given you an example, that ye should do as I have done to you" (John 13:13-15). Even if it were an act of hospitality, its observance is still commanded. Whatever meaning a church may try to impose on this act, it cannot overlook the fact that Jesus commanded it.

This lesson was needful, for it was at this very time during the Last Supper that there had arisen a contention among the disciples about which of them would be accounted the greatest (Luke 22:24). Jesus admonished them and said, "The kings of the Gentiles exercise lordship over them; and they that exercise authority upon them are called benefactors. But ye shall not be so: but he that is greatest among you, let him be as the younger; and he that is chief, as he that doth serve. . . . I am among you as he that serveth" (Luke 22:25-27). Without question, these words were immediately followed by the solemn demonstration of this truth when He rose from supper and began to wash the disciples' feet. The depth of Jesus' love was exemplified in His washing even of Judas' feet, whom He knew would shortly betray Him.

This ordinance is meaningful yet today, because a Christian cannot kneel before his brother or sister without coming into a deep consciousness of his love for that person. The Lord sealed the meaning of His lesson with the words, "A new commandment I give unto you, that ye love one another; as I have loved you, that ye also love one another. By this shall all men know that ye are my disciples" (John 13:34-35). Just as baptism symbolizes the washing of regeneration, the washing of the saints' feet could also symbolize the believers' need of a constant cleansing by the water of the Word as they walk through the world? Finally, this humble ministry to the members of the body symbolizes that this cleansing is accomplished in the context of body ministry.

Chapter Seven
The Doctrine of Last Things: Eschatology

The final aspect of the study of the doctrines of the Christian faith is called *Eschatology*, the *Doctrine of Last Things*. Several areas will be examined, including death, the intermediate state, Antichrist, the Second Advent, the millennium, the resurrection, judgments, the Kingdom of God, and the eternal state.

Death

With reference to mankind, the word *death* is used to describe three different experiences: spiritual death, physical death, and the second death. The Apostle Paul spoke of *spiritual death* which is the present state of all the unsaved. "And you hath he quickened, who were dead in trespasses and sins" (Ephesians 2:1). In Genesis 2:17 and 3:3, *physical death* is described as the separation of the body from the spirit. God said to Adam, "Dust thou art, and unto dust shalt thou return" (Genesis 3:19). The most awesome aspect of death is the second death (Revelation 20:13-15). "And the sea gave up the dead which were in it; and death and hell [Hades] delivered up the dead which were in them: and they were judged every man according to their works. And death and hell

[Hades] were cast into the lake of fire. This is the second death." Those who have rejected Christ are already dead spiritually, and have only to look forward to physical death, as well as the second death (the lake of fire) and all the torments associated with eternal alienation from God.

When the unsaved person dies, his body goes to the grave, and his spirit goes into Hades. This truth is portrayed in Luke 16:19-31 where the rich man died and was in torments; but when Lazarus died, he was in a place of comfort in heaven.

What is the underlying cause of physical death? What was the cause of Lazarus' death? Some would say he died because of his poor diet and sickness, and they would probably surmise that the rich man died of old age or natural causes. But the answer to these questions is found beyond the obvious agents which usher men to their graves, such as sickness, accident, war, miscarriage, and so forth. As commonplace as these things are, they are quite unnatural. According to the Bible, *physical death is the result of sin.* "Wherefore, as by one man sin entered into the world, and death by sin; and so death passed upon all men, for that all have sinned" (Romans 5:12). Men die because of sin, not because they grow old and their bodies wear out. Death is passed upon all men as the consequence of Adam's fall into sin.

Most unsaved people look upon the death of the body simply as cessation of existence. Or if they think there is life after death, they think that God, if there is a God, will somehow take care of them. They do not see death as the Bible teaches it, as the end of all hope, with no second chance, no future relationship to God, just eternal punishment. One moment after death the rich man discovered that he was in Hades suffering torments, and that there was a great gulf separating Hades and heaven.

The Christian no longer fears death, because death has been conquered for him. It is no longer a mystery. In his death there is no separation from God or Jesus. On the contrary, Romans 8:38-39 proclaims that nothing shall separate the believer from the love of Christ—*not even death*. Paul raised the question, "O death, where is thy sting? O grave, where is thy victory?" He continued by answering that Christ has provided victory over death for the redeemed (I Corinthians 15:55-57). Death is merely the doorway into the presence of Christ. On the Cross, Jesus comforted the repentant thief, "Today shalt thou be with me in paradise" (Luke 23:43). Paul said in Philippians 1:23, "to depart" is "to be *with Christ*," and in II Corinthians 5:8, "to be absent from the body" is "to be present with the Lord."

The Intermediate State

The existence of a person between death and the resurrection is called the *intermediate state*. The question may be asked, "Where are the dead?" Obviously, the body is in the grave, but where is the spirit, the person himself? Some teach *annihilation* of the wicked; others teach *soul sleep*, believing that between the death of the body and the resurrection, the soul is asleep. There are others who teach the unscriptural doctrine of *purgatory*, which they say is a place where sins are purged before a person can go to heaven. Of course there is no basis in Scripture for any of these, as will be shown later in this study.

Even though there are different terms both in Hebrew and Greek for grave, for hell, and for the place of departed spirits, the King James Version mistranslated the place of the departed dead with the English word "hell." The Hebrew term "Sheol" was mistranslated as "hell" thirty-one times, and as "grave" thirty-one times. The Greek term for the place of departed spirits is "Hades," mistranslated as "hell" nine times and "grave" one time. In some of the later versions, Sheol and Hades are correctly translated.

Both Testaments affirm that the grave is the place for the body during the intermediate period. The English term "hell" is also used in the King James Version for the final place of punishment for the wicked after judgment. "Gehenna" and "the lake of fire" are also terms used in the New Testament for the final place of the wicked.

The Old Testament did not give a full revelation of the final state, although it was suggested. For example, Isaiah 24-27 speaks of a final day of judgment, and Daniel 12:2 tells of the final punishment of the wicked and of blessing for the righteous. Daniel's writings predict two resurrections—one of the just and one of the unjust. In Mark 9:43-44 Jesus said, "If thy hand offend thee, cut it off: it is better for thee to enter into life maimed, than having two hands to go into hell [literally "Gehenna"] into the fire that never shall be quenched:

Where their worm dieth not, and the fire is not quenched." It is evident that Jesus obtained this imagery from Isaiah 66:24 to describe the final place of punishment of the wicked.

In the Septuagint, which is the Greek translation of the Hebrew Old Testament, "Sheol" was translated with the Greek "Hades" twenty-one times. Apparently, the translators believed they were synonymous terms.

The departed dead, both wicked and righteous, are described in the Old Testament as being in Sheol. The wicked are in "the pit," and "the nether parts of the earth," according to Ezekiel 32. They are in "lowest Sheol" in a place of punishment (Deuteronomy 32:16-22); in the "depths of Sheol" (Proverbs 9:18); or in "the sides of the pit" (Isaiah 14:15). The same imagery is used in Revelation 20:3, which says that Satan is cast into the bottomless pit.

The righteous are also said to be in Sheol. For example, in Genesis 37:35 Jacob said he would go down to the grave (Sheol); that is, he would die grieving, because he thought Joseph was dead. The righteous dead are said to be at rest and in comfort (Daniel 12:13), and in the glorious presence of God (Psalm 23:6; 73:24,26). Moses and Elijah, who appeared to Jesus in Matthew 17, were not awakened from sleep in order to minister to Him, nor were they abiding in some limbo between death and the resurrection. Even after their death they were joyfully serving God. The Old Testament gives wonderful assurances to the righteous that when they die they can have hope after death (Proverbs 14:32), and will not go to a place of punishment, torment, purgatory, or soul sleep.

The New Testament clearly describes a separation between the righteous and wicked in their death, although they both go to the place of departed spirits. This is seen, for example, in Luke 16:19-31, where the rich man found himself in Hades, in torments or punishment; but Lazarus was in paradise—*Abraham's bosom*—in a place of comfort. Abraham told the rich man that there was a great gulf fixed between the righteous in Hades and the wicked in Hades.

In Philippians 1:21-23 and II Corinthians 5:8, Paul said that when the Christian is absent from the body in death, he is present with the Lord. Although the righteous go to the place of departed spirits, they are not being punished or purged of sin, nor are they asleep. In Luke 23:43 Jesus said to the repentant thief, "Today shalt thou be with me in paradise." The fact that the righteous are said to be at rest, present with the Lord in glory and in paradise, lends significance to Jesus' statement in Matthew 16 where He declared that the gates of Hades could not prevail against the church. He further said in Revelation 1 that He has the keys to death and Hades. Neither the experience of death nor the realm of the dead have any hold on the Christian.

The Doctrine of Antichrist

In close connection with the return of Christ is the rise of a sinister figure called the *Antichrist*. His rise *precedes* the Second Advent, and the whole world, including the religious world, will bow down before him. Those who do not worship him will be martyred, but some will be caught away (Revelation 3:10). Actually, anything against Christ is antichrist. This was not a new doctrine to the church because I John 4:3 says, "And every spirit that confesseth not that Jesus Christ is come in the flesh is not of God: and this is that spirit of antichrist, whereof ye have heard that it should come; and even now already is it in the world." There is a *spirit of antichrist* already at work in the world, and there will be a *man, Antichrist,* who shall come.

There are several designations for the Antichrist in Scripture: 1) the Antichrist (I John 2:18); 2) a beast (Revelation 13:1-8); 3) the man of sin, son of perdition—actually a man who personifies sin (II Thessalonians 2:3); 4) the wicked or lawless one (II Thessalonians 2:8); 5) the little horn (Daniel 7:8); 6) the king of fierce countenance (Daniel 8:23); 7) the prince that shall come (Daniel 9:26); 8) the willful king (Daniel 11:36); 9) the worthless shepherd (Zechariah 11:17).

In regard to the *personality* of Antichrist, he and his kingdom are described as being entirely different from all others (Daniel 7:19,24). He will be highly intelligent and have great worldly wisdom (Daniel 8:23). He will be a great orator (Daniel 7:8,11) and a crafty politician (Daniel 8:25). He will endear himself to the world with a dominating, captivating personality (Daniel 7:20; 8:23). He will be a military genius (Daniel 7:20-23; Revelation 13:4) and the last wonder of the world (Revelation 13:3-4).

The Bible suggests that the *racial origin* of Antichrist is Jewish. "Neither shall he regard the God of his fathers, nor the desire of women, nor regard any god: for he shall magnify himself above all" (Daniel 11:37). With regard to his *national origin*, he will rise out of the Roman empire, which Daniel's vision presents as the last kingdom (Daniel 2:44; 7:7-8; 8:20-24). His *political origin* will be out of the nations, expressed as "seas" in Scripture (Daniel 7:2-3; Revelation 13:1). His *spiritual origin* is from Satan and the pit (Daniel 11:36-38; II Thessalonians 2:9; Revelation 13:2).

The Antichrist's *moral character* will be the personification of sin, pride, blasphemy, rebellion, selfish ambition, and arrogance. Religiously, he will "magnify himself above every god" (Daniel 11:36-39). He will be beyond compare in blasphemy (Daniel 11:36; II Thessalonians 2:4). He will be the great antinomian (against law); and he will change times and laws (Daniel 7:25), making his own laws in order to fulfill his own will. He will glorify himself as deity. "Who opposeth and exalteth himself above all that is called God, or that is worshipped; so that he as God sitteth in the temple of God, shewing himself that he is God" (II Thessalonians 2:4).

Who is Antichrist? Church history has birthed many views. Some of the *non-personal* theories are: 1) the Roman empire, 2) the papal system, 3) Russia, 4) Germany, because of the persecution of the Jews, 5) the antichristian spirit, 6) the system of liberalism and modernism because of its denial of the deity of Christ. There have been several *personal* theories: 1) Nero in the first century, 2) Emperor Caligula, who called himself a god and made an image of himself to be worshiped,

3) Hitler, 4) Stalin, 5) the Kaiser, 6) the Pope, and many more.

The Scriptures do not reveal the identity of Antichrist; but they clearly suggest that he is not a religious system, an antichrist system of government, or an individual of the past. He will be a *man* who is yet to be revealed (Daniel 8:23-24; Revelation 13). His humanity is implied because he has eyes and he speaks (Daniel 7:8). He will not appear until certain events occur, such as a great falling away (II Timothy 3-4) and chaotic times of plagues, famine, and death (Matthew 24; Revelation 6).

Antichrist will appear as an insignificant figure—*a little horn* (Daniel 7:8), but he will begin to extend his power and will put down three other kings (vss. 20,24). When finally established in his place of power, he will make a covenant with Israel. There will be a confederacy of ten kings (Revelation 13:1) with him as head, and they will give power to him (Revelation 17:12-13). He will be successful in his military attempts to overthrow many nations (Daniel 11:40-43). As monarch of the world he will rule in the temple in Jerusalem on the holy mount (Daniel 11:45; II Thessalonians 2:4), and will receive worship from nearly all of humanity. "And it was given unto him to make war with the saints, and to overcome them: and power was given him over all kindreds, and tongues, and nations. And all that dwell upon the earth shall worship him, whose names are not written in the book of life of the Lamb slain from the foundation of the world" (Revelation 13:7-8).

There are several factors which will aid in the rise of Antichrist. The world conditions will be in such a state of chaos that men will be willing to accept a leader who promises relief. Other reasons for his rise to power will be his great personal attraction, the support of the Jews, the backing of apostate Christendom (Revelation 17:11-18), and the satanic power and authority which the devil will give him.

Several significant events will take place during the seven years of Antichrist's reign. In the beginning he will permit the Jews to restore their form of worship, including animal sacrifice; but after three and one half years, he will stop the temple worship and set himself up as god (Daniel 9:27; 12:11; Matthew 24:15; II Thessalonians 2:4; Revelation 13:14-15). At this point the Jews will recognize who the Antichrist really is. He will put to death the two witnesses that God sends (Revelation 11:3-7).

The great personal attraction and supernatural powers of the Antichrist will cause people to follow him (Revelation 13:11-13). In fact, his following will be universal (vs. 8), and the economic system of the world will be in his control (vs. 17). Eventually, he will make war with the saints who were not caught away in the manchild rapture (Revelation 12:5), and will overcome them because they refuse to worship him (Daniel 7:21-22; Matthew 24:15; Revelation 13:5-7). Finally, when all earthly powers are in the hands of Antichrist, God will overthrow him and his kingdom (Daniel 7:25-26; 11:45; Revelation 18:1-24), and he will be personally judged by Jesus Christ (Daniel 8:25; 11:45; II Thessalonians 2:8; Revelation 17:14; 19:19-20; 20:10).

The Second Advent

The Second Advent refers to the second coming of Jesus Christ to this earth. When He came the first time, not everyone saw Him; but when He returns, He shall be seen by all men. It will be a literal, personal, visible, bodily return to this planet. His First Advent was His *incarnation* as the suffering servant and Redeemer; His Second Advent will be His *manifestation* as King and Lord. When Jesus walked upon this earth as a man, only a few knew that He was to be a King; but in His manifestation, all mankind will know that He is King of kings and Lord of lords!

In the Old Testament dispensation the Jews did not have sufficient revelation to understand that the Messiah would appear twice. In some passages the Messiah was seen as a reigning King (Isaiah 9, Jeremiah 23, Zechariah 14), but in other passages He appeared as a suffering servant (Psalm 22, Isaiah 53). After Jesus' death and resurrection, He appeared to two of the disciples and explained that the First Advent fulfilled the prophecies concerning His suffering and death (Luke 24). Obviously, He would have to return to earth again to fulfill the prophecies which spoke of His glory and His reign as King (Matthew 24).

The term used in the New Testament of the Second Advent is "parousia," which means "advent, arrival, or presence." This term can be used of anyone's arrival, but it becomes a technical term in the New Testament referring to Christ's second appearance upon the earth. There are 318 verses in the New Testament which refer to the Second

Advent, and the subject is mentioned in almost every book of the New Testament. Jesus frequently mentioned His Second Advent (Matthew 24:30; Luke 19; John 14:3). The apostles spoke of His return in their writings (I Corinthians 1:7; I Thessalonians 4:16; II Thessalonians 2; James 5:7-8; I Peter 1:7; the Book of Revelation). The angels announced His First Advent in Luke 1 and His Second Advent in Acts 1:10-11).

The Time of Christ's Return

Jesus said, "But of that day and hour knoweth no man, no, not the angels of heaven, but my Father only" (Matthew 24:36). Although the Scriptures clearly say no one knows the time of Christ's return, this has not prevented men from speculating or inventing theories about the time.

The Jehovah's Witnesses contend that Christ returned invisibly in 1874, that the beginning of World War I in 1914 marked the beginning of the end of time, and that Satan was then expelled from heaven and Christ was enthroned. They also say that Christ came to His temple (Malachi 3:1) in 1918, signifying His coming to the Jehovah's Witnesses to indwell them as the temples of the Holy Spirit.

Another view regarding the time of Christ's return is held by the Seventh Day Adventists who derived their name from the erroneous Second Advent prophecies of William Miller, and from their emphasis upon observance of the Jewish Sabbath (Saturday). Miller prophesied that Christ would return by March 21, 1843. His gullible followers closed their businesses, abandoned their occupations, left their crops standing in the fields, and waited for Christ's return. When the great day passed uneventfully, another date was predicted, October 22, 1844, which was also wrong. Miller later admitted he had been in error, but one of his undaunted disciples allegedly had a vision revealing where Miller had missed it. He said that Christ did not return to earth on that date, but He entered the heavenly sanctuary to complete His atoning work in preparation for His Second Advent on earth.

Others say that the Second Advent is past, and that the Scriptures which foretell it actually had reference to the Holy Spirit's coming on the day of Pentecost. This is called the *Holy Spirit theory*, and is supposedly based on John 14:16-17,26, where Jesus said that after His departing the Father would send the Holy Spirit. However, Peter made it very clear in Acts 2:32-33 that Jesus was exalted at the right hand of God, and it was He who had sent the Holy Spirit on the day of Pentecost, as He had promised in John 16:7. So it was not Jesus who came at Pentecost, but the Holy Spirit. Christ's second coming is still future.

Another erroneous theory concerning the return of Jesus Christ is the *conversion* or *new birth theory*. Its perpetrators say that Jesus comes to the believer's heart when he is born again—that this is the Second Advent. They cite such passages as Revelation 3:20, where Jesus said, "Behold, I stand at the door, and knock: if any man hear my voice, and open the door, I will come in to him." This view is refuted in many passages, such as Philippians 3:20-21 and Acts 1:11.

The *death theory* is another view concerning the Second Advent. The supporters of this view contend that Christ's Second Advent is when He comes to the Christian at death and receives him. They cite Psalm 23:4, "Yea, though I walk through the valley of the shadow of death, I will fear no evil: for thou art with me." Paul refuted this view in I Thessalonians 4:13-18 when he said that Jesus will return visibly and receive, at that time, both the living and the dead unto Himself.

The *manifested sons theory* is supposedly based upon Romans 8, where Paul spoke of the future manifestation of the sons of God. There are some groups which have superimposed their own extreme ideas and doctrines upon the promise that one day God will manifest His matured sons to this creation. Adherents to this teaching say that Christ is returning in His matured sons and will more and more manifest Himself in them, but will not literally return in visible, bodily form. Since He will not actually return, they say, He will overthrow Satan and his kingdom through those in whom He is appearing—the matured sons or overcomers; and He will reign and rule on this earth through them.

Furthermore, they teach that there will be no literal rapture of overcomers, but that they will be "caught up in spiritual maturity." They contend that there will be no millennial kingdom established on this earth; that the matured sons of God are the Bride and the New Jerusalem of Revelation 21:2; and that there will be no literal city called New Jerusalem. They have fallen into the snare of spiritualizing the literal truths of the Bible to fit their own ideas. They misinterpret the Lord's announcement that He will return in the clouds in great power and glory, saying instead that believers are the clouds, and He is now appearing in them. They conclude that there will be no bodily resurrection of believers because they are being resurrected now by the Holy Spirit, resurrected from death to life or from immaturity to spiritual maturity.

Such teachings are totally out of line with the Word of God, and are obviously designed by Satan to try to turn people's eyes away from the truth of Romans 8. Verses 19-21 clearly teach that God will one day manifest His sons to this groaning creation, and that they will be instrumental in its deliverance from the bondage of corruption. The enemy's apparent intention in this view is to hinder the spiritual preparation required of those who will be counted as sons—who are enjoined to overcome in Revelation 2 and 3. This preparation is discussed at length in the author's book, *Deeper Life in the Spirit*.

In another view the Second Advent is equated with some great event in history, for example, the destruction of Jerusalem in 70 A.D., which Christ predicted in Luke 21. This view says He returned in judgment. Others believe that the Second Advent is to be equated with the spread of the gospel throughout the world, reasoning that Christ is the Word, so when the Word is preached, then Christ is present.

Signs of Christ's Return

Although the time of Christ's return is unknown, there are several passages in the Scriptures which show that the general period can be known. Each generation has seen events which could have been the fulfillment of some of the signs of the Second Advent, but certain things were lacking. Some predicted incidents could only happen one time. For example, Jesus said in Luke 21:24 that Israel would be scattered and Jerusalem would be in the hands of the Gentiles "until the times of the Gentiles be fulfilled." At no other time in history has this prediction been fulfilled—only in this present generation! Israel became a sovereign nation once again in 1948, and Jerusalem was back in the hands of the Jews in 1967.

In Matthew 24 Jesus mentioned several things which would be indications of His soon return. He said false messiahs will arise (vs. 5). There will be an increase of wars, floods, earthquakes, and pestilences (vss. 6-8). Persecution will intensify (vss. 9-10). False prophets will increase (vs. 11). The gospel of the kingdom will be preached in all of the world (vs. 14). The abomination of desolation will stand in the holy place (vs. 15; Daniel 9), which presupposes the rebuilding of the temple, because there is no holy place without a temple. Christ also predicted that His return will be after the Great Tribulation (vss. 29-30), and at a time when few will be expecting it (vss. 36-39; cf. I Thessalonians 5:2). There will be unusual signs in the heavens and earth (vs. 29; cf. Luke 21:25-32).

The Second Advent in Relation to the Millennium

The *amillennial* view of the Second Advent says that there will be no literal, earthly millennial reign of Christ with His saints on earth. Augustine was the father of this view. He insisted that the church was the Kingdom of Christ and that the millennial kingdom had already started. Since he lived in the first half of the first millennium after Christ, he could safely say that the millennium started with the Cross or with the establishment of the church at Pentecost, and would last a literal thousand years. However, not all amillennialists follow Augustine's theory that the church and the kingdom are to be equated.

Amillennialists believe that Christ is now reigning from His throne in heaven, and Christians are reigning with Him. But the Scriptures give evidence that He will reign on earth, and both the Old and New Testaments say He will reign from Zion (Isaiah 2; Zechariah 2; Revelation 20; Matthew 24). They also believe that the first resurrection is the new birth, and that most of the prophecies concerning Israel and the millennium are now being spiritually fulfilled through the church, which they contend is spiritual Israel.

The failure of Augustine's amillennialism to agree with the facts of history led to the rise of *postmillennialism*, which says that Christ will return after the millennium. According to this view, the "gospel age" is the millennium. Postmillennialists believed the church would have such a positive influence on the world that evil would be put down and wars would cease. They were optimistic about man and history; but they discovered that man is not getting better, and the world is not and will not become Christianized. As a result, postmillennialism lost its followers, and amillennialism became popular again.

Premillennialism is the belief that Christ will return to the earth with His saints at the beginning of the millennium rather than at the end. A study of early church history reveals that this view, also called chiliasm, was the prevailing view of the church until the introduction of Augustinian amillennialism in the fourth century A.D. If one interprets the Bible literally, he will be premillennial.

Summary of End-Time Events

Some of the major events surrounding the Second Advent are listed here, but not necessarily in chronological order. 1) World conditions will get worse just prior to Christ's return (Matthew 24). 2) Antichrist will literally appear on the scene as the world's messiah, a great religio-political leader. He will bring peace and solve economic problems for a while (II Thessalonians 2). 3) Israel will make a covenant with Antichrist, who will permit her to dwell securely in her land (Ezekiel 38:8; Daniel 9:27). 4) A great falling away of the church will occur (II Thessalonians 2:1-3; I Timothy 4; II Timothy 3). 5) There are various stages of the rapture, but overcomers will be caught away just prior to the Great Tribulation (Revelation 12:5-6,13-17). 6) There will be a seven year period of Great Tribulation. 7) The king of the north, Gog, and his allies will invade Palestine to gain Israel's riches and natural resources (Ezekiel 38:10-13; Joel 2:1-21). The invaders will be destroyed on the mountains of Israel (Ezekiel 39:1-4). 8) Then Antichrist will break his covenant with Israel and set up his seat of rule in Palestine (Daniel 11:44-45). 9) Israel will be restored and saved, and the covenant promises will be fulfilled (Zechariah 12:10f.; Romans 11). 10) After the Tribulation Christ will return and institute His visible kingdom on the earth (Matthew 24-25). 11) When Christ returns He will bring with Him the saints who were caught up as I Thessalonians 4:17 says. 12) Satan will be bound during the thousand year millennial reign of Christ (Revelation 20:1-3). 13) After the millennium, Satan will be loosed for a short world-wide rebellion, and God will send fire from heaven to destroy him and those he has deceived (Revelation 20). 14) When all the nations are gathered to destroy Palestine and Jerusalem, the Lord will return and fight for Israel in the battle of Armageddon (Zechariah 14; Revelation 19). 15) The wicked dead will be resurrected and judged at the great white throne (Revelation 20; Daniel 12). 16) The millennial kingdom will be given to the Father by the Son (I Corinthians 15), so that God may be all in all.

The Millennium

The term *millennium* is derived from the Latin "mille," meaning "a thousand," and "annum," meaning "year." Although the word does not occur in the Bible, it is used by all of Christendom, saying that they do not believe it will occur, or that they believe some view of it.

According to both Old and New Testaments, the millennium will be a time of peace, prosperity, and righteousness because Satan will be bound in the pit, and Jesus Christ will rule from Jerusalem over the entire world for a thousand years (Zechariah 14:9; Revelation 20:2,4,6). Christ will teach His ways, and men will walk in His paths (Isaiah 2:3; Micah 4:2).

Ideal conditions will prevail. It will be a time of peace (Isaiah 2:4; cf. Micah 4:3). The effects of the curse will be lifted (Isaiah 11:6-9; cf. Romans 8:17-23). Sickness and infirmity will be removed (Isaiah 35:5-6). There will be longevity (Isaiah 65:20; Revelation 20:4). Prosperity will be restored (Isaiah 30:23; Amos 9:13-14; cf. Joel 3:18). There will be no more weeping (Isaiah 65:18-19). Holiness will be prevalent (Isaiah 35:8; Zechariah 14:20-21).

During this period the covenants and promises made to Israel will be fulfilled. First, God will fulfill His covenant with Abraham and his descendants concerning the land of Palestine. Repeatedly in the Book of Genesis, God promised that land to Abraham and his seed as an eternal possession (Genesis 13:14-16; 15:1-21; 17:1-8). He later confirmed those promises to Israel in other passages such as Psalm 105:8-11; Ezekiel 36; Amos 9:14-15. In fact, there are over 140 promises to Israel in the Word of God regarding her restoration and the eternal possession of her land.

Second, there will be a fulfillment of the promises made to David concerning his throne and kingdom (II Samuel 7:12-16; Luke 1:31-33). The Messiah, David's descendant, will rule on His throne over His kingdom.

Third, the promise of Israel's salvation will be fulfilled. During tribulation, God will pour out the spirit of grace upon Israel. They will look upon Him whom they have pierced, and they will turn to the Lord and be saved (Zechariah 12:10f.; Romans 11:25-29).

Fourth, Israel's temple will be rebuilt, and worship will be restored to her during the millennium (Ezekiel 40-48). The author's book *An Introduction to the Old Testament Prophets* gives further details about this fact of Scripture.

The Doctrine of Resurrection

The concept of resurrection was not new during the time of Christ but had been foreshadowed, typified, and predicted in the Old Testament. Job, for example, raised the question in Job 14:14, "If a man die, shall he live again?" In chapter 19 he answered his own question when he confessed that he would live again. He said, "Yet in my flesh shall I see God." David spoke by prophecy in Psalm 16:10, "Thou wilt not leave my soul in hell [Sheol]; neither wilt thou suffer thine Holy One to see corruption." The king was not only speaking from his own heart, but the Spirit was saying through him that Jesus Christ would be raised from the dead. Isaiah also prophesied of the resurrection: "Thy dead men shall live, together with my dead body shall they arise. Awake and sing, ye that dwell in dust: for thy dew is as the dew of herbs, and the earth shall cast out the dead" (Isaiah 26:19). Daniel spoke of the resurrection of the just and of the unjust (Daniel 12:2). Resurrection was typified in the Old Testament when Elijah and Elisha raised the dead (I Kings 17; II Kings 4).

In the New Testament the resurrection of the body was predicted, promised, confirmed, and proven. The Lord said in John 2:19-22, "Destroy this temple, and in three days I will raise it up," obviously *predicting* the resurrection of His own body from the dead. Resurrection was *promised* in Romans 8:11-13 where Paul stated that the same Spirit that raised Jesus from the dead will make alive all who have died in Christ. Resurrection was also promised by Jesus in John 5:28-29, where He said, "Marvel not at this: for the hour is coming, in the which all that are in the graves shall hear his voice, And shall come forth; they that have done good, unto the resurrection of life; and they that have done evil, unto the resurrection of damnation." Christ's words to Martha were a promise of the resurrection. "He that believeth in me, though he were dead, yet shall he live" (John 11:25). He was speaking there, not only of the resurrection, but of the believer's hope of eternal life. Resurrection was *confirmed* when Jesus raised Lazarus from the dead (vss. 43-44). Resurrection was *proven* in I Corinthians 15, where Paul cited the many witnesses who actually saw Jesus after His resurrection. The apostle rehearsed in great detail the resurrection of Christ's body in that chapter to prove the ultimate resurrection of all believers.

Theories Concerning Resurrection

As with every other major doctrine of Scripture, there are some who attempt to pervert the clear teaching on this subject. Therefore, it would be appropriate to mention two erroneous theories concerning *resurrection*.

Those who propose the *new creation view* deny the physical, bodily resurrection. They say that when a person is born again, that is the resurrection, because the person is re-created from being dead in sins and trespasses. They cite Ephesians 2:1, "You hath he quickened [made alive] who were dead in trespasses and sins" with II Corinthians 5:17, "If any man be in Christ, he is a new creation." In order to formulate such an error, they have evidently overlooked the passages concerning bodily resurrection.

Another view is that of the liberals who teach a *spiritual resurrection*. They deny the bodily resurrection, saying that man is resurrected spiritually, in the sense that the spirit survives after death. They, too, ignore the many passages in the New Testament which show a literal resurrection of the physical body. Jesus Himself had a bodily resurrection, proven in Luke 24:39 where the disciples thought they saw a spirit when they saw Jesus after the resurrection. But He said, "Behold my hands and my feet, that it is I myself: handle me, and see; for a spirit hath not flesh and bones, as ye see me have." His invitation for the disciples to touch His new, glorified body—a body of flesh and bones—was to affirm to them that it was truly He before them and not a spirit.

Most churches today say there will be one *general res-urrection,* but the Scriptures teach a separate resurrection of the righteous and of the unrighteous, with a thousand years intervening between the two. According to Revelation 20:4-6 the righteous will be resurrected and will reign with Christ for a thousand years. "This is the first resurrection. Blessed and holy is he that hath part in the first resurrection." This implies that there will be a second resurrection—that of the wicked.

The Doctrine of Judgment

At the end of the age there will be a period of great judgment when God will ultimately overthrow all evil. Judgment will affect all of mankind as well as all evil spiritual powers, including fallen angels and the devil. The present world will be destroyed, being replaced by a "new heavens and a new earth, wherein dwelleth righteousness" (II Peter 3:9-13; Revelation 21-22).

God has placed the administration of judgment in the hands of His Son, the Lord Jesus Christ (John 5:22; Acts 17:31; Romans 2:16). People who now reject Jesus Christ as Lord, one day will have to face Him as Judge. The idea held by most Christians of one final or one general judgment actually has no basis in Scripture. The Word of God states that there are at least five distinct judgments. They are described below, but not necessarily in chronological order.

1) There will be a *judgment* of the *fallen angels* who took part in the rebellion against God with Satan (Jude 6; II Peter

2:4). These angels are to be judged by Christ with His saints (I Corinthians 6:1-3).

2) The Scriptures speak of the *judgment* of the *nation* of *Israel*, which is predicted in Ezekiel 20:33-44 and Malachi 3:1-6. The rebels will be purged from the nation before she is permitted to enter into the millennial kingdom. See Ezekiel 40-48.

3) There will also be a *judgment* of the *Gentile nations*. At the close of the Great Tribulation, when Christ comes in His glory, those on the earth who survive the judgments of Revelation 6-19 will be brought before Him and separated as sheep and goats. Only the sheep—the righteous—will be allowed to enter the millennial kingdom, according to Jesus' promise. He will say, "Inherit the kingdom prepared for you from the foundation of the world." See Matthew 25:31-46.

4) The Scriptures teach that there will be a *judgment* of *believers* for their *works*. This judgment refers only to believers. It does not concern their sins, for they were judged at Calvary, according to John 5:24 and Hebrews 10:10-14. This judgment will result either in the gain or the loss of eternal rewards and privileges, based upon their works from the time of their conversion (I Peter 4:17; Romans 14:10). II Corinthians 5:10 says, "We must all appear before the judgment seat of Christ; that every one may receive the things done in his body." I Corinthians 3:11-15, addressed particularly to ministers, also speaks of judgment concerning one's works.

5) The *judgment* of the *unsaved dead* is often referred to as the *Great White Throne Judgment* (Revelation 20:11-15). The unsaved dead will be raised, and they will stand before the throne of God to be judged out of the books. Then they will be cast into the lake of fire. This judgment will include all the unsaved out of every generation of history and will occur at the end of the millennium.

This judgment should not be confused with the judgment of the living nations which occurs at the close of the Tribulation period at the Second Advent and prior to the millennium (Matthew 25). Remember that by this time the righteous have already been resurrected and judged for their works, and have enjoyed a thousand years of peace on the earth. Two classes of people are mentioned in Matthew 25:33—the righteous and the wicked—but only the wicked are referred to in Revelation 20.

The Destination of the Wicked After Death

Where do the *wicked* spend *eternity*? Basically, there are three views: universalism, annihilationism, and the biblical view of everlasting punishment.

Universalism, an ancient heresy rejected by the early church, taught that God's nature is love and that He will ultimately triumph in the salvation of all men. The universalist says, "If only part of the human race is saved or if the wicked will suffer eternal punishment, it would constitute a triumph of evil and a failure by God." Therefore, they say that judgment and punishment are remedial and will ultimately lead all men to repentance and final harmony with God. This heresy arose in the early history of the church, then was neglected during the middle ages, only to be revived again in the eighteenth century. It underlies the theology of the unitarian and universalist churches of today.

The error of *ultimate reconciliation* constitutes a present-day restatement of the heresy of universal salvation, but is adhered to by groups outside the universalist and the unitarian churches. Like the universalists, they contend that God will ultimately reconcile the whole world, including the eventual salvation of the devil and the demons.

According to the teachers of universalism or ultimate reconciliation, which are essentially the same, God is not angry with His creation, for He "loved the world" (John 3:16), and He "was in Christ, reconciling the world unto himself" (II Corinthians 5:19). They say all creation will be delivered (Romans 8:21), and all men will eventually be drawn to Christ, because of Jesus' promise in John 12:32. "And I, if I be lifted up from the earth, will draw all men unto me." I Corinthians 15:22 is also quoted, "In Adam all die, even so in Christ shall all be made alive."

Quoting such passages to prove universal salvation changes their intended meaning and ignores the scores of passages which teach the eternal punishment of the wicked. Those who teach this error cite John 3:16 in an attempt to prove that all the world will be saved, but they ignore the condition that a person must believe on Christ. "Whosoever

believeth in him should not perish, but have everlasting life."
Jesus did not say He will save those who do not believe. He
actually said, "He that believeth on the Son hath everlasting
life: and he that believeth not the Son shall not see life; but
the wrath of God abideth on him" (John 3:36). If the sinner
shall not see life, and if the wrath of God abides on him;
obviously, John 3 cannot be used to prove universal salvation.

The issue is clearly settled by the abundance of Scripture which sets forth the fact of the eternal punishment of the
lost. Jesus Himself taught that hell is a place where the fire
shall not be quenched and where the worm dieth not (Mark
9:43-48). He also taught that hell is a place of eternal torment
(Revelation 14:9-11; 20:10-15; 21:8).

Contrary to the error that such punishment in hell is
remedial and that the lost will see their error and repent, the
Scriptures not only declare that their punishment is eternal,
but also state that a sinner does not change his character in
hell. Revelation 22:11 says, "He that is unjust, let him be
unjust still: and he which is filthy, let him be filthy still." The
wicked are forever forbidden access to the eternal city of God
(Revelation 22:14-15). There is a great gulf fixed between the
saved and the lost so they cannot pass from hell to heaven or
from heaven to hell (Luke 16:19-31).

In Revelation 9, which depicts the punishment of the
wicked during the Great Tribulation, man's misery does not
lead him to repent. "And the rest of the men which were not
killed by these plagues [of the tribulation] yet repented not of
the works of their hands, that they should not worship devils,

and idols of gold, and silver, and brass, and stone, and of wood: which neither can see, nor hear, nor walk: Neither repented they of their murders, nor of their sorceries, nor of their fornication, nor of their thefts" (Revelation 9:20-21).

Another clear example of the subtle nature of universalism's deception is its contention that I Corinthians 15:22 teaches that all men will ultimately be saved and resurrected. The Apostle Paul said, "For as in Adam all die, even so in Christ shall all be made alive." While it is true that in Adam all die because all men have descended from Adam, all men most certainly are not in Christ. Only those who believe on Him are said to be "in Christ" and have eternal life with the hope of being "made alive" at the resurrection of the righteous.

Another argument used by the proponents of universalism is based upon the so-called *fatherhood of God*. God is the Father of all men, they say, and He would not punish His children forever. But Jesus put an end to that lie in John 8:44 when He said that the wicked have a father—but he is not God! "Ye are of your father the devil, and the lusts of your father ye will do." The world truly has a father, but he is the god of this world, the devil. God is the Father only of those who are *in Christ*, and Satan is said to be the father of all others.

A second major error regarding the destination of the wicked after death is *annihilationism*. Those who hold to this error teach that at death the wicked are annihilated—they cease to exist. But in the Bible "death" or "die" are never

313

used to mean cessation of existence. Teachers of this doctrine believe that Malachi 4:3 predicts that the righteous will walk upon the ashes of the wicked, so they surmise it must mean they are annihilated. Even taken literally, that verse could only be speaking of the ashes of the physical body, since the soul is spiritual and cannot give off any ashes.

Even within the ranks of the annihilationists there are differences. 1) Some believe that the wicked will be annihilated at death. 2) Others, including the Seventh Day Adventists, believe that the ungodly will be annihilated at the time of judgment. They will be resurrected as shown in Revelation 20 and then cast into the lake of fire and burned up. 3) Another group believes that the unsaved will be annihilated at some future time after suffering punishment for a long time in the lake of fire. They contend that the lake of fire was created by God for the devil, the apostate angels, and the wicked; and it cannot exist forever because only God is eternal. Therefore, the wicked must be annihilated after millions of years.

The Bible shows that punishment is eternal, and that the wicked are at no time annihilated. For example, Revelation 14:9-11 reads, "The third angel followed them, saying with a loud voice, If any man worship the beast and his image, and receive his mark in his forehead, or in his hand, The same shall drink of the wine of the wrath of God, which is poured out without mixture into the cup of his indignation; and he shall be tormented with fire and brimstone in the presence of the holy angels, and in the presence of the Lamb: And the smoke of their torment ascendeth up for ever and

314

ever: and they have no rest day nor night, who worship the beast and his image, and whosoever receiveth the mark of his name." There it is plainly stated that they are tormented "for ever and ever" as punishment and have no rest day or night. The same Bible that teaches eternal life for the righteous also teaches eternal punishment for the lost. In Matthew 25:46 Jesus said, the wicked "go away into everlasting punishment: but the righteous into life eternal."

The Scriptures describe the abode of the wicked after death as a place of outer darkness where there will be weeping and gnashing of teeth (Matthew 8:12; 25:30). Jesus spoke of it as everlasting fire (Matthew 25:41). It is a place of eternal destruction and punishment (Matthew 25:46; II Thessalonians 1:9), a place of unquenchable fire (Mark 9:43f.), the lake of fire (Revelation 19:20; 20:14), a place of torment with fire and brimstone (Revelation 14:9-11), a furnace of fire (Matthew 13:42), and the second death (Revelation 20:6,14; 21:8). To dwell there is described as abiding under the wrath of God (John 3:36; Romans 2:5; Revelation 14:10). It is an eternal, unchangeable state (Matthew 25:41,46; Mark 9:48; Luke 16:26; II Thessalonians 1:9; Revelation 14:11; 20:10).

The liberals imagine that hell is a spiritual state where the lost suffer remorse, burning forever with unfulfilled lust and desire, which is their punishment. However, the texts which have been cited indicate that hell (Gehenna or the lake of fire) is not a mere spiritual state or condition, but is an actual place into which the wicked are thrust.

315

The Kingdom of God

Both Old and New Testaments present revelation on the *Kingdom of God*, a topic which was central in the teaching of Jesus. Many of His parables, for example those recorded in Matthew 13, give insight into the nature of the kingdom. In the Sermon on the Mount, Jesus made mention of the kingdom nine times, including His classic injunction in Matthew 6:33, "But seek ye first the kingdom of God, and his righteousness; and all these things shall be added unto you." In Matthew 6:10 He instructed His hearers to pray for His kingdom to come on the earth. When the Bible speaks of the *Kingdom of God* and the *Kingdom of Heaven*, it is not suggesting two kingdoms; they are one and the same.

Views of the Kingdom

There are several different views of the kingdom. 1) Some believe the *heavenly view*, a very elemental concept that when a Christian dies he enters the Kingdom of Heaven, which is God's dwelling place. 2) The *visible church view* equates the Kingdom of God with the church which presently exists on the earth. 3) The *social view* (Social Gospel) is held by those who erroneously believe that the Kingdom of God will be manifested as a result of educational and social improvements. They contend that through political reforms, economic prosperity, and education of the people the Kingdom of God will be established on the earth. 4) *The spiritualized view* is the prevailing belief of most denominational churches. They spiritualize the kingdom and say that the Kingdom of God is only the reign and rule of God in the hearts of His people.

While some of the above views contain elements of truth, they do not paint the whole picture of this comprehensive doctrine regarding God's vast kingdom. Thus, a thorough study of the *biblical view* of the Kingdom of God and its three-fold nature will follow. As a *present possession* the kingdom is spiritual and is within the believer (Luke 16:16; 17:20-21; John 3:3; Colossians 1:13). The *future realization* will be visible and millennial. At the First Advent, Christ came in humiliation, having neither throne nor kingdom; but when He returns in the Second Advent, He will establish His kingdom here on the earth (Luke 19:11-27; 21:24-31; 22:28-30). The kingdom is an *eternal hope*, and in this sense it is eschatological (Isaiah 65:17-25; 66:22-24; Revelation 21-22).

The denominational amillennial teachers contend that there will be no literal, earthly kingdom. They cite Luke 17:20-21: "And when he was demanded of the Pharisees, when the kingdom of God should come, he answered them and said, The kingdom of God cometh not with observation: Neither shall they say, Lo here! or, lo there! for, behold, the kingdom of God is within you." The phrase "within you" could also be read as "among you" or "in your midst." Jesus was emphasizing the spiritual aspect of the kingdom because the Jews were looking for a Messiah who would be a political leader—one who would set up a political kingdom (John 6:14-15). His sudden departure was evidence that He had no such aspirations. He did not come in the First Advent as a civil ruler, but as a suffering servant.

317

John 18:36 is also cited in an attempt to prove that the kingdom is not an earthly kingdom. "Jesus answered, My kingdom is not of this world: if my kingdom were of this world, then would my servants fight, that I should not be delivered to the Jews: but now is my kingdom not from hence." The Greek text literally says that Christ's kingdom is not *out of* or *from* this world, meaning that it is from heaven.

There is much teaching in both Testaments on the Kingdom of God. In the Old Testament there were many prophecies which spoke of a future king and kingdom; and the New Testament continues this emphasis, more often stressing its earthly aspect. This kingdom would be spiritual, but it would also be outwardly visible in its ultimate aspect. The Old Testament predicted a future kingdom on the earth which would be eternal (Isaiah 9:6-7; Daniel 7:13-14). Daniel 2:44 states that the kingdom will stand forever. There will be a king who will reign over Israel and over all the earth (II Samuel 7:12-13; Jeremiah 23:5-6; Daniel 7:13-14; Zechariah 14:9; Matthew 2:1-6 with Micah 5:2; Luke 1:31-33). Jesus said in John 18:37 that it was to this end—as King—He was born. The earthly aspect to this kingdom is predicted in Isaiah 2:1-4. Also see Isaiah, chapters 11; 24-28; 65:17.

From her vantage point in the Old Testament, Israel did not know how to distinguish between the First and Second Advents. For that reason it seemed strange, even to the apostles, that Jesus did not set up a kingdom. It took time—until after the resurrection—for them to realize that Jesus had to suffer and die. Even very late in Christ's ministry, Peter's attempt to deter Jesus from the Cross (Matthew

16:22-23) proved that the disciples did not have a complete revelation.

The Old Testament saints could not distinguish between the two advents because they did not have adequate revelation. Therefore, they were confused by prophecies that mixed the two advents, as well as by prophecies that combined elements of the eternal state with the millennium. The truths revealed in the New Testament clarified the differences.

God's Universal Kingdom

The doctrine of the Kingdom of God is best understood by examining its two essential aspects: the universal and the mediatorial. The *universal Kingdom* of God is the eternal, unlimited, and sovereign reign of God over all things, whether visible or invisible. Jesus clearly taught that His mission was to establish the Kingdom of God on this earth. When He preached, He said, "The kingdom of God is at hand." In fact, many of His parables were related to the kingdom. The mediatorial kingdom is an aspect of the universal.

God's kingdom is *eternal*; it has always existed. "For thine is the kingdom, and the power, and the glory, for ever" (Matthew 6:13). David said in Psalm 10:16, "The Lord is King for ever and ever." The prophet stated in Jeremiah 10:10, "The Lord is the true God, he is the living God, and an everlasting king." God's throne is *perpetual*. "Thou, O Lord, remainest for ever; thy throne from generation to generation" (Lamentations 5:19). God's kingdom is *unlimited* in its scope.

319

"All that is in the heaven and in the earth is thine; thine is the kingdom, O Lord, and thou art exalted as head above all. Both riches and honour come of thee, and thou reignest over all; and in thine hand is power and might" (I Chronicles 29:11-12).

God not only rules, but He also "setteth up over" this earthly kingdom the leaders He chooses (Daniel 4:17,25,32). Paul admonished the church in Romans 13:1, "Let every soul be subject unto the higher powers. For there is no power but of God: the powers that be are ordained of God." He further stated in Colossians 1:16-17 that God reigns over all things, visible and invisible.

God's Method of Ruling

With reference to heaven and the universe, God is ruling *directly*. In Matthew 6:10 Jesus taught His followers to pray, "Thy kingdom come. Thy will be done in earth, as it is in heaven," indicating that God's perfect will is already being done in heaven.

At the present time God is ruling on the earth *indirectly* in four basic ways. 1) He rules through His providential control of the laws of nature (Psalm 148:8; 104). 2) He rules through secondary causes. For example, He may use one nation to punish another (Isaiah 10:5-15). Isaiah 44:24 to 45:7 tells of God's dealings with Cyrus so that he would initiate the rebuilding of Jerusalem. "Thus saith Cyrus king of Persia, The Lord God of heaven hath given me all the kingdoms of the earth; and he hath charged me to build him an house at

Jerusalem, which is in Judah" (Ezra 1:2). 3) God also rules indirectly through mediators. In the case of Israel, He ruled through kings and spoke to her through the prophets. 4) He rules in the world through the elected or appointed leaders.

God is reigning at present over all humanity. He rules over the *saints*, who gladly yield to His authority, through Jesus Christ, the head of the church (Colossians 1; Ephesians 3). He also rules over the *rebellious*. This is evident in Exodus 9:16 which describes God's dealings with Pharaoh. "For this cause have I raised thee up, for to shew in thee my power." God reigns over those He uses as instruments, even though they are not aware of it. He used Assyria to punish Israel for her sins. In Daniel 4:34 King Nebuchadnezzar was compelled by his humiliating experience to acknowledge that God is King and His dominion is everlasting.

God's Mediatorial Kingdom

God's purpose was to establish His kingdom on the earth where He would reign and rule. From the beginning He has had chosen representatives who speak and act for Him. These mediators occupy an intermediate place between God and man to bring reconciliation. The mediatorial aspect of God's kingdom actually began in the Garden of Eden when He gave Adam dominion over all the earth (Genesis 1:26), but after Adam sinned God took away much of that authority. Many generations lived and died without the leadership of a mediator; but following the Flood, God once again established His rule—this time through Noah (Genesis 9:1-2).

The rulers and leaders that God has chosen have been invested with divine dominion and authority; therefore, God has been ruling through them in a mediatorial way. In fact, when God chose Abram, He said to him, "I will make of thee a great nation" (Genesis 12:2). When God delivered the Israelites from their bondage in Egypt, He chose Moses as His mediator and spoke to him face to face. He told Moses that He had made him a god to Pharaoh, and Aaron was to be Moses' prophet. Moses was God's representative to the Israelites until their entrance into the promised land. After the death of Moses, God said to Joshua, "There shall not any man be able to stand before thee all the days of thy life: as I was with Moses, so I will be with thee" (Joshua 1:5). God bestowed such authority on Joshua that he commanded, and "the sun stood still, and the moon stayed" (Joshua 10:13).

God's Rule: Judges

The judges were also appointed by God, and the Israelites looked to them for counsel and leadership. Israel repeatedly fell into a pattern of sin, judgment, and repentance. Whenever the nation strayed away from the obedience God required, He delivered them into the hands of their enemies. They would repent and cry out to Him and He would raise up "judges, which delivered them out of the hand of those that spoiled them" (Judges 2:16). Samuel was both a judge and a prophet. He served as a transitional figure between the judges and the kingship (I Samuel 3:19—4:1).

God's Rule: The Kingship

It has always been God's intention to have a kingdom with a king ruling over His people. He told Abraham that there would be kings in his lineage. "And I will make thee exceeding fruitful, and I will make nations of thee, and kings shall come out of thee" (Genesis 17:6). This is seen again in Genesis 35:9-11 where God repeated the promise to Jacob, "Kings shall come out of thy loins." Having predestinated that a kingship would eventually be established, God listed certain principles and regulations for the king to follow (Deuteronomy 17:14-20), even though the kingship did not begin until hundreds of years later.

God was grieved that the Israelites asked for a king, not because the kingship and kingdom were violations of His will, but because their motives were wrong and their timing was premature. Why were God and Samuel displeased when the people asked for a king?

1) The Israelites sinned in asking for a king because they did not wait on God's time. Saul was not God's first choice—David was—but at that time David was only a little boy, so God gave them Saul. Saul was a failure from beginning to end, and much oppression came because the people demanded a king. If they had waited on God's timing, He would have given them David, who was His choice and a type of the Messiah to come.

2) They sinned in asking for a king because they wanted to be like the other nations, which God never

323

intended. "For thou art an holy people unto the Lord thy God: the Lord thy God hath chosen thee to be a special people unto himself, above all people that are upon the face of the earth" (Deuteronomy 7:6).

3) In asking for a king, the Israelites were actually rejecting the rule of God (I Samuel 8:7). God's will was to establish a monarchy; God would reign through a righteous king. As recompense for their sin, He gave them an oppressor for forty years, a disobedient king.

The Division of the Kingdom

After Solomon began to reign, he multiplied wives, went to Egypt and bought horses, and did all those things God forbade in Deuteronomy 17:14-20. After the wives turned his heart to other gods, God said He would take the kingdom away from him. He did not do this in Solomon's lifetime because of David; but during the reign of Solomon's son, the kingdom was divided and only the tribe of Judah was left in David's kingdom. The other tribes followed Jeroboam and were called Israel. After the division of the kingdom, the rule of God became less direct. The kings often took the throne by force or obtained it by inheritance and not by divine appointment. There were only a few good kings.

During this period the prophets came on the scene with prophecy and prediction concerning a future age when God would raise up a King after His own heart. The prophets pointed to the failures of the kings, and repeatedly stated there would eventually come a righteous King, who would reign from Zion and do God's will. His name would be called *the Lord is our righteousness* (Jeremiah 23:6; 33:16). The close of the kingdom period came when Israel fell to Assyria and Judah was overtaken by Babylon.

The Kingdom in Prophecy

There has been no kingdom since the downfall of Judah. Although Israel is restored today as a political entity, she has no God-appointed king or kingdom and certainly is not a theocracy in which God is ruling. However, the prophets predicted a day when that kingdom will be restored (Isaiah 9:6-7; Jeremiah 23:5-6; Daniel 2 and 7). The Scriptures have much to say about the kingdom. Before the death of Jacob, he called his sons together and prophesied over them, saying to Judah, "The sceptre shall not depart from Judah, nor a lawgiver from between his feet, until Shiloh come; and unto him shall the gathering of the people be" (Genesis 49:10).

Balaam was hired to curse Israel but he could not, because the Spirit of the Lord came upon him, compelling him to bless the ones he intended to curse. He prophesied, "There shall come a Star out of Jacob, and a Sceptre shall rise out of Israel" (Numbers 24:17). God promised that He would establish the kingdom through David's son, referring to Solomon, but also to Christ, David's son (II Samuel 7:1-16). "Thine house and thy kingdom shall be established for ever before thee: thy throne shall be established for ever" (verse 16).

The Nature of Kingdom Prophecy

The nature of kingdom prophecy, like the nature of much Old Testament prophecy, is two-fold. The prophet would deliver a prophecy that applied to his present time and circumstances, but many of the prophecies also looked to the future and had a second fulfillment in the time of the Messiah. Not all kingdom prophecies were fulfilled at the First Advent. Some kingdom prophecies are: Psalm 2; Isaiah 2:1-4; Ezekiel 20:33-42; 40-48; Daniel 2 and 7; Hosea 3:4-5; Amos 9:11; Obadiah 21; Micah 4:1-5; and the entire Book of Zechariah.

The modern church with its amillennial viewpoint denies the literal kingdom and spiritualizes the kingdom prophecies; however, the Bible clearly shows that they are to be taken literally. Exact details are given, such as locations, rulers, and nations—facts which would make no sense if they were not to be taken literally. In Ezekiel 40-48 God gave exact measurements of the future city, the temple, its furnishings and fixtures, and He described the nature of the worship.

Since the future kingdom will destroy other literal kingdoms on the earth, the prophecies which predict it cannot be spiritualized. "And in the days of these kings shall the God of heaven set up a kingdom, which shall never be destroyed: and the kingdom shall not be left to other people, but it shall break in pieces and consume all these kingdoms, and it shall stand for ever" (Daniel 2:44). God's kingdom will destroy what is remaining of those other kingdoms in the latter days, which a spiritualized kingdom could not do. The revived kingdom which the Bible predicts is a continuation of the literal, historical, Davidic kingdom. It would be nonsense to insist that a spiritual kingdom could replace a real kingdom. When Gabriel appeared to Mary, he said, "Thou shalt conceive in thy womb, and bring forth a son, and shalt call his name Jesus. He shall be great, and shall be called the Son of the Highest: and the Lord God shall give unto him the throne of his father David: And he shall reign over the house of Jacob for ever; and of his kingdom there shall be no end" (Luke 1:31-33).

Jesus Himself said He would return in all of His glory with His holy angels and would sit upon the throne and rule in Zion (Matthew 25:31). He also told the apostles they would sit on twelve thrones judging the twelve tribes of Israel (Matthew 19:28). In Acts 1:6-7, when Christ was asked when He would restore the kingdom to Israel, He told the disciples it was not for them to know, but it was in the Father's hand. That would have been an excellent opportunity to inform them if there would be no literal earthly kingdom, but He did not.

The Prophetic Kingdom in Relation to the New Testament Kingdom

What is the relationship between the Kingdom of God which John the Baptist proclaimed and the kingdom of prophecy in the Old Testament? The present-day amillennial teachers say that there is no direct relation and that Jesus reinterpreted the Old Testament, changing the emphasis from an earthly, political kingdom to a spiritual one. They

327

quote Luke 17:20-21 which says the Kingdom of God is within the believer. However, the kingdom announced by Christ in the Gospels was identical with the kingdom which was predicted by the Old Testament prophets. In fact, the entire New Testament supports that statement.

Jesus did not begin His teaching with a message about the church, but He opened and closed His ministry with the message of the kingdom. His mission on the earth was to establish His kingdom, yet the stress by most ministers is that He came merely to establish His church. In the Gospels, Jesus mentioned the church only two times, but He spoke of the kingdom repeatedly. Obviously, it was in God's plan to set up His church, but it was not to be an end itself. It was to be the door into the kingdom during the New Testament period until the return of Christ.

Mark 1:14-15 describes the early part of Christ's ministry. "Jesus came into Galilee, preaching the gospel of the kingdom of God, And saying, The time is fulfilled, and the kingdom of God is at hand: repent ye, and believe the gospel." Likewise, Jesus closed His ministry with the message of the kingdom. After His crucifixion and just prior to His ascension, it is recorded, "He shewed himself alive after his passion by many infallible proofs, being seen of them forty days, and speaking of the things pertaining to the kingdom of God" (Acts 1:3).

John the Baptist preached the kingdom, exhorting his listeners, "Repent ye: for the kingdom of heaven is at hand" (Matthew 3:2). Furthermore, Jesus sent out the twelve disciples and said to them, "And as ye go, preach, saying, The kingdom of heaven is at hand" (Matthew 10:7). When He appointed seventy of His followers and sent them out, He said to them, "Heal the sick that are therein, and say unto them, The kingdom of God is come nigh unto you" (Luke 10:9).

The Scriptures clearly show that Jesus Christ came to fulfill the kingdom prophecies of the Old Testament. In Micah 5:2 the prophet predicted that a ruler in Israel would be born in Bethlehem, which was fulfilled at the birth of Jesus Christ (Matthew 2:1-6). When Jesus entered into Jerusalem just before His crucifixion, He entered as a King (Matthew 21:1-10), fulfilling Old Testament prophecy. "Thy King cometh unto thee: he is just, and having salvation; lowly, and riding upon an ass, and upon a colt the foal of an ass" (Zechariah 9:9). Moreover, the death of Jesus is related to Old Testament kingdom prophecy (Matthew 26:24 with Psalm 16:10) as was His resurrection (Acts 7:54-56; Psalm 110:1). These are just a few of the many examples which could be cited.

Jesus appealed to the prophets in support of His kingdom message. In His first sermon He quoted Isaiah 61:1, then said, "This day is this scripture fulfilled in your ears" (Luke 4:21). He declared in Luke 4:43, "I must preach the kingdom of God to other cities also: for therefore am I sent." In Matthew 11:2-6 John the Baptist sent two of his disciples to Jesus to see if He was the promised Messiah, to whom Jesus replied, "Go and shew John again those things which ye do hear and see: The blind receive their sight, and the lame walk, the lepers are cleansed, and the deaf hear, the dead are raised up, and the poor have the gospel preached to them." These were signs of the Kingdom of God. The fact that sickness, defeat, and suffering are prevalent in the world today is evidence that the Kingdom of God has not yet been established, and that "the whole world lieth in wickedness" (I John 5:19).

Christ never suggested that His conception of the kingdom was different from that of the prophets. In fact, He taught about the law and the kingdom in the same discourse (Matthew 5:17-20), explaining that He had not come to destroy the law or the prophets but to fulfill them.

Israel's Rejection of the Kingdom

The unfolding of God's plan is seen in Israel's rejection of the King and His message of the kingdom from the very beginning of Christ's ministry. After Jesus' first message, "All they in the synagogue, when they heard these things, were filled with wrath, And rose up, and thrust him out of the city, and led him unto the brow of the hill whereon their city was built, that they might cast him down headlong" (Luke 4:28-29).

In order for God to provide an atonement for sins, God's wise plan and purpose included Israel's rejection of the King and the kingdom at the First Advent (Acts 2:22-23; 4:27-28; Ephesians 1:11). Therefore, it was no surprise to Jesus that the kingdom He offered to the Jews was rejected. When He left the Father's side and came into the world, He knew He would be crucified as the Lamb of God. "From that time forth began Jesus to shew unto his disciples, how that he must go unto Jerusalem, and suffer many things of the elders and chief priests and scribes, and be killed, and be raised again the third day" (Matthew 16:21). He knew that rejection was a part of His coming into the world. If He were not rejected, He could not die; and if He did not die, He could not redeem mankind.

There is a positive side to Christ's rejection by the Jews—the salvation of the Gentiles. Because Israel scorned God's offer of the kingdom, He turned to the nations with the same offer of hope which the Jews had refused. Thus, the church throughout history has largely been Gentile. God's plan, however, is not to cast off His chosen people forever; but He will grant them repentance and mercy, and will "graft them in" again (Romans 11:23).

In order to fulfill God's plan, the kingdom had to be offered first to Israel. When Jesus sent out the twelve disciples before Him, He instructed them, "Go not into the way of the Gentiles, and into any city of the Samaritans enter ye not. But go rather to the lost sheep of the house of Israel. And as ye go, preach, saying, The kingdom of heaven is at hand" (Matthew 10:5-7). He confirmed this plan in Matthew 15:24 where He said, "I am not sent but unto the lost sheep of the house of Israel." But to their own detriment they refused God's Son, their Messiah, and thus the kingdom. Only then did God offer the gospel to the Gentiles.

The certainty of Israel's rejection of the kingdom is evident in the unique nature of Jesus' teaching after He was rejected. He began to teach in parables which could not be understood without an interpretation. "And with many such parables spake he the word unto them, as they were able to hear it. But without a parable spake he not unto them: and when they were alone, he expounded all things to his disciples" (Mark 4:33-34). Jesus deliberately spoke to Israel about the kingdom in a mystery so they could not understand, purposely insuring that they would reject Him. When great multitudes were gathered to hear Jesus, some of the disciples inquired of Him, "Why speakest thou unto them in parables? He answered and said unto them, Because it is given unto you to know the mysteries of the kingdom of heaven, but to them it is not given" (Matthew 13:10-11). It is a fact of both Scripture and history that when people receive His Word, He will give them more; but if they reject it, He will take away what they have.

In the Old Testament God told Isaiah to go and make the people's eyes blind and their ears dull of hearing (Isaiah 6:8-10). Nations or individuals can reach the place where there is no further opportunity for repentance. When the Jews rejected Jesus and His message, they were fulfilling the prophecy of Isaiah (Matthew 13:14). The meaning of the kingdom parables was a mystery to the Jews because God was judging them for perpetually rejecting His prophets and finally their King when He came. The Apostle Paul, in his day, affirmed that God deals in this stern fashion with people when they reject the true Word of God. "They received not the love of the truth, that they might be saved. And for this cause God shall send them strong delusion, that they should believe a lie: That they all might be damned who believed not the truth, but had pleasure in unrighteousness" (II Thessalonians 2:10-12).

Between the rejection of the original offer of the kingdom and its visible establishment at the Second Advent, there is a *parenthesis in time*—the church age. After His rejection Christ began to unfold the mystery of His "ekklesia" or assembly. This was such a mystery to Peter that he had to receive a repeated vision in Acts 10 in order to understand that Gentiles would be included in this assembly. Paul also spoke of this mystery in Ephesians 3:1-9. In Matthew 16:18-19 Jesus related the church to the kingdom when He proclaimed, "Upon this rock I will build my church; and the gates of hell shall not prevail against it. And I will give unto thee the keys of the kingdom of heaven."

The church was as much a mystery to the apostles as the kingdom had been to the Jews when Jesus spoke to them in parables (Romans 16:25-26; Colossians 1:24-27). The church was not directly revealed in the Old Testament, although the prophets repeatedly spoke of God taking a people out of the Gentiles. Yet God established this church, which had been a mystery to the Jews, as the way into His kingdom, offering hope to the whole world by faith.

With the formation of the assembly of believers in Christ, which included both Jews and Gentiles, the visible kingdom was temporarily set aside, and Israel as a nation was rejected for a time. Entrance into the kingdom would subsequently come through the "ekklesia." In I Corinthians 12:13 Paul said, "For by one Spirit are we all baptized into one body," and that one body is the church. Before this church age draws to a close, an innumerable host out of all nations will be saved (Revelation 7:9).

Just prior to His crucifixion, Jesus gave a preview of the kingdom to His disciples in Matthew 16:18-19, when He said He would build His church. He spoke of the "keys of the kingdom of heaven," referring to the preaching of the gospel through the "ekklesia." To several of them He offered an even deeper glimpse of His kingdom when He said, "There be some standing here, which shall not taste of death, till they see the Son of man coming in his kingdom" (verse 28). He did not mean that His hearers would still be living many years later; but He was obviously alluding to His transfiguration which would occur six days later in the presence of Peter, James, and John, who would see Him briefly in the glory of His kingdom. At His ascension eleven of those disciples saw Him ascending to the right hand of God and entering into His kingdom.

Jesus' disciples "thought that the kingdom of God should immediately appear" (Luke 19:11); therefore, He began to prepare them for His long absence. He also offered Himself as King one final time when He rode into Jerusalem on a donkey in fulfillment of Zechariah 9:9. As he approached the city the people gladly received Him as Messiah and cried, "Hosanna to the son of David"; but the chief priests and scribes were sore displeased and continued to reject Him (Matthew 21:1-15). Then, in verse 43, Christ officially sealed their rejection of the kingdom when He said, "Therefore say I unto you, The kingdom of God shall be taken from you, and given to a nation bringing forth the fruits thereof." Thus, the kingdom has been set aside temporarily until it will be visibly established upon earth at Christ's return. "Now is come salvation, and strength, and the kingdom of our God, and the power of his Christ" (Revelation 12:10).

During this present age the church must be obedient to its commission to preach the Kingdom of God, not failing to preach the whole counsel of God. Paul said to the Ephesians, "I know that ye all, among whom I have gone preaching the kingdom of God, shall see my face no more" (Acts 20:25). In verse 27 he told them that he had declared unto them "all the counsel of God."

The present age should be designated in the hearts of all believers as a period of preparation for the kingdom. God is in the process of developing a nucleus out of the earth, a firstfruits people, who are called in Scripture the sons (children) of the kingdom (Matthew 13:38). All believers are said to be citizens of the kingdom, but some of them will be *overcomers* who will reign and rule over the nations with God. Every Christian is an overcomer in the sense of I John 5:4, but there are those who will overcome in all things and inherit all things (Revelation 21:7).

During this time in which God is preparing sons for His kingdom, He is also allowing the development of other sons within His kingdom—the sons of Satan (Matthew 13:38). Jesus spoke of the kingdom in relation to the end of the world, saying that the angels will gather out of His kingdom those who do iniquity and will cast them into a furnace of fire (verses 40-42).

The mediatorial kingdom during the millennium will be the visible manifestation of the kingdom on earth when Christ will reign for a thousand years (Revelation 20). Paul said that when the last enemy of God is put down, the purpose for the mediatorial kingdom will cease, and it will be merged into the eternal state. "Then cometh the end, when he shall have delivered up the kingdom to God, even the Father; when he shall have put down all rule and all authority and power. For he must reign, till he hath put all enemies under his feet" (I Corinthians 15:24-25). Verse 28 shows that the kingdom will be merged into the kingdom of the Father; but that does not mean it will cease to exist, because Jesus will continue reigning over His people. "But unto the Son he saith, Thy throne, O God, is for ever and ever: a sceptre of righteousness is the sceptre of thy kingdom" (Hebrews 1:8).

Jesus will subject Himself to the Father, speaking of relationship. Of course, Jesus is God and is equal with God. Revelation 3:21 indicates that Jesus will reign with the Father. "To him that overcometh will I grant to sit with me in my throne, even as I also overcame, and am set down with my Father in his throne." That does not mean a *single* throne, but that the dominion and authority is equally shared by the Father and Son.

Satan will be bound during the thousand year perfect reign of Christ, but will be loosed at the end and will go out to deceive the nations (Revelation 20:7-8). They will gather for a great, final battle; but fire will come down from God out of heaven and will devour them. The devil, who deceived them, will be cast into the lake of fire and brimstone, along with the beast and the false prophet, where they will be tormented day and night for ever and ever (Revelation 20:9-10).

God's first man, Adam, failed to fulfill God's purpose, but Jesus will vindicate and validate God's perfect plan when He reigns. He will rule over a kingdom of righteousness and will represent the Father on earth, perfectly performing God's original intention.

The New Heavens, New Earth, and New Jerusalem

Just as God created the present heavens and earth by a direct act of creation, the Bible reveals that He will create another heaven and earth. "For, behold, I create new heavens and a new earth: and the former shall not be remembered, nor come into mind" (Isaiah 65:17). "For as the new heavens and the new earth, which I will make, shall remain before me, saith the Lord, so shall your seed and your name remain" (Isaiah 66:22). "The heavens shall pass away with a great noise, and the elements shall melt with fervent heat, the earth also and the works that are therein shall be burned up" (II Peter 3:10). "Nevertheless we, according to his promise, look for new heavens and a new earth, wherein dwelleth righteousness" (II Peter 3:13). "And I saw a new heaven and a new earth: for the first heaven and the first earth were passed away; and there was no more sea" (Revelation 21:1).

Many people within the church have a misconception that their salvation ensures them a place for eternity in a so-called "heaven" somewhere. The Scriptures, however, indicate that the righteous will forever inhabit New Jerusalem, a totally new city created by God, which will come down upon the new earth. This city will be the seat of His power; "the throne of God and of the Lamb shall be in it" (Revelation 22:3).

Just prior to Christ's crucifixion He comforted His eleven faithful disciples with the words of John 14:1-3. He eased their troubled hearts with the revelation that they would some day be restored to Him in a wonderful place which He was going to prepare for them. New Jerusalem will be a spiritual city; that is, it will not be composed of wood, stone, and steel; but it will be real, even as the saints' new glorified bodies will be real and also spiritual.

Life in the Eternal State
Things Which Will Be Absent

The eternal state is described in Scripture according to what will be there or will not be there. Some things which will not be found in this realm are as follows:

1) *The seas* (Revelation 21:1). The seas set the boundaries of nations, keeping them separated both culturally and

physically. In the present world, if there were no oceans separating the nations, there would be many more wars and
conquests; but in the eternal ages there will be no more division because there will be no religious and ethnic separation
in the hearts of earth's redeemed inhabitants.

2) *Death* (Revelation 21:4). Death reigns in the world at
present, according to Romans 5:14. When Adam sinned,
death passed upon all men, binding all of humanity to the
miserable surety that physical life would conclude in the
grave in corruption and dishonor (I Corinthians 15:42-43).
John 3:16 promises eternal life to those who believe on the
Lord Jesus Christ, guaranteeing them victory over death's
sting, a triumph which will be perfectly realized in this final,
eternal state where death has been abolished.

3) *Sorrow, crying, and pain* (Revelation 21:4). Sorrow is
mental or emotional suffering which is caused by loss,
trouble, or disappointment, and results in weeping. However, when the causes for tears are removed, there will be no
more sorrow or crying, "and God shall wipe away all tears
from their eyes" (Revelation 7:17). Pain will be non-existent.
There will be nothing in that peaceful place that could hurt or
cause pain.

4) *Darkness* (Revelation 21:25; 22:5). There will be no
darkness because "the glory of God did lighten it, and the
Lamb is the light thereof" (Revelation 21:23). The light
spoken of here is not a figure of speech; it is light for the spiritual dimension. God is called the Father of lights in James
1:17, and John said that Jesus is the true Light in John 1:9. On

the road to Damascus at his conversion, Paul saw a great light, brighter than the noonday sun (Acts 9). Christians are called children of the light; they are children of God who is Light. Satan counterfeits this light by appearing as an angel of light (II Corinthians 11:14). He is really not light; he is darkness because he has rule over the powers of darkness.

The Scriptures repeatedly contrast light and darkness and draw spiritual lessons from these two realities. Jesus came into the world that He created, and His own received Him not (John 1:11) because men loved darkness rather than light (John 3:19). Jesus said of Satan and to the religious leaders that came to arrest Him, "This is your hour, and the power of darkness" (Luke 22:53).

Night and darkness also speak of spiritual ignorance. "The people that walked in darkness have seen a great light: they that dwell in the land of the shadow of death, upon them hath the light shined" (Isaiah 9:2; Matthew 4:16). "To open the blind eyes, to bring out the prisoners from the prison, and them that sit in darkness out of the prison house" (Isaiah 42:7).

5) *Sin* (Revelation 21:27). Only those whose names are written in the Lamb's book of life will be in this joyful place— all sinners having been separated at judgment. The new heavens and new earth will be righteous (II Peter 3:13). Conditions will be even better in the eternal state than they were in the Garden of Eden before the Fall, because the tempter will have been cast into the lake of fire. It will be an eternity without temptation or sin of any kind.

6) *The curse* (Revelation 22:3). The curses of Deuter-onomy 28 will not be in effect upon the inhabitants there. While it is true that believers today by their faith are free from the curse of the law (Galatians 3:13), this redemption will be fully and effortlessly realized in eternity.

Things Which Will Be Present

1) *Fellowship with Jesus Christ.* It will be an eternity of personal communion with Jesus Christ. The Lord told His disciples, "I will come again, and receive you unto myself; that where I am, there ye may be also" (John 14:3). He prayed, "Father, I will that they also, whom thou hast given me, be with me where I am" (John 17:24). Also see I Corinthians 13:12; II Corinthians 5:6-8; Revelation 2:26-27; 3:21; 21:3; 22:3-5.

2) *A time of entrance into full knowledge.* "For now we see through a glass, darkly; but then face to face: now I know in part; but then shall I know even as also I am known" (I Corinthians 13:12). This does not imply that the redeemed will know everything, because only God is omniscient. However, those things that were mysteries to man, such as creation, the flood, certain biblical accounts, God's plan, and aspects of His nature will be unveiled as man is able to absorb them. In this life believers must make considerable effort to study and learn some of these truths, but there they will enjoy an eternity of acquiring God's wisdom.

3) *An eternity of glory.* The emphasis here is not so much the believer's glorified body which will be his forever (discussed under the Doctrine of Resurrection), but the glory

the saints will enter into is God's glory which He will share with them. Although God is invisible, He manifests His glory visibly unto His creation. The day will come when the redeemed will behold the glory of the Son of God. Jesus prayed in John 17:24, "Father, I will that they also, whom thou hast given me, be with me where I am; that they may behold my glory." God's glory is the revelation of Himself in His wisdom, power, holiness, love, mercy, truth, and grace.

There is more to partaking of God's glory than simply having the resurrection body. When John wrote about the Messiah in John 1:14-18, he spoke of *beholding His glory*. What the disciples had seen was a carpenter, Jesus of Nazareth; but John's thought here was deeper, speaking of seeing Him in the demonstration of His heavenly powers, hearing Him speak of the wisdom of God, and learning of the knowledge and truth of God. They beheld His glory in His life and in all His works, a privilege which will belong to the elect for eternity.

While all believers will be glorified (Colossians 3:4), there apparently will be greater degrees of glory which some will enjoy, based on their suffering with Christ (Romans 8:17-18; II Corinthians 4:17), soulwinning (Daniel 12:3; I Thessalonians 2:19-20), etc.

4) *An eternity of service to the Lord.* It is not likely that the comical representation of a saint in heaven will ever be fulfilled—that of a robed figure reposing in the clouds playing a harp. On the contrary, the Bible shows that the redeemed will be occupied for eternity in glorious service to the Lord. "The throne of God and of the Lamb shall be in it;

342

and his servants shall serve him" (Revelation 22:3). This verse does not refer to the cherubim, seraphim, or angels, who constantly minister to Him, but to the redeemed among humanity who are His servants. There will be new challenges, fresh experiences, and new things for the elect to learn.

5) *An eternity filled with unspeakable joy.* The atmosphere of the eternal state will be one of abounding, unspeakable joy (Revelation 21:4). The believer in the present realm may have the joy of salvation, but things often enter in to mar that joy. As one draws closer to Jesus he can know a greater experience of joy, but it is still only partial—a small foretaste of what will prevail in eternity. In the personal presence of Christ, there will be supreme, unmarred joy, the joy of the Lord.

> *Therefore the redeemed of the Lord shall return, and come with singing unto Zion; and everlasting joy shall be upon their head: they shall obtain gladness and joy; and sorrow and mourning shall flee away (Isaiah 51:11).*

> *His lord said unto him, Well done, thou good and faithful servant: thou hast been faithful over a few things, I will make thee ruler over many things: enter thou into the joy of thy lord (Matthew 25:21).*

> *Then shall the King say unto them on his right hand, Come, ye blessed of my Father, inherit the kingdom prepared for you from the foundation of the world (Matthew 25:34).*

Index

Notes Regarding the Use of This Index:

This index is intended as a guide which will enable the reader to quickly locate topics of interest. While it is as comprehensive as is practical, it would have been nearly impossible for the editors to cross reference every term. For example, there is no listing under *First Advent*, so related headings should be checked, such as *Birth of Christ*, and *Incarnation*.

This listing does not discriminate between an incidental mention of a subject and a lengthy discussion. For example, the topic of Judgment is cited in the index on several pages within the book, including page 308; however, that page is only the first of many pages on the subject. In cases where the topic continues for more than one page, only the beginning page number is listed; therefore the reader should examine subsequent pages if he is attempting to glean all he can about a matter.

The names of personalities mentioned in the book, from *Aaron* to *Zilpah*, are also listed. Names which were used repetitiously, such as the Apostle Paul's, have not been cited, except where the text refers to their lives and experiences. To cite the page number for every occurrence of "Paul said in the Book of . . ." would have no particular value to the reader.

Aaron 322

Abel 170

Abelard 177

Abimelech 30

Abomination of Desolation 300

Abortion 23

Abraham 24, 30, 99, 104, 113, 120, 181, 183, 207, 209, 290, 304, 323

Abram 322

Absorption 86, 215

Accepting vs Receiving Christ 190

Adam 23, 24, 51, 112, 135, 285, 337

Adam's Fall 5, 13, 146, 159, 175, 181, 211, 286, 313, 321, 339

Adoption 104

Adoption, Doctrine of 218

Adultery 164, 243, 250

Advent, Second 129, 146, 231, 290, 295, 317, 327, 333, 335

Advocate, Christ as 124

Agape Love 102

Agape, the Meal 278

Agnosticism 52

Ahab 29

Ahaz 133

Alexander the Great 92

Amillennial View 301, 317, 326

Amos 40, 44

Ananias and Sapphira 149, 164

Angel of Light 340

Angel of the Lord 72, 127

Angels 22, 32, 80, 84, 85, 95, 112, 114, 126, 138, 146, 164, 227, 268, 296, 314, 327, 335, 343

Angels, Fallen 164, 308, 314

Animal Sacrifice 108, 124, 131, 169, 174, 182, 186, 207, 278, 294

Animals 28, 62, 67, 88

Animals, Distinction from Man 19

Animals, Man's Rule Over 18

Animals, Souls of 19, 21

Animism 56

Annihilationism 287, 313

Anointing of H.S. 148, 151, 153, 156, 267

Anointing with Oil 157

Anselm 61, 177, 179

Anthropological Argument 62

Anthropomorphic 68

Antichrist Judged 294

Antichrist, Names of 291

Antichrist, the Man 290, 302

Antichrist, the Spirit 246, 250, 291

Antinomianism 292

Apollinarians 111

Apostasy 10, 161, 167, 187, 202, 220, 246

Apostle, Office of 145, 238, 255

Apostle, Qualifications 261

Apostle, Selection of 138

Appearances of Christ 139, 140, 142, 328

Appearances of God 68, 72, 105, 127

Appellations of Christ 112

Aquinas, Thomas 58, 177

Archaeology 35

Archbishop 231, 236

Arianism 111

Ark of the Covenant 68, 124

Ark, Noah's 100

Armageddon, Battle of 303

Arminianism 78, 189, 194,

Arminius, Jacobus 190

Ascension of Believers 145

Ascension of Christ 33, 115, 142, 328, 334

Ascension of Christ Predicted 144

Assembly, New Testament 224

Assembly, the Term 224

Assyrian Captivity 7, 325

Athanasius 176, 179

Atheism 52, 53

Atheistic Communism 54

Atonement 101, 122, 186, 246, 278, 330

Atonement in Hell Theory 131, 180, 208

Atonement, Doctrine of 173

Atonement, the Term 71, 173, 174

Attribute: Eternalness 75

Attribute: Faithfulness 99

Attribute: Glory 107

Attribute: Grace 106, 182

Attribute: Holiness 95

Attribute: Immutability 79

Attribute: Infinity 94

Attribute: Love 101

Attribute: Mercy 106

Attribute: Omnipresence 83

Attribute: Omniscience 88

Attribute: Patience 100

Attribute: Righteousness 97

Attribute: Sovereignty 77

Attributes of Christ 129

Attributes of God 74

Attributes of the H.S. 149

Attributes, Metaphysical 95

Attributes, Moral 95

Augustine 59, 176, 301

Authority, Believer's 219

Authority of Local Church 238

Babylonian Captivity 80, 325

Balaam 43, 325

Baptism into One Body 228

Baptism of Christ 111, 152

Baptism of Fire 116

Baptism of the H.S. 74, 116, 143, 151, 155, 156, 215, 233, 253, 274, 274

Baptism of the H.S. Promised 33, 74, 144, 150, 155

Baptism, John the Baptist 203

Baptism, Immersion 276

Baptism, in What Name? 274, 275

Baptism, Infant 212, 233, 273

Baptism, Symbolism of 217, 218, 275, 284

Baptism, Water 116, 149, 212, 215, 232, 253, 273, 276
Baptismal Regeneration 212, 236
Baptismal Sanctification 212
Barnabas 240, 267
Baruch 35
Bathsheba 183
Battle of Armageddon 303
Beast 337
Beast, Mark of 314
Believism 196, 198, 220
Betrayal by Judas 10, 161, 167, 202, 284
Bigamy 324
Biological View 172
Birth of Christ 64, 82, 111, 117, 120, 126, 127, 128, 132, 152, 327
Bishop, Office of 231, 233, 236, 258
Blasphemy 220, 292
Blasphemy of the H.S. 153, 187
Blessings and Curses 82, 106, 325
Blindness, Spiritual 221, 332, 340
Blood of Christ 121, 124, 131, 139, 143, 174, 186, 207, 208, 210, 212, 230, 277
Blood Sacrifice 124, 131, 169, 174, 182, 186, 207, 278, 294
Body Ministry 225, 232, 252
Body of Christ 225, 226, 227, 228, 229, 242, 252
Body, Soul, and Spirit 19
Book of Life 188, 227, 293, 340
Born Again 42, 131, 155, 171, 185, 197, 199, 202, 204-206, 216, 227, 232, 233, 297, 307
Bottomless Pit 289
Breath of Life 23

Bride of Christ 298
Buddhism 215
Burnt Offerings 108
Cain 170
Caligula 292
Calling 182
Calling, Effectual 191
Calling, General 191
Calling, Special 191
Calvin, John 61, 189
Calvinism 189
Campbell, J. M. 179
Catholicism 58, 61, 130, 172, 173, 177, 178, 212, 220, 223, 225, 231, 234, 236, 238
Causative Decrees 13
Charismatic Gifts 37, 108, 156, 233, 253, 267
Chastening 93, 183, 186
Chemosh 55
Child Discipline 93, 259, 313,
Chiliasm 302
Choice, Freedom of 6, 13, 29, 191
Christ as Advocate 124
Christ as Creator 15, 74, 109
Christ as Head of Church 144, 321
Christ as High Priest 116, 117, 121, 174
Christ as Judge 146, 308
Christ as King 125, 295, 304, 317, 327, 336
Christ as Lamb of God 124, 130, 132, 169, 188, 330, 339
Christ as Light of the World 60
Christ as Messiah 72, 116, 122, 200, 230, 329
Christ as Priest 123
Christ as Prophet 122

Christ as Redeemer 74
Christ as Resurrection and Life 116
Christ as Savior 116, 135, 140, 144, 253
Christ as Son of God 69, 112, 224
Christ as Son of Man 125
Christ's Mission on Earth 328
Christian Liberty 185
Christian Perfection 213, 214
Christian Science 250
Christian Theology 58
Christianity 1, 2, 3, 249
Christmas 130
Christology 109
Church Age 333
Church Councils 110
Church Discipline 238, 242
Church Offices 254
Church, a Mystery 333
Church, Definition 232
Church, Doctrine of 223
Church, Its Creator 153
Church, Its Government 231, 236
Church, Its Practice 239
Church, Nature of 223, 224
Church, Organization of 231
Church, Origin 223, 224, 229, 333
Church, the Term 223, 224
Churches, House 224
Circumcision 207, 240
Clergy 238
Commercial Theory 177
Commission, Great 149, 274, 329, 335
Communion of the Bread and Cup 130, 216, 217, 234, 238, 276
Communion with God 14, 19

Communism, Atheistic 54
Concepts of God 51, 52
Concurrence 29
Confession of Faith 115, 137, 154, 195, 198, 253, 291
Confession of Sin 106, 186
Congregational System 236
Conscience of Man 62, 162, 167
Consequences of Sin 165
Constantine 234, 235
Continuous Creation View 26
Control, Determinative 32
Control, Directive 31
Control, Parental 30
Control, Permissive 31
Control, Preventive 30
Control, Providential 29
Conversion 203, 205
Conversion Theory 297
Conviction of Sin 153, 191, 274
Cornelius 275
Cosmological Proof 58
Councils, Church 110
Covenant 174, 278
Covenant Love 101
Covering 174, 215
Covetousness 260
Creation 211
Creation by Christ 15, 74, 109, 127
Creation by God 15, 25, 59, 62, 63, 77, 80, 83, 107, 151, 337, 341
Creation by H.S. 148
Creation of Man 17, 19
Creation Out of Nothing 15, 16
Creationism 22
Criticism 245, 249, 254

Cross of Christ 58, 111, 131, 139, 177, 185, 208, 230, 277, 287, 301, 318

Cross, the Believer's 162, 198, 217

Crowns 222

Crucifixion of Christ 138, 328, 330, 334, 338

Crucifixion Predestinated 8, 12

Crucifixion with Christ 218

Curse of the Law 166, 171, 209

Curses 40, 43, 304, 325, 341

Cyprian 233

Cyrus 320

Dagon 55

David 48, 152, 160, 163, 183, 186, 304, 305, 323, 324

Davidic Kingdom 304, 324, 325, 327

Deacon, Appointment 268

Deacon, Duties 268

Deacon, Family Relations 270

Deacon, Gender 270

Deacon, Number of 264, 269

Deacon, Office of 256, 257, 261, 268,

Deacon, Origin of 268

Deacon, Qualifications 256, 257, 270

Deaconess, Office of 271

Dead Sea Scrolls 35

Death 285, 313, 339

Death of Christ 118, 128, 130, 131, 230

Death of God Theologies 54

Death Theory 298

Death, Premature 280

Death, Second 285

Death, Spiritual 24, 161, 175, 181, 188, 189, 203, 285

Deceit 149, 291

Deceivers 246

Decrees of God 5, 14, 65

Decrees, Causative 13

Decrees, Permissive 13

Degrees of Punishment 166

Degrees of Sin 166

Deism 56, 80

Deity of Christ 69, 111, 143, 246, 327

Deity of the H.S. 149

Deliverance from Demons 86, 153, 215, 274

Democratic Government 237, 254, 265

Demon Possession 86

Demons 64, 215, 311

Denial of Christ 118, 246, 247, 292

Denial of God 51, 52, 64, 69, 70, 99, 110, 133, 142, 187, 193

Denominationalism 173, 197, 213, 223, 233, 252, 256, 265, 273, 317

Departed Spirits, Place of 84

Depravity 97, 165, 170, 175, 189, 196, 203, 206, 212

Determinative Control 32

Dictation Theory 43

Directive Control 31

Discernment 90

Discipline of Children 93, 259, 313

Discipline, Church 238, 242

Discovery, Religion of 33, 181

Disobedience 82, 93, 100, 162, 186

Dispensation of Grace 182, 184

Dispensation of Law 182, 184

Divine Nature of Christ 110, 118, 120, 127, 131

Divorce 18

Docetic Gnosticism 111

Doctrine 1, 2, 3, 51

Doctrine of Adoption 218

Doctrine of Antichrist 290, 290

Doctrine of Atonement 173

Doctrine of Christ 109

Doctrine of Crucifixion with Christ 218

Doctrine of Election 11

Doctrine of Eternal Security 219

Doctrine of Faith 194

Doctrine of Grace 180

Doctrine of Imputation 209

Doctrine of Judgment 308

Doctrine of Last Things 285

Doctrine of Redemption 169

Doctrine of Regeneration 203

Doctrine of Repentance 201

Doctrine of Resurrection 305

Doctrine of Sanctification 211

Doctrine of Sin 159

Doctrine of the Church 223

Doctrine of the H.S. 147

Doctrine of Union with Christ 215

Dominion of Christ 125

Dreams 30, 36

Drunkenness 164, 260

Dual Fulfillment of Prophecy 160, 326

Dualism 19

Dynamic View 45

Earnest of the H.S. 156

Ears of God 68

Earthquakes 28, 300

Ebionism/Ebionites 111

Ecclesiastical Theory 231

Edict of Milan 234

Effectual Call 191

Elder, Discipline of 250

Elder, His Authority 262

Elder, His Calling 265

Elder, His Duties 261

Elder, His Family Relations 259

Elder, His Gender 260, 261

Elder, His Ordination 267

Elder, His Permanence 265

Elder, His Qualifications 259

Elder, Number of 263

Elder, Office of 257, 258

Election 6, 9, 101, 183, 187, 189, 192, 220

Election Love 101

Election, Doctrine of 11

Elijah 122, 208, 289, 306

Elisha 85, 123, 306

Embalming 139

Emmanuel/Immanuel 114, 128, 133

Empowering of the H.S. 151, 154, 155, 153, 157,

Emptying, Self- 82

End-time Events 285

Enoch 214

Episcopal System 236

Equality of God 71

Equality with God 69, 112, 114, 126, 130, 149

Esau 20, 24

Eschatology 285

Essentialism 135

Establishment of the Church 143

Esther 28

Eternal Plan of God 5

Eternal Security 219

Eternal State 336
Eternalness of God 75, 94, 314
Eternity 76, 88, 170, 341
Eucharist 276
Eutychianism 111
Evangelism 230, 233, 299, 300
Evangelist, Office of 145, 255, 266
Eve 23, 64, 128, 182
Evolution 63
Evolution, Naturalistic 17
Evolution, Theistic 18
Exaltation 218
Exaltation of Christ 115, 136, 144, 297
Exaltation of Christ Predicted 144
Example Theory 178, 180
Excommunication 244, 245, 246
Exhortation 260, 263
Exile of Israel & Judah 80, 325
Existence of God 51, 54, 57
Existence of God Assumed 63
Exodus from Egypt 14, 36
Eyes of God 68
Faith 106, 143, 233
Faith for Salvation 9, 58, 115, 173, 253
Faith in Christ 99
Faith vs Reason 199
Faith, Doctrine of 194
Faith, the Term 195
Faithfulness 79, 80, 95, 291
Faithfulness of God 99, 186
Fall of Adam 5, 13, 146, 159, 175, 181, 211, 286, 313, 321, 339
Fall of Creation 165
Fall of Israel & Judah 325
Fall of Man 164, 169, 189, 340

Fall of Nations 5
Fall of Satan 160, 161
False Messiahs 300, 302
False Prophets 300, 325
Fame 107
Family Relations 259
Famines 28, 293
Fasting 240, 258
Fatalism 14, 190
Fate 14
Fatherhood of God 216, 313
Fathers 93
Fear of Death 287
Fear of God 222
Feet Washing 130, 217, 281
Fellowship with God 66, 176, 231, 277, 282
Fetishism 57
Filling vs Fulness of H.S. 157
Fire of God 107
First Cause 58
Five-fold Ministry 254
Flood, the 100, 182, 321, 341
Floods 28, 29, 300
Foolishness of Man 51, 52, 64
Foot Washing 130, 217, 281
Foreknowledge 11
Foreordination 5
Forgiveness 101, 115, 171, 174, 176, 182, 183, 186, 196, 198, 201, 206, 236
Forms of God 68
Fornication 164, 238, 313
Forsaken by God 52
Franklin, Benjamin 56
Fraud Theory 140
Freedom of Choice 6, 29, 31, 92

Freedom of Worship 234
Freedom, Man's 6, 12, 92, 93, 185
Fruits of the Spirit 154, 196, 205, 214
Fulfillment of Prophecy: Dual 160
Fulness of the Spirit 156, 157
Gabriel 112, 327
Galerius 234
Gandhi 42
Gehenna 288, 315
General Calling 191
General Resurrection View 308
General Revelation 57, 59
Gentiles in Church 331, 333
Gentleness 259
Gift of Miracles 108, 108
Gift of Prophecy 108, 253, 267
Gift vs Gifts of H.S. 155, 156
Gifts of Healing 108
Gifts of the H.S. 37, 41, 106, 108, 145, 154, 196, 233
Giving 245, 253
Glorification 108, 218
Glorified Body 21, 84, 129, 338, 341, 342
Glorified, Christ 84
Glory of Christ 144
Glory of God 63, 66, 107, 341
Gnosticism 111
God as Creator 15, 59, 216
God as Designer of the Universe 59
God as Father 216, 313
God as First Cause 59
God as King 27, 319
God as Light 339
God as Messiah 72
God as Provider 28

God as Self-conscious 66
God as Self-determining 67
God as Self-limiting 92
God as Source of Life 66
God as Spirit 67
God as the Living God 67
God is Dead Theory 54
God, Doctrine of 51
God-breathed 38, 47
God-consciousness 60
Godhead 69, 70, 73, 105, 107, 109, 111, 119, 150, 170, 208
Godhead, Distinctions 74
Gog 302
Gospel of Salvation 143
Government of the Church 231, 236
Government Theory 178
Government, God's 27
Grace of God 106, 182, 196, 230
Grace, Dispensation of 182, 184
Grace, Doctrine of 180
Graven Images 57
Great Commission 149, 274, 329, 335
Great Tribulation 221, 300, 302, 309, 312
Great White Throne 303, 310
Greek Philosophy 80, 249
Gregory I, Pope 236
Grotius, Hugo 178
Guilt 62, 163, 167, 169, 170, 176, 179, 202, 206, 208, 209, 211
Hades 287
Hallucination Theory 139
Hardness of Heart 31, 183
Healing 93, 114, 194, 274, 329

Healing, Gifts of 108
Heart of God 68
Heaven 84, 286, 287, 338
Heavenly View 316
Hell 84, 167, 286, 288, 312
Henotheism 55
Heresy & Heretics 110, 116, 118,
    131, 180, 187, 208, 246, 247,
    249, 310
Herod 8
High Priest, Christ 116, 117, 121
Hinduism 55, 86, 215
History, God in Control 5, 13
Hitler 92, 166, 293
Holidays 130
Holiness 97, 175, 212, 304
Holiness of God 95
Holy of Holies 124
Holy Spirit as Agent in Evangelism
    153
Holy Spirit as Agent in
    Regeneration 74, 150, 153, 155
Holy Spirit as Creator 148, 149, 151
Holy Spirit as Creator of Church
    153
Holy Spirit as God 149
Holy Spirit as Intercessor 154
Holy Spirit as Power 147
Holy Spirit as Teacher 148, 152
Holy Spirit in the N.T. 152
Holy Spirit in the O.T. 151
Holy Spirit Promised 33, 74, 144,
    150, 155
Holy Spirit Theory 297
Holy Spirit, Anointing of 148, 151,
    153, 156, 267
Holy Spirit, His Attributes 149
Holy Spirit, His Deity 149

Holy Spirit, His Work 151
Homosexuality 164
Honor 107, 320
Horses 85, 324
Hospitality 260, 281, 283
House Churches 224
Humanity of Christ 110, 116, 118,
    120, 127, 131
Humility 96, 194, 241, 284, 321
Hyper-Calvinism 190
I AM 65, 66, 75
Idolatry 34, 52, 57, 63, 67, 70, 249,
    291, 313, 324
Ignatius 136
Illumination by H.S. 37, 154
Illumination Theory 44
Image of God in Man 17, 19, 21,
    215
Immanuel/Emmanuel 114, 128, 133
Immorality 244
Immortality 76
Immutability of God 79
Impatience 323
Imputation 176, 181, 182, 206, 208,
    218
Imputation, Doctrine of 209
Incarnation of Christ 46, 63, 64, 82,
    111, 117, 120, 126, 127, 246,
    295
Incarnation Predicted 127
Infallible Revelation 39, 46
Infant Baptism 212, 233, 273
Infinity 61
Infinity of God 94
Inspiration 36, 152
Intellect, Man's 58
Intellectual View 172
Intercessor, Christ as 124, 144

Intercessory Prayer 80, 121, 124, 144

Intertestamental Period 229

Intuition Theory 42

Invisible God 64, 342

Invisible Mystical Church 227, 232

Irenaeus 136, 176

Isaac 104, 113

Isaiah 40, 42, 44, 96, 128, 133, 332

Ishmael 113

Israel 66, 69, 103, 127, 183, 202, 212, 229

Israel's Restoration 147, 300, 303, 304

Jacob 7, 20, 24, 104, 289, 323, 325

James 88, 142, 334

Jefferson, Thomas 56

Jehoiakim 35

Jehovah's Witnesses 140, 250, 296

Jeremiah 24, 35, 47

Jeroboam 324

Jesus as Creator 15, 74, 109

Jesus as Head of Church 144, 321

Jesus as High Priest 117, 121

Jesus as Judge 146, 308

Jesus as King 295, 304, 317, 327, 336

Jesus as Lamb of God 124, 130, 132, 169, 188, 330, 339

Jesus as Light of the World 60

Jesus as Lord 94, 295

Jesus as Messiah 72, 116, 122, 200, 230, 329

Jesus as Priest 123

Jesus as Prophet 122

Jesus as Redeemer 74

Jesus as Resurrection and Life 116

Jesus as Savior 116, 135, 140, 144, 253

Jesus as Son of God 69, 112, 224

Jesus as Son of Man 125

Jesus Died Spiritually Error 131, 180, 208

Jewish Theory 141

Job 32, 214, 305

John the Apostle 40, 43, 114, 140, 142, 261, 334

John the Baptist 116, 122, 124, 130, 172, 203, 327, 328, 329

Joseph 7, 13, 14, 134, 289

Joshua 322

Joshua, High Priest 123

Joy of the Lord 343

Judaism 233

Judaistic Heresy 111

Judas 10, 138, 161, 167, 202, 284

Judges 322

Judgment 81, 97, 101, 146, 166, 175, 180, 186, 201, 207, 242, 285, 288, 303, 321, 337, 340

Judgment, Doctrine of 308

Justice of God 98, 100, 175

Justification 128, 181, 206, 207

Justification by Faith 226

Justification of Sinners 91

Justin Martyr 136, 176

Kenosis 82, 117, 128

Keys of the Kingdom 334

King, Christ as 125, 295, 304, 304, 317, 327, 336

Kingdom Divided 324

Kingdom of God 126, 187, 193, 204, 225, 316

Kingdom of God on Earth 146

Kingdom of Heaven 126, 316

Kingdom Prophecy 326

Kingship in Israel 257, 322, 323

Kingship of Christ 125

Koinonia 277

Laban 20

Lake of Fire 286, 288, 310, 312, 314, 315, 336, 337

Lamb of God 124, 130, 132, 169, 188, 330, 339

Lamb's Book of Life 188, 227, 293, 340

Last Supper 229, 283

Law of God 91, 99

Law of God in Man's Heart 62

Law, Dispensation of 182, 184

Laying on of Hands 253, 267, 269

Lazarus 286, 290, 306

Leah 20

Legal View 172

Legalism 186

Levi 24

Liberalism 180, 292, 315, 316

Lies, Lying, Liars 30, 149, 159, 166, 332

Life After Death 289

Life Principle, Spirit 21

Light 87, 339

Limiting God 95

Living God 67

Logos 82, 111, 112, 118, 119, 120, 121, 126, 127, 128, 131, 132, 135

Lord's Supper 278, 280

Lordship of Jesus 94

Love 98

Love Feast 279

Love of Brethren 280, 284

Love of Christ 284

Love of Enemies 102, 183

Love of God 101, 170, 176, 206, 311

Love of Money 149, 260, 270

Love, Agape 102

Love, Covenant 101

Love, Election 101

Love, Self-giving 105

Love, Unconditioned 101

Loving-kindness 101

Luther, Martin 206, 226, 61

Mahershalalhashbaz 133

Man as God? 54, 292, 294, 322

Man's Distinction from Animals 19

Man's Foolishness 52

Man's Freedom 6, 12, 92, 93, 185

Man's Nature 19, 21, 163, 165

Man's Wisdom 52, 90

Manchild 294, 298, 302, 335

Manifested Sons Theory 298

Marduk 55

Marijuana 164

Mark of the Beast 314

Marriage 18, 103, 259

Martyrdom 291

Marx, Karl 54

Mary Magdalene 142, 139

Mary, Mother of Christ 112, 120, 126, 128, 327

Materialism 53

Mediatorial Kingdom 321, 336

Mediators 123, 321

Medieval Period 177

Melchisedec 24

Mercy of God 100, 101, 106

Mercy Seat 68, 124

Merit Theory 177

Messiah 334

Messiah, Jesus as 72, 116, 122, 200, 230, 329

Messiahs, False 300, 302

Metaphysical Attributes of God 95

Millennium 146, 298, 301, 303, 310, 317, 319, 336

Miller, William 296

Miracles 25, 36, 51, 93, 108, 114, 116, 123, 135, 211, 322

Miracles, Gift of 108

Mission of Christ 328

Mistaken Woman Theory 139

Modalism 73, 150

Modernism 179, 292, 316

Money 320

Money, Love of 149, 260

Monolatry 55

Monophysitism 111

Monotheism 54, 70

Monotheletism 111

Moral Argument 62

Moral Attributes of God 95

Moral Decline 18

Moral Influence Theory 177, 180

Morality 172

Mormonism 250

Moses 34, 35, 43, 47, 65, 68, 75, 103, 122, 123, 152, 186, 208, 214, 289, 322

Murder 183, 199, 202, 220, 313

Mystical Invisible Church 223, 226

Mystical Theory 231

Names of Christ: Emmanuel 114, 128, 133

Names of Christ: Father of Eternity 114

Names of Christ: God 112

Names of Christ: Holy One 114

Names of Christ: Image of God 114

Names of Christ: Lord 114

Names of Christ: Mighty God 114

Names of Christ: Only Begotten Son 113

Names of Christ: Son of God 112

Names of God: Holy 96

Names of God: I AM 65, 66, 75

Names of God: Jesus 276

Nathan 183

National Gods 55

Nations Used as Judgment 7

Natural Theology 58

Naturalism 55

Naturalistic Evolution 17

Nature of God 65, 69, 95, 105, 110, 112, 175, 217

Nature of Man 19, 21, 60, 163, 170, 175, 196, 203, 207, 212, 216

Nature of Sin 162

Natures of Christ 110, 111, 118, 119, 120, 127, 131

Nebuchadnezzar 92, 321

Nehemiah 27

Neo-Orthodox View 180

Nero 292

Nestorianism 111

New Birth 106, 150, 171, 185, 197, 198, 199, 202, 204, 205, 210, 216, 217, 219, 232, 307

New Birth Theory 297

New Creation View 307

New Heavens & Earth 308, 337

New Jerusalem 87, 298, 326, 338

Nietzsche, Friedrich 54

Noah 100, 182, 214, 321

Oaths 98, 183

Obedience 82, 100, 106, 129, 135, 171, 178, 184, 186, 198, 207, 237, 239, 255, 322, 335

Object of Sin 163

Objects, Worship of 57

Offerings 245, 253

Offices, Church 254

Omnipotence, God's 90

Omnipotence, Holy Spirit's 149

Omnipresence, God's 68, 83, 94

Omnipresence, Holy Spirit's 149

Omniscience, God's 88, 94, 341

Omniscience, Holy Spirit's 149

Oneness Error 73, 150

Oneness of God's Nature 69, 70

Ontological View 60

Ordinance, Communion of Bread & Cup 276

Ordinance, Feet Washing 281

Ordinance, Water Baptism 273

Ordinances 232, 238, 253, 272

Ordination to Ministry 255, 257, 258, 264, 267

Organization of the Church 225, 252

Origen 136, 176

Origin of Man 17, 54

Origin of the Soul 22

Original Sin 135, 165, 166, 167, 170, 175, 189, 212, 213, 233

Overcomers 294, 298, 299, 302, 335, 336

Paganism 130, 249

Paine, Thomas 56

Pantheism 55, 66, 84

Papal System 236, 292

Parables 316, 319, 332, 333

Paraclete 148

Paradise 290

Parental Control 30

Partial Providence Theory 28

Passover 134

Pastor, Office of 145, 256, 257, 258, 263

Pastor, Qualifications 257

Pastors, Number of 264

Patience 259

Patience of God 100, 208

Patristic Period 176

Paul 44, 48, 51, 119, 142, 148, 165, 172, 184, 217, 222, 238, 240, 246, 253, 255, 258, 261, 267, 280, 340

Peace of God 171

Penal Substitution 179

Penance 236

Pentecost 138, 142, 151, 153, 155, 230, 297, 301

Perfection, God's 66

Perfection, Christian 213, 214

Perfections of God 74, 75, 97, 101, 107

Permissive Control 31

Permissive Decrees 13

Persecution 102, 120, 138, 234, 250, 291, 300, 331

Perseverance 189, 220

Personality of Christ 110, 118, 120

Personality of God 66

Personality of the H.S. 147

Peter 8, 39, 44, 142, 149, 161, 195, 224, 229, 261, 274, 281, 318, 333, 334

Peter, First Pope? 236

Pharaoh 31, 103, 321

Pharisees 135, 317

Philip 255
Philosophy, Greek 80, 172
Phoebe 271
Pilate 8, 31
Pit, Bottomless 289
Plan of God 65, 130, 321, 323, 330
Plan of God, Eternal 5
Plan of God, Unconditional 5, 9
Plato 42
Plenary Verbal Inspiration 47
Plurality of the Godhead 72
Polytheism 55, 70
Pope 231, 235
Pope Gregory I 236
Postmillennialism 301
Power of God 90, 92, 95, 221
Power of Sin 171
Power of the H.S. 233, 147, 148, 232
Practical Atheism 53
Praise 108
Prayer 14, 80, 215
Prayer for Healing 262, 264
Prayer of Faith 80, 81
Prayers to the "Saints" 236
Predestination 5, 6, 65, 105, 187, 192, 221
Prediction 329
Predictive Prophecy 89, 123, 324
Preexistence 144
Preexistence of Christ 82, 112, 118, 120, 126, 128
Premillennialism 302
Presbyterian System 236
Preservation of Creation 25, 80, 145
Preservation of Israel 29

Preservation of Scripture 34
Preservation of the Elect 80, 99, 154, 220
Preservation of the Soul 20
Preventive Control 30
Pride 90, 161, 194, 292
Priest, Christ as 123
Procreation 23, 27
Promises of God 78, 81, 95, 100, 194, 197, 215, 220, 229, 278, 304, 337
Promises, Receiving God's 14
Prophecy, Gift of 37, 108, 253, 267
Prophecy, Predictive 89, 123, 324, 329
Prophet, Christ as 122
Prophet, Office of 145, 255
Prophetess, Office of 261
Prophets, False 300, 325
Prophets, Period of 324
Propitiation 174, 207
Prosperity 146, 304
Protection 85, 228, 234, 274
Protestantism 178, 206, 212, 225, 226, 231, 238
Providence 24, 80
Providential Control 29, 320
Provider, God as 25
Punishment of Sin 99, 100, 175, 179, 186, 321
Punishment, Borne by Christ 171, 176, 185, 206, 208, 209, 211
Punishment, Eternal 286, 288, 311, 314, 336
Punishment, Place of 288
Punishment, Purgatory 236, 288
Purgatory 236, 288
Purity of God 96

Quakers 272
Qumran 35
Ransom Theory 176
Rapture 291, 294, 298, 302
Reason vs Faith 199
Reason, Man's 56, 58, 60
Reasoning up to God 58, 60, 92
Rebellion 90, 92, 101, 104, 162,
    203, 292, 308
Rebellious Israel 34
Recapitulation Theory 176
Receiving vs Accepting Christ 190
Reconciliation 71, 136, 171, 174,
    176, 178, 208, 311, 321
Redemption 130, 131, 135, 147,
    182, 187, 341
Redemption, Doctrine of 169
Reformation Period 177, 178, 179,
    189, 206, 226
Regeneration 155, 215, 228
Regeneration, Doctrine of 203
Reign of Christ 145
Religion, Biblical 1, 33
Religious Holidays 130
Religious Works 168
Religious Activities 2
Remnant 220
Repentance 100, 106, 171, 186, 191,
    207, 218, 243, 251, 253, 274,
    312, 322, 331
Repentance, Doctrine of 201
Reputation 107
Resurrection of Unsaved 306
Restitution 145
Restoration 145, 146
Restoration of Israel 147, 300, 303,
    304, 325, 327
Resurrection of Believers 136, 137,
    217, 287, 299, 342

Resurrection of Christ 21, 135, 136,
    143, 153, 230, 246, 306, 329,
    331
Resurrection of Unsaved 288, 303,
    308, 310, 314
Resurrection, Doctrine of 305
Resuscitation Theory 139
Return of Christ 129, 146, 231, 290,
    295, 317, 327, 333, 335
Revelation, Doctrine of 33
Revelation, General 57, 59
Revelation, Receiving Today 255
Revelation, Special 57
Rewards 99, 100, 286, 289, 309
Riches of Christ 129, 320
Righteousness by Faith 199, 207
Righteousness of Future Kingdom
    337
Righteousness of God 97, 209, 218
Righteousness of Law 207
Righteousness of Man 135
Righteousness, Imputed 206, 209,
    218
Rock, God as 98
Roman Catholicism 58, 61, 130,
    172, 173, 177, 178, 212, 220,
    223, 225, 231, 234, 236, 238
Rome 234
Russia 302
Sabellianism 73, 150
Sacraments 172, 236
Sacrifice 108, 124, 131, 169, 174,
    182, 186, 207, 278, 294
Sacrifice of Christ 132, 174, 209,
    216, 230, 278
Salvation 106, 135, 136, 196, 198,
    203, 331, 338
Salvation by Works 172, 181, 205

Salvation in the O.T. 171, 174, 172, 206, 208

Salvation, Its Extent 171

Samson 151

Samuel 322, 323

Sanctification 192, 199, 212

Sanctification by H.S. 154

Sanctification, Doctrine of 211

Sanhedrin 257

Sarah 30, 113

Satan 10, 32, 39, 64, 139, 298, 311, 314

Satan as Angel of Light 340

Satan as Tempter 117

Satan Bound 336

Satan's Fall 160, 161, 303

Satan's Power Limited 94

Satan's Sons 335

Satan, as Tempter 159

Satan, Bondage to 165

Satan, Defeated 128

Satan, Father of Unsaved 313, 335

Satan, Judged 308

Satan, Punished 289

Satisfaction 174, 176, 206, 207

Satisfaction Theory 177

Saul of Tarsus 143

Saul, King 323

Saving Faith 9, 58, 115, 173, 253

Savior, Jesus as 116, 135, 140, 144, 253

Schleirmacher, Friedrich 179

Science 53

Scientific Reason 56

Sealing of the H.S. 156, 221

Seared Conscience 63

Second Advent 129, 146, 231, 290, 295, 317, 327, 333, 335

Second Death 285

Secondary Causes 25, 27, 320

Self-abasement 283

Self-condemnation 62

Self-denial 162

Self-emptying 82, 117, 128

Self-exaltation 292

Self-exaltation of Satan 159

Self-existence of God 65

Self-giving Love 105

Self-improvement 178

Self-interest 253

Self-limitation of God 92

Self-sufficiency of God 66

Self-sustained Universe Theory 26

Self-will 162, 242, 259, 292

Selfish Ambition 292

Selfishness 105, 162, 280

Semi-legal View 172

Septuagint 133, 289

Seventh Day Adventists 296, 314

Shakespeare 42

Sheol 83, 288, 289

Shiloh 325

Shintoism 55

Sickness Overcome 80, 304, 329

Sickness, Because of Sin 166, 286, 330

Signs 89, 123, 134, 300, 322

Sin Offering 211

Sin's Effect 164, 286

Sin's Entrance/Origin 5, 24, 146, 159, 161, 175, 181, 211, 286, 313, 321

Sin, Doctrine of 159

Sin, Its Nature 162

Sin, Universal 164

Sin, Unpardonable 153, 187
Sin, Willful 183, 185, 187, 189
Sinfulness 104, 322
Sinless Perfection Error 214
Sinners 104, 175, 181, 183, 191,
    193, 198, 202, 206, 210, 230,
    286, 312, 340
Skepticism 53
Social Gospel View 316
Socinian Theory 178
Socinus, Faustus 178
Socrates 172
Solomon 324, 325
Son of God, Christ as 127, 132, 224
Son of Man, Christ as 125
Sons of God, Believers 112, 155,
    165, 217, 218, 299
Sons of God, Overcomers 335
Sons of Satan 335
Soul of Man 18, 20
Soul Sleep 287
Soul, Origin 22
Soul, When Received 23
Sovereign Plan of God 7
Sovereignty of God 77, 93, 125,
    189, 194
Space 67, 77, 83, 84, 87, 94
Sparrows 15, 28, 88
Special Calling 191
Special Revelation 57
Spirit of Man 21
Spirit, God as 82, 83
Spirit, Nature of 67, 140
Spiritual Blindness 221
Spiritual Body 22
Spiritual Death 24, 165
Spiritual Dimension 85, 86

Spiritual Nature of Man 21
Spiritual Resurrection Theory 140,
    307
Spiritualized View 316
Stalin, Joseph 293
States of Christ 126
Stephen 142
Stolen Body Theory 141
Stubbornness 43, 104, 183
Submission to Authority 254, 320
Substitution 8, 82, 128, 131, 132,
    143, 169, 176, 179, 186, 203,
    208, 210, 246
Substitutionary View 176
Suffering Because of Sin 287
Suffering with Christ 342
Suffering, Abolished 339
Suffering, Eternal 310, 314
Suffering, Human 121, 125, 330
Sufferings of Christ 118, 121, 125,
    129, 131, 132, 139, 209, 295,
    317, 318, 331
Suicide 202
Sun Worship 55
Sunday, as Day of Worship 143,
    232, 234
Superabundant Merit 178
Supererogation, Works of 178
Sustainer, God as 26, 29, 145, 183
Swearing 98
Syria 85
Tabernacle 152
Teacher, Function of 3
Teacher, Office of 145, 255
Teacher, Qualifications for 261
Technology 53
Teleological Proof 59
Temperance 259, 270

Temple Rebuilt 300
Temptation 32, 121, 166, 214, 244, 340
Temptation of Adam 165
Temptation of Christ 117, 125, 129, 131, 132, 136
Tempting God 117
Ten Commandments 48, 164
Tertullian 136, 177, 280
Theism 53, 54
Theistic Evolution 18
Theocratic Government 237, 239, 254
Theophanies 68, 72, 105, 127, 328
Thief on the Cross 287, 290
Thomas 142
Throne of God 68, 128, 144, 319, 327, 336, 338
Time 75, 94, 170
Time Created 76, 77
Tomb, Christ's 139, 141
Tongues, Evidence of H.S. 144, 155, 253
Tongues, Gift of 37
Total Depravity 165, 170, 175, 189, 196, 203, 206, 212
Traditions of Man 130
Traducianism 22, 23
Transcendence of God 74, 75, 96
Transfiguration of Christ 209, 289, 334
Tree of Life 165
Tri-personality of God 70
Trials 32, 121
Tribulation, Great 221, 300, 302, 309, 312
Trinity, the Term 71
Tritheism 71

Triumphal Entry 329, 334
Triune Nature of Man 19, 170
Triunity 66, 69, 70, 107, 111, 150
Truth 2, 3, 39
Truth of God 95, 342
Two Natures of Christ 110, 111, 118, 119, 127, 131
Two Natures Theory 213
Two Witnesses 294
Ultimate Reconciliation 311, 313
Unburied Body Theory 139
Unconditional Plan of God 5, 9
Unconditioned Love 101
Unction of the H.S. 156
Unemptied Tomb Theory 139
Union with Christ 86, 215
Unitarians 69, 71, 172, 311
Unity of Christ 118
Unity of God 68, 151
Universal Body of Christ 223
Universal Invisible Church 223, 226
Universal Invisible Mystical Church 228, 231
Universal Kingdom of God 319
Universal Rule of God 27
Universal Visible Church 223, 225
Universalism 188, 310
Universe, Theories of 56
Unpardonable Sin 153, 187
Unqualified Love 101
Vengeance, Divine 146
Vengeance, Human 14
Vicarious Repentance Theory 179
Virgin Birth 111, 112, 117, 128, 132, 152, 327
Visible Church View 316
Visions 36, 85, 85, 93, 142, 333
Voice of God 35, 62, 63

Vulgate Bible 38, 173
Wars 18, 28, 29, 293, 294, 300, 301, 339
Washing, Feet 217, 281
Water Baptism 116, 130, 149, 212, 215, 217, 218, 253, 273, 276
Wesley 190
Wickedness of Man 101, 330
Widows 282
Will of God 80, 91, 162, 208, 240, 241, 320
Willful Sin 183, 185, 187, 189
Wine 108
Wisdom of God 88, 89, 94, 201, 230, 341, 342
Wisdom of Man 52, 90
Wisdom of the H.S. 148
Wisdom, Worldly 291
Witness of the Spirit 63, 64, 204
Witnessing 144, 147, 153, 154, 157, 230, 232, 233
Women in Ministry 260, 261, 271
Work of Christ 122

Work of the H.S. 150
Works as Basis of Judgment 99
Works by Grace 106
Works of Christ 115, 200
Works of God 11, 51, 108
Works of Men 170
Works of Supererogation 178
Works, as Basis of Judgment 210, 285, 309, 312
Works, as Means of Salvation 172, 173, 178, 181, 186, 194, 196, 236
Works, Proving Repentance 203, 205
World Wars 18, 29, 296
Worship 67, 96, 114, 127, 305
Worship, Day of 143
Wrath of God 80, 82, 97, 100, 101, 175, 207, 312, 314
Wrath of Man 330
Yielding to God 157
Zilpah 20

Bibliography

A book of this scope would normally contain an extensive bibliography. However, this work was compiled from transcriptions of Dr. Freeman's Biblical Theology teaching cassettes, and it would be impossible to assemble a list of the many sources he used in his research.

Hobart Freeman (1920—1984) was a theologian in his own right, and developed these teachings from his own diligent study of God's Word, as well as his examination of the writings of countless Bible scholars who went before him.

If it were possible, he would surely give due credit to those who were instrumental in the shaping of his solid foundation in God's truth.